Sports Law in Serbia

Sports Law in Serbia

Second Edition

Marija Ignjatović
Filip Mirić
Goran Stanković

This book was originally published as a monograph in the International Encyclopaedia of Laws/Sports Law.

Founding Editor: Roger Blanpain
General Editor: Frank Hendrickx
Volume Editor: Michele Colucci

Wolters Kluwer

Published by:
Kluwer Law International B.V.
PO Box 316
2400 AH Alphen aan den Rijn
The Netherlands
E-mail: lrs-sales@wolterskluwer.com
Website: www.wolterskluwer.com/en/solutions/kluwerlawinternational

Sold and distributed by:
Wolters Kluwer Legal & Regulatory U.S.
920 Links Avenue
Landisville, PA 17538
United States of America
E-mail: customer.service@wolterskluwer.com

ISBN 978-94-035-3707-8

e-Book: ISBN 978-94-035-3717-7
web-PDF: ISBN 978-94-035-3727-6

The Authors

Prof. Dr Marija Ignjatović was born in 1974 in Niš, Republic of Serbia. She graduated in 1989 from the Faculty of Law, University of Niš. She received her Master's in 2005 at the Faculty of Law '*Justinijan Prvi*' of the University '*sv. Kiril i Metodij*', in Skopje, Republic of Northern Macedonia. She received her PhD in 2009 at the Faculty of Law '*Justinijan Prvi*' of the University '*sv. Kiril i Metodij*', in Skopje, Republic of Northern Macedonia. She has published a large number of scientific and professional papers. She has participated in numerous scientific and professional conferences of national and international importance in the country and abroad. She is the Vice President of the Balkan Association for Roman Law and Roman Legal Tradition (*SIR*). She is a member of the World Association of Historians of Ancient Rights (*SHIDA*). She is the Vice President of the Supervisory Board of the Science Fund of the Republic of Serbia. She is a member of the *Lex sportiva* Sports Association (Macedonia). She is a visiting professor at the State Law Faculties in Skopje, Republic of Northern Macedonia, Sofia, Republic of Bulgaria, Parma, Republic of Italy. She is a full professor at the Faculty of Law, University of Nis, Republic of Serbia.

Dr Filip Mirić was born in 1981 in Niš, Republic of Serbia. He graduated in 2008 from the Faculty of Law, University of Niš. He received his doctorate in 2014 at the Faculty of Law, University of Niš. He has published a large number of scientific and professional papers. He has participated in several scientific and professional conferences of national and international importance in the country and abroad. He is a President Advisor of Association of Lawyers – *AEPA*, Belgrade, Member of the Criminology Section of the Serbian Association for Criminal Justice and Practice, Belgrade, Active member of Victimology Society of Serbia, Belgrade, Member-Establisher of City Center for Independent Living of People with Disabilities, Niš, Member of City Union of Cerebral and Infantile Palsy, Niš. He has a large number of scientific papers in the field of sports law, the most important of which are: *Holistic approach to adapted physical activity: theory and practice/*

The Authors

Bojan Jorgic, Marko Aleksandrovic, Filip Miric, Hristina Colovic, Lidija Dimitrijevic – Niš: Faculty of Sports and Physical Education, University of Nis, 2020.

The holistic approach of adaptive physical exercise: textbook for students master academic studies/Marko Aleksandrovic, Bojan Jorgic, Filip Miric – Niš: Faculty of Sport and Physical Education, 2016.

Goran Stanković, MSc, was born in 1974 in Niš, Republic of Serbia. He graduated from the Faculty of Law, Security and Management in Niš '*Konstantin Veliki*'. He received his Master's degree in 2020 from the Faculty of Law '*Justinijan Prvi*' University '*sv. Kirili Metodij*' in Skopje, Republic of Northern Macedonia. He is a member of the *Lex Sportiva* Sports Law Association (Macedonia). He is a member of the Management Board of the Association of Sports Journalists of Serbia and a long-term president of the Sports Organization '*Sports Journalist*'. He is a professional sports journalist with twenty-five years of experience as an editor, journalist, presenter in local, regional and state media (TV5 Niš, TV Copernicus, Public Service Radio Television of Serbia, List 'Sport', TV Zona Plus). He is also the author of a large number of television shows, documentaries and publications in the field of sports journalism and sports law (TV shows '*Sports Zone*', '*Sports of Southeast Serbia*', '*Local Sports Idols*', publications '*Sports in Serbia*' of the Association of Sports Journalists of Serbia, '*Sports Bulletin of the Sports Association of Nis*'). He is the holder of the award of the best sports journalist in the city of Niš for 2020.

Table of Contents

List of Abbreviations

ADAS	Anti-doping Agency of the Republic of Serbia
CC	Criminal Code (KZ Krivični zakonik)
CEV	European Volleyball Confederation
Constitution	Constitution of the Republic of Serbia (Ustav Republike Srbije)
EHF	European Handball Federation
IOC	International Olympic Committee (Međunarodni olimpijski komitet)
IPC	International Paralympic Committee (Međunarodni paraolimpijski komitet)
LAPV	Law on Determining Certain Competencies of the Autonomous Province of Vojvodina (ZAPV Zakon o utvrđivanju određenih nadležnosti Autonomne pokrajine Vojvodine)
LCIT	Law on Corporate Income Tax (ZPD Zakon o porezu na dobit pravnih lica)
LCRR	Law on Copyright and Related Rights (ZASP Zakon o autorskim i srodnim pravima)
LCT	Law of Contract and Torts (ZOO Zakon o obligacionim odnosima)
LDPD	Law on the Prevention of Discrimination against Persons with Disabilities (ZDOSI Zakon o sprečavanju diskriminacije osoba sa invaliditetom)
LFAI	Law on Free Access to Information of Public Importance (ZSPI Zakon o slobodnom pristupu informacijama od javnog značaja)
LHI	Law on Health Insurance (ZZO Zakon o zdravstvenom osiguranju)
LID	Law on the Legal Protection of Industrial Design (ZID Zakon o pravnoj zaštiti industrijskog dizajna)
LL	Labour Law (ZOR – Zakon o radu)
LoA	Law on Advertising (ZO Zakon o oglašavanju)
LoAss	Law on Associations (ZU Zakon o udruženjima)

List of Abbreviations

LoM	Law on Ministries (ZM Zakon o ministarstvima)
LoMis	Law on Misdemeanours (ZOP Zakon o prekršajima)
LoP	Law on Patents (ZP Zakon o patentima)
LoT	Law on Trademarks (ZŽ Zakon o žigovima)
LPDI	Law on Pension and Disability Insurance (ZPIO Zakon o penzijskom i invalidskom osiguranju)
LPDS	Law on the Prevention of Doping in Sports (ZSDS Zakon o sprečavanju dopinga u sportu)
LPIT	Law on Personal Income Tax (ZPDOH Zakon o porezu na dohodak građana)
LPOP	Law on Public Order and Peace (ZJRM Zakon o javnom redu i miru)
LPT	Law on Property Tax (ZPI Zakon o porezu na imovinu)
LPVMS	Law on the Prevention of Violence and Misconduct at Sports Events (ZSNNP Zakon o sprečavanju nasilja I nedoličnog ponašanja na sportskim priredbama)
LRECDS	Law on the Ratification of the European Convention against Doping in Sport (ZREKDS Zakon o ratifikaciji Evropske konvencije protiv dopingovanja u sportu)
LRECVS	Law on the Ratification of the European Convention for the prevention of Violence and misconduct at Sports events, especially football matches (ZREKNS Zakon o ratifikaciji Evropske konvencije sprečavanju nasilja i nedoličnog ponašanja na sportskim priredbama, posebno fudbalskim utakmicama)
LS	Law on Sports (ZS Zakon o sportu)
LSA	Law on State Administration
LSRS	Law on Public Ski Resorts (ZJS Zakon o javnim skijalištima)
MPK	International Paralympic Committee
NPE	Order Declaring an Epidemic of an Infectious Disease
NZO	Order on the prohibition of gatherings in the Republic of Serbia in public places indoors and outdoors
OKS	Olympic Committee of Serbia (OKS Olimpijski komitet Srbije)
OPO Čair	Decision on opening a temporary facility for accommodation and treatment of persons suffering from infectious disease COVID-19 caused by the SARS-CoV-2 virus – 'Čair Hall'
PKS	Paralympic Committee of Serbia (PKS Paraolimpijski komitet Srbije)
PSA	Permanent Sports Arbitration
PSO	Rulebook on the Nomenclature of Sports Occupations and Titles (PSZ Pravilnik o nomenklaturi sportskih zanimanja i zvanja)

RDC	Rulebook on the Doping control at sports competitions and out of Competitions (PDK Pravilnik o doping kontrolinasportskimtakmičenjimaiizvantakmičenja)
REM	Regulatory Body for Electronic Media
RGI	Rulebook on Detailed Criteria for Determining the General Interest in the Field of Sports (POI Pravilnik o bližim kriterijumima za utvrđivanje opšteg interesa u oblasti sporta)
RNCS	Rulebook on the National Categorisation of Sports (PNKS Pravilnik o nacionalnoj kategorizaciji sportova)
RPW	Rulebook on the Supervision of Professional Work in the Field of Sports (PSR Pravilnik o nadzoru nad stručnim radom u oblasti sporta)
RSF	Rulebook on the Use of Public Sports Facilities and the Performance of Sports Activities in Public Sports Facilities (PSO Pravilnik o korišćenju javnih sportskih objekata i obavljanju sportskih aktivnosti u javnim sportskim objektima)
RTA	Rulebook on Detailed Conditions and Criteria for Scholarships for Top Athletes and for Financial Assistance to Top athletes (PVS Pravilnik o bližim uslovima i kriterijumima za stipendiranje vrhunskih sportista i za novčanu pomoć vrhunskim sportistima)
SAA	Stalna Sportska Arbitraža
TUE	Therapeutic Use Exemption
UFP	Regulation on establishing the programme of financial support to sports organizations in difficult economic conditions due to the COVID-19 pandemic caused by the SARS-CoV-2 virus
ULEB	Union of European Leagues of Basketball
WADA	World Anti-Doping Agency
ZZSZB	Law on the Protection of the Population from Infectious Diseases

List of Abbreviations

Foreword

The Monograph '*Sportsko pravo u Republici Srbiji*' was created as a result of many years of experience of the author. It was written, on the one hand, in order to acquaint the scientific and professional public with the development of sports law in the Republic of Serbia, its basic institutes and its public and private regulations, and on the other hand, it is intended as part of a large project '*International Encyclopedia of Laws*' within *Wolters Kluwer*. In addition, this monograph can be helpful to students from colleges and universities where sports law is studied. Although the monograph is intended for the scientific and professional public, as well as students who show greater interest in sports law in the Republic of Serbia, it may be the subject of interest to a wider readership interested in the development of sports and its regulations in the Western Balkans.

The purpose of this monograph determined its content and the way of presenting the material. Using primarily the normative method, the method of synthesis and analysis, induction and deduction, as well as the use of the sociological method, it presents the necessary knowledge about the organization of sports, the legal status of athletes, the prohibition of doping in sports and knowledge about the use of sports for commercial purposes.

Since there are not enough papers in the field of sports law in the domestic literature, this monograph is an attempt and an expression of efforts to unite in one place the basic institutes of sports law in the Republic of Serbia and their legislation. Because it is quite clear that the normal functioning of the state depends on a healthy society (*mens sana in corpore sano*), the subject of the monograph is, first of all, the organization of sports in the Republic of Serbia. Given that sport is a large system of social activities, it is clear that this requires a very elaborate management mechanism. Observed from the point of view of the organization of sports, the monograph emphasizes, given the different legal jurisdictions in the Republic of Serbia, that the competence in the field of sports is divided between the Republic of Serbia, the Autonomous Province of Vojvodina and local governments.

The subject of this monograph is also the legal status of the athlete, a very important issue on whose legal regulation depends on a number of factors of importance for sports law. In order to better define the legal status of athletes in the Republic of Serbia, the paper pays special attention to the qualifications of athletes, their rights and obligations, the relationship between labour and sports law, employment status of athletes, social, health and pension insurance and tax treatment of athletes.

The monograph also deals with the issue of banning the use of doping in sports, unfortunately, the increasingly frequent occurrence at sports competitions. In the

Republic of Serbia, where sport is defined as an activity of special importance, very restrictive anti-doping legislation is in force. Its consistent application aims to ensure the protection of the health of athletes, the regularity of sports competitions and results, as well as the preservation of the reputation of sport in society.

The final part of the monograph is dedicated to the use of sports for commercial purposes. Sport is a primordial need, but sport has become a lucrative business today. The inflow of money in sports, however, increases inequality between big and small clubs, between rich and poor athletes. Making a distinction between athletes and '*first and second order*' sports events is not only not in accordance with the rules of fair play, but is also the basis of discrimination because it is clear that in this case, athletes do not have the same starting points:

> The monograph makes a significant contribution to interdisciplinary scientific research, explanation and interpretation of the institute of sports law in the Republic of Serbia. Thanks to a thorough analysis and a significant amount of material, the work can be considered a stable basis on which to develop further scientific research of this multidisciplinary discipline in modern law. …
>
> The study is also reflected in the fact that it treats a special type of athlete, i.e., the sports law of persons with disabilities, which, unfortunately, is insufficiently taken into account both in practice and in the professional public.

Prof. Dr Goce Naumovski
Prof. Dr Marko Aleksandrović

General Introduction

Chapter 1. General Background

1. In general, sport can be defined as 'free physical human activity oriented towards development of psychophysical abilities'.[1] Defined like this, sport can be viewed as: (1) top sport (sport with the goal of achieving top competitive results); (2) school sport (represented in a class of physical education in schools, aiming at the development of children and youth); and (3) sport for everyone (recreation, which is defined as 'an area that includes engaging in sports activities for relaxation and recreation, improving health or improving our own results in all segments of the population').[2] Awareness of the importance of sport for human health contributes to the global adoption and implementation of health promotion strategies that emphasize sport and its important role in preserving human health.[3]

2. Physical activity is a significant area of research. Sport is a multidisciplinary activity for the study of which numerous scientific disciplines are interested (medicine, biology, psychology, sociology, law, as well as many other natural and social-humanistic sciences and scientific disciplines), and due to its importance for society, the state itself.

3. Since ancient times, people have competed in various sports, and the winners have enjoyed the status of heroes. In the Middle Ages, under the strict influence of religion and the realization that life is only a moment, and that real life begins after death, the human body was the shackles of the soul, and sport was often a rough, brutal and cruel physical activity. In civil and modern society, the traditional understanding of sport, according to which it represents an educational social institution imbued with play, whose goal is the physical and spiritual improvement of personality, changes its essential significance.

4. Modern sport is an elastic concept that speaks more about the one who practices it than about the sport itself. From the point of view of athletes, sport is an uncompromising fight for victory or for a record and from the point of view of a

1. *See* Branimir Nešić, *Sportsko pravo*, Sportska akademija, Beograd, 2020, 70.
2. *See* Branimir Nešić, *supra*, 71–72.
3. *See* Bojan Jorgić, Marko Aleksandrović, Filip Mirić, Hristina Čolović, Lidija Dimitrijević, *Holistički pristup adaptiranoj fitičkoj aktivnostim*, Fakultet sporta i fizičkog vaspitanja Univerziteta u Nišu, Niš, 2020, 8.

coach, it is a kind of way of life. Visitors to sports competitions describe sport as the uncertainty of the outcome of the fight between rivals, while sociologists and social psychologists see sport as a means of meeting the needs during the sport battle, but also an opportunity to realize and express various aggressive instincts. Using drugs, fixing the outcome of sports competitions, abuse of young athletes for personal enrichment of many coaches and sports managers are just some of them. Hence, the task of modern society is to prevent and suppress negative activities as much as possible, and to return all positive aspects to sports, as an organized activity. An important instrument for achieving this goal is recognized in the legal regulation of sports as a social activity.

5. The need for normative regulation of sports and sports activities today is increasingly imposed as an imperative to modern society. It is, above all, conditioned by the presence of a large number of 'negative phenomena' in sports ('education' of young people in stadiums and sports halls, dilemmas about abuse of position by athletes and sports organizations) and efforts to reduce them to socially acceptable frameworks. Conversely, the progressively challenging process of European integration assigns the responsibility to both potential and existing European Union Member States to undertake specific actions aimed at aligning regulations in the domain of sports law.

6. At the same time, the legal regulation of sports has imposed the need to develop a special branch of law (sports law), which is increasingly imposed on the scientific public, and above all, legal thought in order to determine its place in the legal system and legal practice. This further raises a number of additional questions, primarily the question of the nature of sports law.

7. The basic dilemma of legal theorists is whether sports law is a branch of public or private law. According to most legal theorists, sports law is, given the broad social influence and public function of sport, a branch of public law. According to the second opinion, sports law is a legal discipline sui generis (in itself, independent), which aims to emphasize its multidisciplinary approach, which has a goal to indicate the equal influence of public and private law in the development of sports law as a separate branch of law.

8. In the Republic of Serbia, sports law is primarily defined as a branch of public law, taking into account the importance of sports for the development of society and its individuals. Sports law bears all the hallmarks of the legal system of the Republic of Serbia. The norms that regulate it are of an imperative character, and the scope of freedom of private initiative is determined by legal norms. As this is a 'young' branch of positive law and legal science, there is a lack of relevant legal literature.

9. The monograph Sports Law in the Republic of Serbia will seek to contribute to the elimination of this shortcoming, through a comprehensive analysis of all sources of sports law and scientific criticism of all aspects of sports law in the Republic of Serbia. The wish of the author of the monograph is to present sports law in the Republic of Serbia in more detail by reviewing the sources of sports law, and in that sense, the subject of analysis is different norms of sports law through legislative activity and through their practical application.

Chapter 2. Development of Sports Law

10. In the Republic of Serbia, sport[1] is defined as a part of physical culture that includes every form of organized and unorganized performance of sports activities and sports activities by individuals and legal entities in the sports system, in order to meet human needs for creativity, affirmation, physical exercise and competition with others, while sports law is most often defined as a set of legal rules that regulate social relations in sports. There is a dilemma about whether the term sports law or law in sports is used. The first term is more accepted in legal science, and the second in sports science.

11. Sports law is one of the newer branches of the legal system of the Republic of Serbia, which due to its complexity, is characterized by mixed legal features. It includes basic principles and specific normative solutions that belong to different legal areas (spheres of constitutional, civil, criminal, administrative and other classical branches of law) combining different legal segments into a single entity within sports law, which is motivated by practical needs. Sport has become a highly profitable business activity in the Republic of Serbia, as well as in other societies of modern times. In this regard, numerous questions were raised that equally affect the domain of public and private law (there was a need for new types of contractual and commercial agreements, for specific regulation of criminal and material responsibility, etc.).

12. In the Republic of Serbia, which has adopted an interventionist approach to regulating the rules of conduct in sport,[4] sports law is defined as a predominantly branch of public law, taking into account the importance of sport for the development of society and its individuals. Such a codified approach has certain technical advantages because it is easier to find and interpret not only legal norms but also political ones because, in this way, it sends a clear message that the state shows appropriate attention to the position of sport in its legal system. Both advantages

---

4. In order to be able to talk about the roles and significance of sport in the legal context, the question of the origin and meaning of the term sport itself necessarily arises as a preliminary question. The term sport as a generic term, has a wide modern practical use and is generally accepted in modern speech, and has its origin in Latin (from the Latin verb *dispotare*, which could be translated as entertainment, leisure), as well as many others today words and expressions, with an emphasis on leisure, play. The medieval Latin term *dispotare* was used in archaic Italian as '*to have fun*', '*to entertain*', while the *prent* in archaic French meant '*fun*', and in Anglicism, from more than a hundred years ago in the term *sport* (created by shortening the hitherto valid term *disport*), which is accepted and is in regular use to this day. The cradle of modern sport, which aims to win, strengthen the body and develop a competitive spirit is England. Hence, it is not surprising that the term sport is from the English language. Thus, this term can be heard in: Albania, Belarus, Bosnia, Bulgaria, Denmark, Estonia, Ireland, Italy, Hungary, Norway, Germany, Poland, Russia, Serbia, Northern Macedonia, Slovakia, Slovenia, Ukraine, France, Croatia, Czech Republic. Only in a certain number of countries has the traditional term *sport* remained alive, so in Spain and Galicia the term *deporte* has been retained, while in Portugal the term *esporte* is in use.

increase the level of legal certainty in the field of sports because all persons to whom the norms apply can more easily see their rights and obligations.[5]

13. In the objective sense, sports law is a set of legal norms provided by a special law, which regulates social relations in the field of sports. By defining sports law in an objective way, the public segment is clearly visible. Viewed through the prism of public regulation, sports law is viewed as:

(1) A special branch of law which includes a systematic set of regulations on the sports system and sports activities.
(2) Science aimed at studying legal norms, concepts of sports, sports organizations, sports activities, athletes, sports infrastructure, as well as procedures related to the realization of rights in sport.

14. In a subjective sense, where the autonomous private segment of sports law is clearly recognized, sports law is defined as a set of rules of conduct prescribed by sports organizations, represented by the term sports rules.[6]

15. These segments of sports law have a significant place in the regulation of sports and the analysis of their role in regulating social relations in sports is essential for a proper understanding of sports law in the Republic of Serbia.

16. The basic terms and concepts of sports law in the Republic of Serbia are contained in the Law on Sports (LS).[7] They will be exhaustively listed and defined here:

(1) sports activities are all forms of physical and mental activity that, through unorganized or organized participation, aim to express or improve physical fitness and spiritual well-being, create social relationships or achieve results in competitions of all levels;

---

5. For many centuries, the rules of conduct in sports have been the result of the autonomy of the will of the subjects of sports activities, without the essential influence of the state and its regulations on the management of these relations. However, starting from the second half of the twentieth century, the state has shown great interest in this area of social relations, through the inclusion of sports in constitutional provisions, the adoption of special laws on sports, and the ratification of certain norms of international law within international conventions. Depending on the way of regulating the rules of conduct in sports, it is possible to divide countries into interventionist and non-interventionist. In the interventionist approach, most of the legal norms that regulate national sport and its basic elements are contained in a special law. *See* Dejan Šuput, *Reform of Legal Framework Regulating Sports in the Republic of Serbia, Serbian Law in Transition: Changes and Challenges* (Belgrade 2009), 142.
6. *See* Dejan Šuput, *supra*, 142.
At the same time, the name *lex sportiva* can often be heard for these rules. There is a special danger in the case of identifying the term lex sports with the term sports law, insisting on its autonomous and supranational character. In this way, attention is diverted from the norms of national legislation and the norms of international public law, which in recent years have become increasingly important in regulating social relations in sports. *See*, Miloš Galantić, *Lex sportiva* – Origin and Meaning of the Term, Themes, XXXIX, edition 2, Niš, 2015, 559–577.
7. *See* Law on Sports ('Official Gazette of RS', No. 10/2016) hereinafter: LSRS.

(2) sports activities are activities that provide conditions for performing sports activities, i.e., enable their performance, in particular: organizing participation and conducting sports competitions, including international competitions; training for sports activities and planning and conducting sports activities; sports trial; organization of sports preparations and sports events; provision and management of sports equipment and facilities; vocational education, training, advanced training and information in the field of sports; scientific research and research-development work in sports; sports mediation, organization of business organizations in the field of sports;
(3) sports recreation (recreational sports, sports for all, mass sports) is an area of sports that includes voluntary physical exercise, i.e., sports activities for rest, refreshment, entertainment, health improvement or improvement of one's own results and to meet the needs for movement, play and socializing, aim all segments of the population;
(4) top sport is an area of sport that includes sports activities that result in exceptional (top) results and sports qualities;
(5) children's sport is an organized form of physical exercise, i.e., sports activities, harmonized with the anthropological characteristics of children's age;
(6) sports organization is an organization established for the purpose of performing sports activities and sports activities, in accordance with this law;
(7) an athlete is a person who engages in sports activities;
(8) an amateur athlete is an athlete whose earnings are not the goal of engaging in sports activities and does not engage in these activities in the form of occupation;
(9) professional athlete is an athlete who engages in sports activity as the only or basic occupation and another athlete who has the status of a professional athlete in accordance with the sports rules of a competent international sports federation;
(10) Athlete who competes is an amateur athlete and professional athlete who participates in a sports competition, as a member of a sports organization or independently, in accordance with this law and sports rules;
(11) top athlete is an athlete who, based on the achieved top sports results at sports competitions and other ways of achieving them in accordance with the sports rules of the competent international sports federation, is ranked, in accordance with the National Categorization of Athletes, in the category of top athletes;
(12) promising athlete is a minor athlete who, based on the achieved sports results, is ranked, in accordance with the National Categorization of Athletes, in the category of promising athletes;
(13) talented athlete is an adult athlete who, based on the achieved sports results, is ranked, in accordance with the National Categorization of Athletes, in the category of talented athletes;
(14) categorized athlete is an athlete who is based on the achieved sports results ranked in accordance with the National Categorization of Athletes;
(15) organization in the field of sports is any legal entity and entrepreneur engaged in organizing sports activities and performing sports activities in accordance with the law;

(16) professional sports club is a sports organization (club) that has this status in accordance with sports rules or in which at least 50% of registered senior athletes have the status of professional athletes in relation to the number of registered senior athletes registered with the competent national branch sports federation for the competition season;
(17) sports team is an organizational unit of a sports organization that brings together athletes and sports experts from a particular branch of sport who participate in a particular range of competitions organized by the competent national branch sports federation;
(18) national sports federation is a sports federation (branch, for the field of sports or territorial) whose goals, tasks and activities in the field of sports are directed to the territory of the Republic of Serbia and which is open for membership of persons from the territory of the Republic of Serbia;
(19) the competent national branch sports federation is the national branch sports federation that regulates the performance of sports activities and sports activities in a certain branch of sport through sports rules, in accordance with this Law;
(20) competent international sports federation is an international sports federation that is a member or recognized by the International Olympic Committee (IOC) and the International Paralympic Committee (IPC) when it comes to sports for persons with disabilities or an international sports federation that is globally responsible for a particular branch or field of sport and which is a member of the competent national sports federation;
(21) a sports event is a specific, planned and conducted, time-limited sporting event, for which there is a public interest and in which several athletes participate;
(22) a sports competition is a sporting event that takes place according to predetermined and known sports rules, which may be generally valid for a specific branch of sport or only for a specific sporting event and whose goal, which each participant strives for, is either winning the opponent or achieving a certain predetermined sports score;
(23) national sports competition is a sports competition organized for the territory of the Republic of Serbia by the competent national branch sports federation, in accordance with this law and sports rules;
(24) amateur sports competition is a sports competition that has this status in accordance with the sports rules of the competent national branch sports federation and in which a maximum of 20% of professional athletes can participate;
(25) professional sports competition is a sports competition that has this status in accordance with the sports rules of the competent national branch sports federation and in which, in accordance with this law and sports rules of the competent national branch sports federation, at least 75% of professional athletes compete, unless of the International Sports Federation otherwise;
(26) professional sports league is the highest national professional sports competition (open or closed type) of sports organizations, i.e., sports teams of sports organizations, organized as companies, which compete against each other according to a predetermined schedule and sports rules;

(27) the organizer of a sports event is a person who decides on his own responsibility for the organization and implementation of a certain sports event, ménages it and leads it, in accordance with the law and sports rules;
(28) sports rules are rules determined by general acts of the competent national sports federations, which regulate the performance of sports activities and activities and the achievement of established sports goals;
(29) professional sports supervisor is a person who supervises professional work in the field of sports, monitors and proposes measures taken by the organization in the field of sports, or sports expert to eliminate deficiencies, and notifies the Minister responsible for sports (hereinafter: Minister).

17. Determining the basic concepts of sports law, according to the normative framework of the Republic of Serbia, is extremely important for understanding its basic institutes.

Chapter 3. Sources of Sports Law

18. The basic sources of sports law in the Republic of Serbia are: The Constitution, the LS and ratified international conventions.

19. Constitution of the Republic of Serbia (Constitution),[8] as an act of the highest legal force that regulates the basic and most important relations in the state, indirectly regulates relations in the field of sports. The Constitution contains several provisions of importance for sports and recreation. Freedom of political, trade union and any other association and the right to remain outside any association are guaranteed (Article 55, paragraph 1). The Republic of Serbia supports the development of health and physical culture (Article 68, paragraph 4). The Republic of Serbia provides: a system in the areas of health, social protection, veterans and disability protection, child care, education, culture and protection of cultural goods, sports, public information; system of public services (Article 97, paragraph 1, item 10).

20. The most important legal source that contains legal norms that regulate national sport and its basic elements is the LS.[9] The need to regulate by law a part of the matter of sports law arises from the fact that the Constitution of the RS regulates basic issues and the LSRS regulates them specifically. LSRS regulates the largest number of rules of conduct in sports, but at the same time, formally confirms the traditional practice of state recognition of sports autonomy. The law recognizes the adoption of sports rules by national federations and the Olympic Committee of Serbia (OKS). It explicitly allows for the possibility of excluding the jurisdiction of national courts in the field of resolving disputes in the field of sport and entrusting them to sports arbitrations. Also, the Law accepts the existing pyramidal organizational structure in the field of sports and adds to it certain organizational forms in order to improve social relations that are not regulated by international sports organizations and are of interest to the Republic of Serbia. It is necessary to emphasize here that in addition to a number of legal norms related to the autonomy of sports and sports organizations, the Law also provides for the restriction of autonomy, which indicates that the Republic of Serbia has opted for an interventionist model. In addition to the LS as the most important legal source in the field of sports, the Law on Prevention of Doping in Sports was passed in the Republic of Serbia[10] and the Law on Prevention of Violence and Misconduct at Sports Events has been passed in the Republic of Serbia.[11]

8. *See*, Constitution of the Republic of Serbia ('Official Gazette of RS', No. 98/2006).
9. *See*, Law on Sports ('Official Gazette of RS', No. 10/2016).
10. *See*, Law on Prevention of Doping in Sports ('Official Gazette of RS', Nos 111/2014 and 47/2021).
11. *See*, Law on Prevention of Violence and Misconduct at Sports Events ('Official Gazette of RS', Nos 67/2003, 101/2005 – other law, 90/2007 – other law, 111/2009, 104/2013 – other law and 87/2018).

21. On the Basis of ratified international conventions and documents important for the field of sports in the Republic of Serbia, the Law on Ratification of the European Convention against Doping in Sport and the Law on Ratification of the European Convention for Prevention of Violence and Misconduct at Sports Events, especially Football Matches.[12]

22. Considering the interventionist model of sports regulation in the Republic of Serbia, there are numerous legal regulations that directly or indirectly regulate issues of importance for the field of sports, so they are among the additional sources of sports law. These include laws, regulations, statutes and other by-laws.[13]

---

12. *See*, Law on Ratification of the European Convention for the Prevention of Violence and Misconduct at Sports Events, Especially Football matches ('Official Gazette of SFRJ – International Agreements', No. 9/1990).
13. More in the part of Public Regulation of Organizations in Sports.

Part I. Organization of Sport in the Republic of Serbia

Chapter 1. General Issues

23. The sports system in the Republic of Serbia is very complex and consists of three constitutive elements:

(1) The first contains: Olympic and Paralympic sports, non-Olympic sports and sports of persons with disabilities (which are not part of Paralympic sports).
(2) The second constitutes sport in institutions (schools, universities, army, police, etc.).
(3) The third is the activities of individuals who are not strictly institutionally connected, such as family sports, mass sports, health sports, fitness, recreational sports, extreme sports, sports within housing, etc.[14]

24. Sport is a large system of social activities that requires a very elaborate management mechanism. From the point of view of legal competence, the competence in the field of sports is divided between the Republic of Serbia, the Autonomous Province of Vojvodina and local self-governments. A distinction is also made between legal jurisdiction within the governmental and non-governmental sectors.

25. Sports management in the Republic of Serbia is performed by government institutions, the National Olympic Committee and sports associations.

26. The government sector includes:

(1) Ministry of Youth and Sports – is at the top of the hierarchical pyramid of the sports system, as the main bearer of its definition, monitoring and financing.
(2) The council for Sports and the National Council for the Prevention of Negative Phenomena in Sports of the Republic of Serbia are coordinating expert bodies that ensure the implementation of the strategy for the development of sports while respecting the principles of sports autonomy. This body represents a kind of link between the governmental and non-governmental sectors in the field of sports.

---

14. *See*, Branimir Nešić, Franja Fratrić, *Osnove organizacije sporta*, Edukons, Sremska Kamenica, 2013, 170.

(3) Republic Institute for Sports and Sports Medicine.

27. The non-governmental sector encompasses:

(1) The OKS, which is organized at the national level, is in accordance with the rules of the IOC. The body has an obligation to affirm the values of the IOC, affirm the values of Olympism, organize the preparation of Olympians for the Olympic Games, etc.
(2) The Paralympic Committee of Serbia (PKS) is a national body that aims to promote the sport of persons with disabilities and provide conditions for the participation of the Serbian Paralympic team in the Winter and Summer Paralympic Games.
(3) The Sports Federation of Serbia is a territorial sports federation for the territory of the state (non-governmental, non-partisan and non-profit sports institution). It unites branch sports federations and lower-level associations (city, municipal, provincial). He is in charge of affirming universal sports values and monitoring the development of non-Olympic sports.
(4) National branch federations are the highest form of association in Serbia in the appropriate branch of sport. They are established with the aim of developing a certain sports branch, sports activities and activities in the field of their activities, harmonizing the activities of their members, representing national sports, achieving top sports results, professional work and encouraging the organization of sports competitions. National branch sports federations are obliged to improve the conditions for the development of sports in accordance with the appropriate training and competition programmes.
(5) Professional sports associations are also non-governmental, non-political and non-profit organizations and their main activities and responsibilities are focused on building subsystems related to sports accreditation of members, resolving trade union and professional issues and disputes, as well as issues of continuing improving sport.[15]

§1. Government Institutions in the System of Sports Organization in the Republic of Serbia

I. Ministry of Youth and Sports of the Republic of Serbia

28. The Ministry of Youth and Sports of the Republic of Serbia is at the top of the hierarchy of the sports management system in the Republic of Serbia.

29. The Ministry gives an opinion on whether an activity belongs to a sports activity and to which sports discipline and sports branch, i.e., area it belongs. Also, the Ministry in charge of sports gives an opinion in accordance with the LSRS,

15. *See* Branimir Nešić, *supra*, 74–76.

based on the previously obtained expert opinion of the Sports Federation of Serbia, the OKS and the PKS, which has the status of a competent international sports federation (*see* Article 3 of the LSRS).

30. Also, the Ministry prescribes more detailed conditions of the ways of recognizing forms of abuse, discrimination and violence against minors together with the ministry in charge of internal affairs, justice and the ministry in charge of health (*see* Article 4, paragraph 8 of LSRS).

31. A particularly important issue that falls within the competence of the line ministry is the area of financing projects in the field of sports. Project financing is a complex process and is achieved through the process of financing annual projects. These projects are very important because sport is an activity of great importance for the Republic of Serbia.

32. It is of general interest in the field of sports:

(1) providing conditions for the preparation, participation and achievement of top results of athletes at the Olympic Games, Paralympic Games and other major international sports competitions;
(2) improvement of the sports system and capacity building of the OKS, the PKS and the Sports Federation of Serbia and other competent national sports federations for branches and areas of sports through which the general interest in the field of sports is realized;
(3) construction, equipping and maintenance of sports facilities that are important for the development of sports in the entire territory of the Republic of Serbia, taking into account, the regional coverage and the degree of development of sports infrastructure in local self-government units;
(4) scholarships for sports training of top amateur athletes and financial assistance to top athletes with special merits;
(5) national recognitions and awards for special contribution to the development and affirmation of sports;
(6) activities of sports camps for promising athletes, which are of special importance for the Republic of Serbia;
(7) organization of international and national sports competitions of importance for the Republic of Serbia;
(8) providing conditions for organizing and holding school and university sports competitions at the level of the Republic of Serbia;
(9) promotion of sports recreation, promotion and encouragement of sports for all citizens of the Republic of Serbia, especially children, women, youth and persons with disabilities;
(10) preventing negative phenomena in sports (doping, violence and misconduct, fixing sports results, etc.);
(11) improving the protection of athlete's health, improving professional work and professional training in sports;
(12) interstate and international sports cooperation and development of sports and cooperation with organizations from the diaspora;

(13) scientific conferences, research and development and scientific research projects in sports and publishing sports publications of national importance;
(14) activities and programmes of organizations in the field of sports founded by the Republic of Serbia.

33. Funds in the budget of the Republic of Serbia are provided for the realization of the general interest in the field of sports. Funds that are realized in the budget of the Republic of Serbia by organizing games of chance, in accordance with the Law, are used to achieve the general interest in the field of sports (*see* Article 112 of the LSRS). The branch of sport within which the programme is being implemented should be of special importance for the Republic of Serbia.

34. The proposal of annual programmes is submitted by the OKS, the PKS and the Sports Federation of Serbia, in accordance with this law. Annual and special programmes are submitted by the holders, i.e., proposers of programmes and projects according to the dynamics determined by the Programme Calendar.

35. The annual programme is executed according to the following dynamics:

- 1 June – proposers, i.e., programme holders, submit their proposals for annual programmes to the Ministry.
- 1 July – the Minister forms an expert commission for the selection of programmes and projects that analyses and evaluates the submitted proposals for annual programmes.
- 15 July – The Ministry makes a preliminary decision, on the proposal of the expert commission on the allocation of funds for the next budget year for the implementation of annual programmes that achieve the general interest in the field of sports.
- 15 December – The Ministry revises the proposals for annual programmes and harmonizes them with the funds determined in the budget of the Republic of Serbia for the next year.
- 30 December – The Ministry makes a decision and informs the programme holders about the amount of approved funds for programmes and projects.

36. The proposal of the annual and special programme and project shall include appropriate data on the personality of the person participating in the implementation of the programme, i.e., project.

37. The proposal of the programme or project may exceptionally refer to activities that are implemented over a longer period of time, up to four years, provided that this is necessary given the nature and objectives of the activity, that the proposed programme or project for each year provides the necessary funds and that the annual results of programme implementation are measurable.

38. The continuation of the implementation of the programme or project is approved every year.

39. Realization, i.e., continuation, of the programme, i.e., project, can be approved only if the annual report for the previous budget year has been submitted in accordance with the contract on realization of the programme, i.e., project and if the expected results have been achieved.

40. Approval of annual and special programmes from the article is done in accordance with this law and the Strategy, and in the case of annual programmes and in relation to categorizations in terms of this law and development programmes of the competent national sports federation.

41. The programme is financed in whole or in part and under conditions that ensure that the intended results are achieved with the least expenditure of funds from the budget of the Republic of Serbia.

42. When approving a programme or project that achieves a general interest in the field of sports, priority is given to programmes that are structural and developmental in nature, and between the programmes of organizing or participating in sports events, priority is given to programmes related to higher-level sports events.

43. Programmes and projects are financed once or in instalments, depending on the time period for the implementation of the programme. The Minister regulates in detail: the criteria and manner of approving the programme, i.e., project, and allocation of funds; appearance and content of the programme proposal, i.e., project, and documentation submitted with the proposal; the content and appearance of the report on the implementation of the programme, the manner and procedure of control over the implementation of approved programmes, i.e., projects.

44. The costs of programmes of general interest in the field of sports must relate, as a rule, at least 15% to activities related to children's sports.

45. The Ministry may exceptionally approve a certain programme which realizes the general interest in the field of sports and on the basis of the submitted programme proposal during the year, without a public invitation, in the case of a programme of special importance for general interest in sports, submitted by the programme holders and in the case of a programme that for objective reasons could not be submitted in accordance with the Programme Calendar, and the subject and content of the programme is such that it can be successfully implemented only by a particular programme holder.

46. The special programme is executed by public invitation. The Ministry may determine in the public call for submission of proposals for special programmes, projects or programme tasks for the submission of programmes.

47. One competent national branch sports federation, i.e., one competent national sports federation in the field of sports, may not be approved more than 20% of the total amount of funds from the budget of the Republic of Serbia provided for financing the programmes of competent national sports federations.

48. The Minister shall issue an act determining:

(1) competent national sports federations for sports branches and sports areas in the Republic of Serbia;
(2) sports branches and areas of sports in the Republic of Serbia and sports disciplines within sports branches and areas of sports;
(3) sports branches that are of special importance for the Republic of Serbia.

49. The Minister issues an act on the basis of: organization of the federation, number of member organizations and athletes, economic strength, media and social influence, development of the sports branch, national and international organization and tradition, membership in the competent international sports federation, competition system, fulfilment of prescribed conditions for sports activities and activities, as well as sports results.

50. Prior to the adoption of the act, the Ministry obtains the opinion of the OKS, the PKS and the Sports Federation of Serbia.

51. For the evaluation of annual and special programmes, i.e., projects, the Minister forms an expert commission in which, in addition to representatives of the Ministry, representatives of the OKS the PKS, the Sports Federation of Serbia and the Republic Institute also participate. The Commission performs an expert review and evaluates the submitted proposals, based on this law and the conditions and criteria stated in the public invitation, and submits to the Minister a proposal for approval of the programme.

52. The Ministry decides on the approval of the annual and special programme, i.e., project, by an individual decision.

53. With the holder of the approved programme or project, the Ministry concludes an agreement on the implementation of the programme, i.e., project, which obligatorily regulates: the name and seat of the holder of the programme, i.e., project; type and content of the programme or project; time of realization of the programme, i.e., project, and performance of activities; goals and expected results; the amount of allocated funds; time plan for the use of funds; the manner of supervision over the implementation of the programme, i.e., project; the obligations of the programme holder in terms of submitting a report on the implementation of the programme, i.e., project; proving the realization of the programme, i.e., project, intended use of funds, media presentation of the programme, i.e., project, and participation of the Republic of Serbia in its financing.

54. If the holder of the approved programme or project does not respond to the invitation to conclude the contract within eight days from the date of receipt of the invitation, it will be considered that he has withdrawn from the programme proposal. The contract on the realization of the programme, i.e., the project which realizes the general interest in the field of sports concluded contrary to the provisions of this law, is null and void. The holder of the approved programme, i.e., the project to which the funds were transferred, is obliged to purposefully use the funds obtained from the budget of the Republic of Serbia. The contract on approval of the programme, i.e., the project which satisfies the general interest in the field of sports in the Republic of Serbia, which was concluded contrary to this law, is null and void (*see* Articles 112–122 of the LSRS).

55. This range of competencies of the Ministry, especially from the aspect of financing, clearly shows its key role in the system of sports development.

56. To perform the tasks within its competence, the Ministry has several sectors: Sector for Sports, Sector for Youth, Sector for International Cooperation and European Integration, Secretariat, as well as the Department for Infrastructure Project Management and the Department for Inspections of Sports Affairs.

57. From the aspect of sports law, the work of the Sports Sector is especially important.

58. The Sports Sector performs activities related to: monitoring and determining the situation in the field of sports; preparation of development strategies and other measures that participate in shaping the Government's policy in the field of sports; initiating and taking measures within the competence of the Ministry in order to improve the situation in the field of sports; preparation and implementation of the Sports Development Strategy; preparation and implementation of action plans for implementation of the Sports Development Strategy; exercising the rights of foreign athletes and sports organizations and federations in the Republic of Serbia; normative affairs within the scope of the Sector; keeping the register of sports organizations and other special records in the field of sports and other activities within the scope of the Sector.

59. The group for normative, legal and operational-analytical affairs in sports performs activities related to: preparation of regulations within the scope of the Sector; prepares opinions on the application of laws and other regulations in the field of sports, as well as opinions on proposals and draft acts prepared by other ministries, from the point of view of the scope of the Sector; cooperation with the Sector for International Cooperation and European Integration in the field of implementation of bilateral and multilateral programmes of cooperation in the field of sports, analysis of harmonization of regulations in the field of sports with EU regulations, harmonization of regulations within the scope of the Sector with Council of Europe standards; cash prizes, scholarships and national recognitions and operational-analytical work in sports; monitoring the situation and preparing analyses, information and notifications within the scope of the Group and other tasks within the scope of the Group.[16]

16. Ministry of Youth and Sports of the Republic of Serbia, Sector for Sports, *See also* https://www.mos.gov.rs/o-ministarstvu/sektor-za-sport, accessed 28 Aug. 2021.

60. Based on the functional competence of certain parts of the Ministry, its importance for the stability and coherence of the sports management system in the Republic of Serbia can be noticed.

II. The Sports Council and the National Council for the Prevention of Negative Phenomena in Sports

61. In order to realize the goals and activities determined by the Strategy and to improve the overall activities, the Ministry established the Sports Council, composed of eminent experts in the field of sports, whose engagement in the Council is of an honorary nature.

62. The Sports Council is a link between the governmental and non-governmental sectors in the sports system.

63. According to the LS, the National Council for Sports proposes and monitors the implementation of measures for the development of Serbian sports, coordinates and establishes communication between all involved parties in order to continue positioning on the international competition scene, assists in the recognition and development of strategic priorities and provides assistance in the interpretation of relevant regulations, while promoting learning in specialized areas of sports development, including management, conducts specialized professional coaching courses and research at various levels of sports. The National Council for Sports is necessary in order to inform the Ministry of Sports and the OKS about the events and discussions of issues concerning all crucial topics of Serbian sports and a detailed analysis of the current situation, as well as work on building the future.

64. The National Sports Council has 35 members, headed by the Minister of Sports in the Government of the Republic of Serbia.

65. The current composition of the Council for Sports, which in the future will have its own subcommittees and expert council, consists of 35 members: the Minister of Sports as president, and as members former athletes, sports experts and experts in sports (state secretaries and special advisors from the Ministry of Sports, president of the OKS, the president of the Sports Federation of Serbia, the president of the PKS, as well as representatives of the Institute for Sports and Sports Medicine of the Republic of Serbia and the Anti-Doping Agency of Serbia, the provincial secretary for sports and youth of the Autonomous Province of Vojvodina, representatives of national branch associations – football, volleyball, basketball, handball, athletics, water polo, shooting, wrestling, judo, taekwondo, boxing, rowing, kayaking, then president of the Association for School Sports of Serbia, representative of the public media service – Radio Television of Serbia, president of the OKS health commission, representatives of higher education institutions, president of the parliamentary subcommittee for sports, as well as several prominent athletes.

66. In order to harmonize activities on prevention of violence and misconduct of spectators at sports events, doping in sports, match-fixing and other negative phenomena in sports, as well as fulfilment of international obligations in these areas, the Government establishes the National Council for Prevention of Negative Events in Sports, tasks and other issues relevant to his work. The National Council consists of representatives of the Ministry responsible for Interior, the Ministry responsible for Justice, the Ministry responsible for Education.

67. On 2 March 2023, the Government of the Republic of Serbia adopted a Decision to amend the Decision on the establishment of the National Council for the Prevention of Violence and Misbehavior of Spectators at Sports Events, Doping in Sports, Match-Fixing and Other Negative Events in Sports.

68. The current Minister of Internal Affairs is appointed as the President of the Council, the Deputy President is the current Minister of Defence, the Vice Presidents are the Minister of Justice and the Minister of Sports, while the current Minister of Education, the Minister of Health, the Public Prosecutor of the Republic, the Director of the Security and Information Agency, the director of the Anti-Doping Agency of the Republic of Serbia (ADAS), the president of the OKS, the president of the PKS, the president of the Sports Federation of Serbia, as well as the presidents of the most numerous branch sports federations - the Football, Basketball, Volleyball, Handball and Water Polo Federations of Serbia, while a seat in the Council is also provided for the president Association of Sports Journalists of Serbia.

III. Republic Institute for Sports and Sports Medicine

69. Professional supervision over activities in the field of sports is performed by the Republic Institute for Sports and Occupational Medicine.

70. The Republic Institute is an institution that performs activities aimed at improving the development of professional work and meeting professional needs in the field of sports.

71. The activity of the Republic Institute includes:

(1) periodic testing, i.e., monitoring of anthropological abilities and characteristics of children, youth and adults;
(2) control of the training of promising and top athletes and providing expert advisory assistance to these athletes and sports experts;
(3) organization and realization of continuous training and final preparations of perspective and top athletes;
(4) keeping national records in the field of sports (data collection and processing) and periodically publishing and publishing aggregate data from national records;

(5) professional training and advanced training of sports experts and experts in the field of sports and sports medicine in cooperation with the appropriate accredited higher education institution, in accordance with the law;
(6) performing supervision over professional work in the field of sports through professional sports supervisors;
(7) evaluation of the health condition of participants in physical activities;
(8) improving the health and functional abilities of promising and top athletes;
(9) organizational and professional assistance to organizations that implement programmes that achieve general interest in the field of sports and organizers of major international sports competitions;
(10) advising on the planning, construction and reconstruction of publicly owned sports facilities and monitoring their utilization;
(11) propaganda, publishing, scientific, research and development and library activities in the field of sports and sports medicine, in accordance with the law;
(12) participation in the development of the Strategy;
(13) giving opinions and professional assistance to participants in the sports system in matters of importance for the development of sports;
(14) international cooperation in the field of sports and medicine sports;
(15) promoting the development of sports for children and youth;
(16) monitoring the planning of construction and utilization of sports facilities;
(17) identification and development of sports talents, in cooperation with the competent national branch sports federation.

72. The Republic Institute for Sports and Occupational Medicine may also perform health care activities, i.e., certain health care activities, in accordance with the law governing health care.

73. The Republic Bureau may also perform other tasks, in accordance with the Statute.

74. The Statute of the Republic Institute is approved by the Government, and the general act regulating the organization and systematization of jobs in the Republic Institute, the financial plan and the annual work programme of the Republic Institute are approved by the Ministry. These jobs are done as entrusted jobs.

75. The Republic Institute has the status of a national training centre and has the exclusive right to perform activities of supervision over sports activities unless, for objective reasons, the organization and implementation of continuous training and final preparations of promising and top athletes are not possible in the Republic Institute (*see* Article 107 LSRS).

76. The bodies of the Republic Institute are: the director and the management board.

77. The Steering Board of the Republic Institute has seven members, of which two representatives of the Ministry, one representative of prominent experts in the field of sports proposed by the Ministry, one representative of the OKS, one representative of the Sports Federation of Serbia and two representatives of the Republic Institute.

78. A person with higher education may be appointed a member of the Management Board and the Director of the Republic Institute. The management Board of the Republic Institute decides by a majority vote of the total number of members of the Management Board.

79. The Director, President and members of the Management Board of the Republic Institute are appointed and dismissed by the Government.

80. Supervision over the legality of the work of the Republic Institute is performed by the Ministry (*see* Article 108 of the LSRS).

81. The regulations on public services shall apply to the organization and work of the Republic Institute unless otherwise determined by the LSRS.

82. Funds for the work of the Republic Institute are provided in the budget of the Republic of Serbia and from other sources, in accordance with the Law (*see* Article 109 of LSRS).

83. The Republic Institute for Sports and Sports Medicine has a key role in conducting supervision and control over sports activities. This competence is rightly within the competence of the Governmental institution, having in mind, its importance for the functioning of sports.

IV. Sports Endowments, Foundations and Funds

84. In order to achieve socially useful goals in the field of sports, sports endowments and foundations may be established.

85. The Republic of Serbia establishes the National Fund for the Development of Sports with the aim of supporting the improvement of sports recreation, promotion and encouragement of sports for all citizens of the Republic of Serbia, especially children, women, youth and persons with disabilities. In order to achieve its goals, the Fund is primarily financed by donations from organizations in the field of sports and other legal entities, as well as from other funds in accordance with the Law (*see* Article 111 of the LSRS).

86. The Autonomous Province and the unit of local self-government may establish their own funds for the development of sports. Funds of territorial units are established as budget funds in accordance with the law governing the budget system.

§2. Non-governmental Institutions in the System of Sports Organization in the Republic of Serbia

I. Serbian Olympic Committee

87. The National Olympic Committees are independent and non-governmental bodies, with the primary goal of promoting Olympic sport in the Member States of the IOC.

88. The National Olympic Committee – The OKS was established in accordance with the Olympic Charter and is recognized by the IOC. The provisions of the law relating to national branch sports federations shall apply according to the establishment, entry in the Register and performance of sports activities, as well as to other issues related to the work and programmes of the OKS unless otherwise specified by the LSRS.

89. There Serbian Olympic Committee may use Olympic symbols within its visual identity, in accordance with the law.

90. The OKS is responsible for the development and promotion of Olympic sports.

91. The OKS performs activities that provide conditions for: monitoring, development and improvement of top sports and the system of top sports in Olympic sports, organization and holding of international sports competitions under the jurisdiction of the IOC, realization of interstate and international sports cooperation and programme implementation; projects in this area that are of general interest to the Republic of Serbia, as well as other activities in accordance with this LSRS.

92. In particular, the OKS performs the following tasks within the scope of its competence:

(1) resolves arbitration disputes for Olympic sports;
(2) participates in the work of the Management Board of the Republic Institute;
(3) on its own behalf, proposes annual and special programmes that achieve the general interest in the field of sports and collects from its permanent members (competent national branch sports federations of Olympic sports) and on their behalf, proposes annual and special programmes that achieve the general interest in the field of sports;
(4) participates in the work of expert commissions that evaluate programmes that are financed in accordance with this law;
(5) give an opinion on the act of the Minister which determines the national branch sports federations whose programmes are financed from the budget of the Republic of Serbia, sports branches and sports facilities of importance for the Republic of Serbia;
(6) participates in the work of the commission for the preparation of the categorization of sports, athletes and sports experts and performs ranking;

(7) gives an opinion regarding the candidacy for the organization of major international sports competitions on the territory of the Republic of Serbia for Olympic sports;
(8) takes care of improving the health protection of athletes and sports experts in Olympic sports and preventing negative phenomena in sports;
(9) temporarily performs the function of the holder of the programme of the competent national branch sports federation of Olympic sports in relation to satisfying the general interest in the field of sports from the member if the competent national branch sports federation is not formed in a certain branch of sport or the national sports federation loses the status of the sports federation or does not function in accordance with this law.

93. The OKS performs its activities in accordance with the principles of the Olympic Movement and the Olympic Charter of the IOC.

94. The Ministry determines by a decision that the conditions are met for the OKS, i.e., the PKS, to temporarily perform the functions of the national branch sports federation.

95. An administrative dispute may be initiated against such a decision of the Ministry, in accordance with the law.

96. The OKS and the PKS are obliged to adopt framework programmes for the development of Olympic and Paralympic sports, within the limits of their competencies determined by the LSRS, for at least four years, and to submit it to the Ministry within fifteen days.

97. The OKS and the PKS have the status of competent national sports federations in terms of exercising their competencies determined by the LSRS. The OKS, the PKS and the Sports Federation of Serbia agree on a code of professional ethics for performing professional work in sports (*see* Articles 103–104 of the LSRS).

98. In addition to the above competencies prescribed by the LSRS and the Statute of the OKS, the ACS is also responsible for the promotion of Olympism as a philosophy of life and value system, which is more than sports competition.

II. Serbian Paralympic Committee

99. Professional sports are an important segment of the lives of many people with disabilities. Paralympics is the realization of a very important idea that even athletes with disabilities can achieve valuable sports results.

100. The PKS[17] is an organization in the field of sports formed in accordance with the Paralympic Charter and recognized by the IPC.

101. The PKS performs activities that provide conditions for: monitoring, development and promotion of sports for persons with disabilities, organization and holding of international sports competitions under the jurisdiction of the IPC, realization of interstate and international sports cooperation and implementation of programmes and projects in the area of sports for athletes with disabilities that are of general interest to the Republic of Serbia, as well as other jobs in accordance with this law.

102. The Ministry determines with a decision the fulfilment of the conditions on the functioning of the PKS as a national branch sports federation. An administrative dispute may be initiated against the decision of the Ministry, in accordance with the law.

103. The OKS and the PKS are obliged to adopt framework programmes for the development of Olympic and Paralympic sports, within the limits of their competencies determined by this Law, for at least four years, and to submit it to the Ministry within fifteen days.

104. The OKS and the PKS have the status of competent national sports federations in terms of exercising their competencies determined by the LS (*see* Article 103 of the LSRS).

105. The PKS is an independent and non-profit body dedicated to the promotion of the Paralympics in Serbia.

106. In the Statute, PKS undertakes to:

(1) in its activities, consistently respect the principles of the Paralympic Charter, as well as the Statute and Decisions of the International Paralympic Committee (MPK), and that it will consistently conduct its activities in accordance with the same, including provisions of the accompanying regulations, which regulate issues related to national Paralympic Committees;
(2) take care of the development and improvement of top sports and the system of top Paralympic sports on the territory of the Republic of Serbia, to participate in activities that help spread peace;
(3) encourage and participate in activities that improve the position of women in sports;
(4) help and encourage the development of sports ethics;

---

17. In our country, athletes with disabilities have been cared for many years by the Sports Association of the Handicapped of Yugoslavia. The Yugoslav Paralympic Committee was established on 9 Sep. 1999, later changing its name to the Paralympic Committee of Serbia and Montenegro, and since 2006 to the Paralympic Committee of Serbia.

(5) fight doping and comply with the provisions of the World Anti-Doping Code and the MPK Anti-Doping Code;
(6) preserve its autonomy and resist all pressures of a political, religious or economic nature, which may prevent it from complying with the above rules;
(7) act responsibly in their actions according to the issues of environmental protection.

107. The special tasks of PKS are:

(1) on its own behalf, propose annual and special programmes which achieve general interest in the field of sports and collect from its permanent members (competent national branch sports federations of Paralympic sports), and on their behalf, propose annual and special programmes which achieve general interest in the field of sports;
(2) participate in the work of expert commissions that evaluate programmes that are financed in accordance with the Sports Law;
(3) give an opinion on the act of the Minister which determines the national branch sports federations whose programmes are financed from the budget of the Republic of Serbia, sports branches and sports facilities of importance for the Republic of Serbia;
(4) participate in the work of the commission for the preparation of the categorization of sports, athletes and sports experts and performs ranking;
(5) prepare an expert opinion – whether an activity belongs to a sports activity and to which sports discipline and sports branch, i.e., area it belongs, as well as which international sports federation has the status of a competent international sports federation in accordance with the Sports Law;
(6) participate in the work of the Management Board of the Republic Institute for Sports and Sports Medicine of the Republic of Serbia (*see* Article 1 of The Statute of PKS).[18]

108. The same provisions regarding rights and obligations apply to the OKS and PKS, which indicates that the Olympians and Paralympians are equal in the normative plan of the Republic of Serbia. In this way, a coherent and functional sports system in the Republic of Serbia was created, largely thanks to the joint work of the Ministry of Youth and Sports of the Republic of Serbia, as the main factor in the sports system in Serbia and the non-governmental sector. The best confirmation of the success of the work and sustainability of the sports system is the numerous successes of athletes in national and international competitions.

109. By investing in sports at all levels, the Republic of Serbia has shown that it recognizes its importance and the role it has in society.

---

18. Statute of the Paralympic Committee of Serbia, *See also* https://paralympic.rs/assets/documents/docs/Paraolimpijski%20komitet%20Srbije%20-Statut.pdf, accessed 28 Aug. 2021.

III. Sports Federation of Serbia and Other Territorial Sports Federations

110. The Sports Federation of Serbia is an important factor in the sports system because it unites the activities of territorial federations of the whole of Serbia, coordinates and directs their work.

111. Organizations in the field of sports from a certain territory establish, for the purpose of regulating and realizing sports issues of common interest, a territorial sports federation (for the Republic of Serbia, an autonomous province, a unit of local self-government, a city municipality).

112. The Sports Federation of Serbia is a territorial sports federation for the Republic of Serbia, which includes the competent national branch sports federations, competent national sports federations for area of sport, national professional and other sports associations, as well as territorial sports federations for the autonomous province, local self-government unit and city municipality.

113. The Sports Federation of Serbia performs activities that provide conditions for monitoring, development and improvement of sports recreation, children's sports, including physical education of preschool children and school sports, university sports, sports in the diaspora and top sports in non-Olympic sports, as well as other activities in accordance with the LSRS and the National Strategy for the Development of Sports (hereinafter: the Strategy), and in particular:

(1) determines, as an entrusted job, the status of a person who independently engages in sports as the only and basic occupation on the basis of criteria for determining that quality, which will be determined with the consent of the Ministry;
(2) resolves arbitration disputes for non-Olympic sports, areas of sport and territorial sports federations;
(3) participates in the work of the Management Board of the Republic Institute;
(4) proposes on its behalf, annual and special programmes that achieve general interest in the field of sports and collect from the competent national branch sports federations through which the general interest in non-Olympic sports is realized, competent national sports federations through which the general interest in certain areas of sports and territorial sports federations and on their behalf, proposes annual and special programmes that achieve in the field of sports;
(5) participates in the work of expert commissions that evaluate programmes that are financed in accordance with this Law;
(6) gives an opinion on the act of the Minister which determines the competent national sports federation for the branch, i.e., field of sports, sports branches and sports disciplines in the Republic of Serbia and sports branches that are of special importance for the Republic of Serbia;
(7) participates in the work of the commission for the preparation of the categorization of sports, athletes and sports experts and performs ranking;

(8) gives an opinion regarding the candidacy for the organization of large international sports competitions on the territory of the Republic;
(9) temporarily exercises the competencies and rights and obligations from Articles 99, 100 and 106 of this Law if the competent national branch sports federation is not formed in a certain branch of sport or field of sport, i.e., the competent national sports federation for the field of sport, or national sports federation loses the status of the competent national branch sports federation, i.e., the competent national sports federation for the field of sports, or the competent national branch sports federation, i.e., the competent national sports federation for the field of sports, does not function in accordance with this Law, unless otherwise prescribed by this Law;
(10) temporarily exercises the competencies of the territorial sports federation of the local self-government unit in which the territorial sports federation has not been formed or it does not function in accordance with this Law;
(11) takes care of improving the health protection of athletes and sports experts in non-Olympic sports and preventing negative phenomena in sports;
(12) monitors the realization of the functions of territorial sports federations in local self-government units and approves and implements programmes, i.e., projects financed from public revenues in local self-government units, and submits a report to the Ministry and local self-government units twice a year.

114. The provisions of the LSRS relating to branch sports federations shall apply according to the establishment, entry in the Register and performance of sports activities, acquisition of funds and realization of income, as well as to other issues related to the work of the territorial sports federation, unless otherwise is determined by this Law.

115. By a decision, the Ministry determines the fulfilment of the conditions for the Sports Federation of Serbia to temporarily exercise the competencies and rights of the national sports federation, i.e., to temporarily exercise the competencies of the territorial sports federation.

116. The Sports Federation of Serbia is obliged to adopt a framework programme for the development of branches and areas of sports within the limits of its competencies determined by the LSRS, for at least four years, and to submit it to the Ministry within fifteen days.

117. The Sports Federation of Serbia has the status of a competent national sports federation in terms of exercising its competencies determined by Law.

118. An administrative dispute may be initiated against the decision of the Ministry, in accordance with the Law (*see* Article 102 of the LSRS).

119. It is important to point out that the Ministry performs administrative and professional supervision over the Sports Federation of Serbia and territorial sports federations.

120. The Minister of Youth and Sports adopts the Rulebook on the National Categorization of National Branch Sports Associations, which determines the criteria for ranking and the rank of competent national branch sports associations in the Republic of Serbia.

121. According to this rulebook, the competent national sports federations are ranked according to the following criteria:

- the rank of the sports branch in accordance with the National categorization of sports branches;
- achieved sports results achieved by athletes, sports organizations and national sports teams of the competent national branch sports federation at international sports competitions;
- number of registered sports organizations, athletes and sports experts with the competent national branch sports federation;
- the national tradition of the branch of sport and the competent national branch sports association;
- the number and type of competitions that are organized within the framework of the competent national sports federation.

Competent national sports federations are classified into six categories:

- first category (Water Polo Federation of Serbia, Rowing Federation of Serbia, Kayaking Federation of Serbia, Basketball Federation of Serbia, Volleyball Federation of Serbia, Swimming Federation of Serbia, Wrestling Federation of Serbia, Handball Federation of Serbia, Serbian Athletics Federation, Shooting Federation of Serbia, Tennis Federation of Serbia, Taekwondo Association of Serbia, Football Association of Serbia, Judo Association of Serbia);
- second category (Cycling Federation of Serbia, Badminton Federation of Serbia, Boxing Federation of Serbia, Aviation Federation of Serbia, Gymnastics Federation of Serbia, Disabled Shooting Federation of Serbia, Karate Federation of Serbia, Kickboxing Federation of Serbia, Bowling Federation of Serbia, National Sports Federation of the Blind and Visually Impaired, Paralympic Committee of Serbia, Mountaineering Association of Serbia, Table Tennis Association of Serbia, Sports Association of the Deaf of Serbia, Table Tennis Association of Persons with Disabilities of Serbia, 'Special Olympics of Serbia', Chess Association of Serbia);
- third category (Sailing Federation of Serbia, Jiu Jitsu Federation of Serbia, Fencing Federation of Serbia, Motorcycle Federation of Serbia, Rugby Federation of Serbia, Dance Federation of Serbia, Savate Federation of Serbia, Federation of Serbia for Body Building, Fitness, Body Fitness and Aerobics, Federation of Serbia for Lifting weights, Federation for Synchronized Swimming of Serbia, Association of Disabled Seated Volleyball of Serbia, Association of Disabled Archers of Serbia, Ice Hockey Association of Serbia, Association of Sports Anglers of Serbia, Association for Equestrian Sports of Serbia for Olympic and FEI disciplines, Sports Car and Karting Association of Serbia, Ski Association of Serbia,

Serbian Association of American Football, Serbian Galloping Association, Serbian Trotting Association, Serbian Triathlon, Archery Association of Serbia, Jet Ski and Motorboat Association of Serbia);
- fourth category (Aikido Association of Serbia, Baseball Association of Serbia, Cycling Association of Persons with Disabilities of Serbia, Bocce Association of Serbia, Bridge Association of Serbia, Go Association of Serbia, Golf Association of Serbia, Kendo Association of Serbia, Kyokushin Kai Association of Serbia, Skating Association of Serbia, Korfball Association of Serbia, National Curling Association of Serbia, Orienteering Association of Serbia, Darts Federation of Serbia, Rafting Association of Serbia, Rugby 13 Federation of Serbia, Sambo Association of Serbia, Association of Underwater Activities of the Republic of Serbia, Diving Association of Serbia, Association for Water Skiing and Wakeboarding of Serbia, Field Hockey Association of Serbia, Sports Association of the Disabled of Serbia, Sports Climbing Association of Serbia, Tug of War Association of Serbia);
- fifth category (Ashihara Kaikan Association of Serbia, Biathlon Association of Serbia, Billiard Association of Serbia, Bobsleigh Association of Serbia, Bowling Association of Serbia, Serbian Kungfu Wushu Association, Cricket Federation of Serbia, Paintball Association of Serbia, Powerlifting Association of Serbia, Association for Practical Shooting of Serbia - I.P.S.C Serbia);
- sixth category (all other competent national branch sports federations for sports branches that are not of special importance for the Republic of Serbia).

IV. Competent Branch Sports Federation

122. Branch sports federations can be established for certain sports branches.

123. The competent branch sports federation represents the highest form of sports association in a certain branch of sports of the Republic of Serbia. The competent national branch sports federation uses Republic of Serbia in its name, in accordance with the Law.

124. The name of the international branch sports federation may be in a foreign language and Latin alphabet (*see* Articles 100–101 of the LSRS).

125. The competent national branch sports federation has an exclusive role in a certain branch of sport for representing the national sport in international competitions and in international sports federations, organizing and conducting national sports competitions and arranging the performance of sports activities through sports rules. The competent national branch sports federation gives an opinion to the Ministry on the existence of interest in admitting to the citizenship of the Republic of Serbia an athlete or sports expert who is a foreign citizen.

126. Only one sports federation can acquire the status of a competent national branch sports federation in one branch of sport, except in the case of sports for persons with disabilities.

127. The President of the Board or a representative of the National Branch Sports Federation or another national sports federation may not be a member of the Board, President or representative of another organization in the field of sports, except the Board of the OKS, PKS, Sports Federation of Serbia, Republic Institute and Provincial Institute.

128. The competent national branch sports federations and other national sports federations, territorial sports federations, professional sports clubs and sports organizations competing in national sports leagues must have an employed or engaged sports expert or a sports expert who has passed the sports professional examination.

129. The professional sports exam is taken before the Commission formed by the Minister from the ranks of prominent experts in the field of sports. The Minister shall prescribe the programme, content, manner and costs of taking the professional sports exam, the form of the certificate of passing the professional sports exam and regulate other issues related to the professional sports exam. Appropriate personal data shall be entered in the certificate of passing the professional sports exam.

130. The competent national branch sports federation is obliged to publish the annual financial report and audit report on the Agency's website.

131. The competent national branch sports federation determines sports rules in the appropriate branch of sport, and in accordance with the Law and sports rules of the competent international sports federation.

132. The sports rules from the paragraph are determined:

(1) system, propositions, rules and calendar of competitions, including determination of amateur and professional sports competitions and leagues;
(2) rules for organizing sports competitions;
(3) conditions and criteria for participation in sports competitions and the procedure for determining their fulfilment, including conditions for the performance of foreign athletes and athletes competing for foreign national teams;
(4) conditions and criteria for participation in the national league sports competition, i.e., professional sports competition, and the procedure for determining their fulfilment (season permit);
(5) manner and procedure of registration of the contract between the athlete, i.e., sports expert, and the organization and general (minimum) conditions for concluding the contract between the athlete, i.e., sports expert, and the sports organization;
(6) conditions for organizing and participating in sports organizations in competitions for the territory of several countries or several regions of different countries;
(7) conditions and manner of registration of athletes and sports experts for a sports organization, including registration of foreign athletes and sports experts;

(8) measures to prevent negative phenomena in sports (doping, violence and misconduct, falsification of sports results, racism and chauvinism, illegal betting, etc.);
(9) medical care of athletes;
(10) disciplinary proceedings and disciplinary sanctions;
(11) status of athletes and sports professionals and transfers of athletes and sports professionals to domestic and foreign sports organizations, including transfers and cede of athletes and sports professionals to domestic and foreign sports organizations, including transfer of athletes between sports organizations;
(12) conditions for mediation in the transfer of athletes and sports experts from one sports organization to another;
(13) status of sports referee, refereeing at competitions, supervision of refereeing and status and competencies of other officials at sports competitions;
(14) performing professional work in sports organizations;
(15) other issues determined by the law and sports rules of the competent international sports federation.

133. The competent national branch sports federation is obliged to submit a copy of these rules to the Ministry, including later amendments to the rules, within fifteen days from the day the sport rules come into force, calculating the deadline separately for each general act establishing sports rules. The competent national branch sports federation is obliged to publish the sports rules from this article on the official website of that federation.

134. The competent national branch sports federation is obliged to adopt a programme for the development of the branch of sport for which it was established, for at least four years, and to submit it to the Ministry within fifteen days from the day of its adoption.

135. The competent national branch sports federation is obliged to submit to the Ministry a certified translation of the statute of the competent international sports federation, including later amendments to that statute. The provisions of the LSRS, which refer to national branch sports federations, shall accordingly apply to international branch sports federations having their seat on the territory of the Republic of Serbia.

V. Sports Associations

136. Sports associations are independent and non-profit associations. Their importance was also recognized by the legislator, so a large part of the provisions of the LSRS is dedicated to their establishment, organization and functioning.

137. A sports association can be founded by at least three founders.

138. The founder of a sports association can be a fully business-capable person or a legal entity.

139. The sports association is established at the founding assembly, by adopting and signing the founding act and statute and by electing or appointing a person authorized to represent it.

140. The founding act of a sports association is made in writing and contains: business name, legal form, registered office and ID number of the founder and signature of the founder's representative if the founder is a legal entity, i.e., personal name, address, unique personal identification number and signature of the founder if the founder is a businessman; name, address, and number and country of insurance of the travel document if the founder is a foreign businessman; basic goals of the sports association; name and seat of the sports association; personal name, address, unique personal identification number of the citizen, i.e., the number and country of insurance of the travel document of the person authorized to represent the sports association; date of adopting of the founding act.

141. The founding act must be certified in accordance with the Law (Articles 38–39 LSRS).

142. The general acts of a sports association are: the statute, the rulebook and the decision which regulate certain issues in a general way.

143. The statute is the basic general act of the sports association. It is obligatory and regulated by the statute:

(1) name and seat of the sports association;
(2) goals, content of activities and determination of sports branch and sports discipline, i.e., area of sports in which sports goals are achieved;
(3) authorities, their powers, the manner of election and dismissal, the duration of the mandate and the manner of decision-making;
(4) the procedure of adoption, i.e., amendments to the statute and other general acts of the sports association;
(5) representation of a sports association;
(6) making the work public;
(7) conditions and manner of membership and termination of membership, determining the amount of membership fees, rights, obligations and responsibilities of members, especially minors;
(8) the manner of acquiring funds for achieving sports goals and disposing of funds;
(9) way of deciding on status changes;
(10) dealing with the property of the sports association in case of termination of the association;
(11) the procedure for adopting financial and other reports;
(12) the form and content of the seal;
(13) economic and other activities that the sports association directly performs;
(14) other issues of importance for the sports association, as well as other issues determined by Law. Every member of a sports association has the right to

receive a copy of the statute of the sports association. The statute and other general acts of the sports association must be in accordance with the sports rules and the LSRS.

144. Individual acts adopted by authorized persons in a sports association must be in accordance with the general acts of the sports association, sports rules and the law.

145. The statute of a sports association is registered and published on the website of the Business Registers Agency (hereinafter: the Agency), in accordance with the law governing the registration procedure in the Agency.

146. The provisions of the general act of a sports association are subject to the assessment of constitutionality and legality in accordance with the Constitution and the law.

147. The Sports Association has a long time to submit an application for entry in the Register within thirty days from the day of delivery of final decisions on annulment of new general acts, i.e., decisions on appropriate amendments to the general act.

148. If the statute of the sports association, i.e., certain provisions of the statute, is annulled, and the sports association does not make a new statute, i.e., the decision on appropriate changes to the statute – the sports association ceases to exist and is deleted from the Register.

149. This provision is accordingly applied in the case when, in accordance with the Constitution and the law, the unconstitutionality, i.e., the illegality of the provision of the general act of the sports association, has been established.

150. Any member of a sports association may initiate proceedings before the locally competent basic court to determine the nullity of the general act of the sports association that was passed contrary to the statute of the sports association or sports rules, in accordance with the law governing the association.

151. The founders of a sports association are jointly and severally liable, with all their property, for the obligations assumed in connection with the establishment of a sports association unless otherwise stipulated by the contract with third parties who have claims on that basis. The sports association is jointly and severally liable for the obligations of the founders from the moment of entry in the Register.

152. The sports association has a name and a seat. The name of the sports association must be in the Serbian language and the Cyrillic alphabet, i.e., in the Serbian language and the Cyrillic alphabet and the languages and scripts that are in official use in the territory where its headquarters are located.

153. The name of a sports association may also be in a foreign language, i.e., it may also contain certain foreign words, if they form the name of the founder, i.e., if they are common in the Serbian language or if there are no appropriate words for them in the Serbian language, i.e., about words in a dead language. The name is determined by the statute of the sports association and is entered in the Register. A sports association may also have an abbreviated name, which is determined by the statute. The abbreviated name is entered in the Register. The sports association for mountaineering may use the word 'society' in the name if the word 'mountaineering' is used in front of the word 'society'.

154. The name and abbreviated name of a sports association are used in legal transactions in the form in which they are entered in the Register. The branch of the sports association in legal transactions appears under the name of the sports association and its name. The name of a sports association can be transferred to another person only within the status change. The name of a newly established sports association must be clearly distinguished from the names of other sports associations that are registered or duly registered for entry in the Register.

155. It must be clear from the name of the sports association that it is a sports organization. The name of a sports association must not be misleading as to the branch or field of sport to which the sports association belongs or what type of legal entity it is or which legal entity it is. Notwithstanding paragraph 1 of this Article, a newly established sports association may use the name or part of the name of a sports association already entered in the Register, provided that the name of the newly established sports association contains the seat of the newly established sports association duly registered for entry in the Register. The name of a sports association may contain the name of the Republic of Serbia, an autonomous province or a unit of local self-government, with the prior consent of the competent authority of the Republic of Serbia, an autonomous province or a unit of local self-government.

156. The name of a sports association may contain the name or part of the name of a natural person, with his consent, and if that person died, with the consent of all heirs of the first hereditary order, consent may be withdrawn.

157. The name of a sports association cannot contain the name of a foreign country or international organization. This does not refer to the adjective use of the name of the domestic or foreign state, territorial unit and international organization, i.e., the indication of the territorial unit as the seat of the sports association. The seat of the sports association must be on the territory of the Republic of Serbia, provided that the seat from which the activities of the association are managed is determined. In business correspondence and in public appearances, the sports association states its seat along with its name.

158. The sports association may have its own sign, logo and other symbols, in accordance with the statute. The symbols of the visual identity of a sports association must be clearly distinguished from the symbols of other sports organizations and must not be misleading as to the objectives of the sports association and its identity. Symbols of the visual identity of a sports association may not contain symbols of a foreign state or international organization. Symbols of the visual identity of a sports association may contain symbols of the Republic of Serbia, an autonomous province or a unit of local self-government, with the prior consent of the competent authority of the Republic of Serbia, an autonomous province or a unit of local self-government. Symbols of the visual identity of a sports association cannot be the subject of a pledge (*see* Articles 40–48 of the LSRS).

159. Members of a sports association are the founders and persons who subsequently join the sports association in accordance with its statute.

160. The sports association keeps a book of members, including data on their right to manage the association. The following data are entered in the book of members of the sports association: name, father's name and surname; date of birth; citizenship; the number of the personal document that serves as a means of identification; address of residence and domicile; contact details; date of membership; date of termination of membership; membership category in accordance with the statute of the association; election to the bodies of a sports association; disciplinary sanctions imposed. The Minister regulates in more detail the content, except for personal data, the form and the manner of keeping the book of members.

161. An individual may be a member of a sports association regardless of age, in accordance with the Law and the Statute. A sports association may, in accordance with the statute, have different categories of members, with different rights and obligations, provided that members of the same category must have the same rights and obligations and that a member of a sports association cannot be deprived of the right to vote by statute. The statement on joining, i.e., joining a sports association for a minor who has not reached the age of 14, is given by a minor with the prior written consent of the parents or guardians.[19]

162. Any person may, under equal conditions determined by the statute, become a member of a sports association. Athletes who are members of a sports association have the right to withdraw from the association at any time, but the sports rules of the competent national branch sports federation may stipulate that notice period in sports, where the rules provide for a transitional period, may last no longer than the beginning of the first subsequent transitional period, and in other sports a maximum of six months.

163. An athlete may not unilaterally withdraw from a sports association in the event that he has contracted to remain a member until the expiration of a certain period, unless, in accordance with the law, the contract is terminated, annulled or its nullity is established. Membership in a sports association cannot be transferred or

19. The amount of the monthly membership fee for minor athletes may not exceed one-tenth of the average salary at the level of the Republic of Serbia determined by the republic body responsible for statistics for the previous budget year.

inherited. A member of a sports association may be expelled from the sports association for reasons and according to the procedure determined by the statute.

164. The general acts of a sports association must provide for the right to appeal the decision of the association's body which decided on the rights and obligations of the members of the association unless the arbitration is competent for making a decision in accordance with this law.

165. A member of a sports association may be subject to disciplinary sanctions in accordance with the law, sports rules and general acts of the sports association, provided that he cannot be punished for a disciplinary offence for which he is not guilty and which was not a general act of the sports association determined as a disciplinary offence and for which no penalty was prescribed unless otherwise provided by law. A member of a sports association has the right in a disciplinary procedure to: conduct the procedure without delay and with as few costs as possible; independence, expertise and impartiality of the authority deciding on responsibility; defence counsel at personal expense; statement and presentation of evidence; written and reasoned decision and appeal. A member of a sports association may not be disciplined for exercising his rights in accordance with the law, sports rules and general acts of the association.

166. The sports association has its own governing bodies and assets.

167. The sports association is managed by its members in a manner determined by the statute of the association. Members manage the sports association directly or through their elected representatives in the bodies of the association. The sports association in sports recreation is directly managed by all members with equal voting rights (Articles 49–52 of the ZS).

168. Every sports association must have an assembly, and sports associations with more than twenty members have a board elected by the assembly of the association, in a manner determined by the statute.

169. The governing body of a sports association (board of directors, presidency, executive board, etc.) has at least three members.

170. A representative of a sports association may be a member of the board of the sports association.

171. Decisions of the management of a sports association are made by a majority vote of the total number of members of the management unless the statute of the sports association determines a different majority (*see* Article 56 of the LSRS). Sports associations are entered in the appropriate register (*see* Article 65 of the LSRS).

172. With regard to the performance of economic activity, it should be noted that a sports association may perform only one economic activity in accordance with the statute, to the extent that corresponds to the goals of the company and that it is registered (*see* Article 72 of the LSRS).

173. A sports association can be terminated in one of the following ways:

(1) if the number of members is reduced below the number required for establishment, and the competent body of the association does not make a decision on the admission of new members within thirty days;
(2) if the competent body of the sports association makes a decision on the termination of the association;
(3) status change and change of legal form leading to the termination of the association;
(4) if a measure of prohibition to perform sports activities has been imposed on him because he does not meet the conditions for their performance, and does not meet those conditions within the period specified in the imposed measure;
(5) if it has been determined by a final decision of the competent court that the registration of the establishment of a sports association was null and void;
(6) if he is forbidden to work;
(7) if it is determined that it has stopped working;
(8) in other cases determined by the law, the founding act or the statute of the sports association which are stated as the basis for the termination of the association;
(9) bankruptcy.

174. The sports association is terminated by deletion from the Register (*see* Article 86 of the LSRS).

175. The importance of sports associations for the development of sports is immeasurable because they enable its continuous development and progress.

176. The Sports Organization itself represents a very complex, dynamic and open system, which consists of certain components and elements, which form a whole.

177. In accordance with the LS and on the basis of the Rulebook on National Records in the field of sports, a database was created, i.e., National record of registered sports organizations on the territory of the Republic of Serbia.

178. According to the latest updated data of the Republic Institute for Sports and Sports Medicine, based on registration in the national records in the Republic of Serbia, a total of 16,121 sports organizations are registered, of which 12,668 are sports clubs, other sports activities are registered in 2,719 cases, while the activity of fitness clubs is predominant at 734 sports organizations.

179. The Sports Organization itself represents a very complex, dynamic and open system, which consists of certain components and elements, which form a whole.

180. In accordance with the LS and on the basis of the Rulebook on National Records in the field of sports, a database was created, i.e., National record of registered sports organizations on the territory of the Republic of Serbia.

181. According to the latest updated data of the Republic Institute for Sports and Sports Medicine, based on registration in the national records in the Republic of Serbia, a total of 16,121 sports organizations are registered, of which 12,668 are sports clubs, other sports activities are registered in 2,719 cases, while the activity of fitness clubs is predominant at 734 sports organizations.

182. According to data from the National Records of the Republic Institute for Sports and Sports Medicine, most sports organizations perform their activities in the City of Belgrade, more than one-fourth or more precisely 26.51% of the total number of registered organizations on the territory of the Republic of Serbia. In addition to the City of Belgrade, the number of sports organizations registered in the territory of four administrative districts - Južnobački, Sremski, Nišavski and Južnobanatski (in total, there are twenty-nine districts in Serbia, including the city of Belgrade) make up about half of the total number of registered sports organizations in the territory of the Republic of Serbia, which can indicate an uneven development of sports depending on the region.

183. According to the data entered by the representatives of sports organizations, sports activities on the territory of the Republic of Serbia are performed in a total of 123 sports bran football - a total of 3501 sports organizations or more than one-fifth, more precisely 21.72%. This information only confirms that football, as a branch of sport, is by far the most popular in Serbia.ches and areas of the country, and the most registered sports branch is Sports organizations registered for the sport of football along with seven other sports (basketball, karate, fitness, fishing, volleyball, chess and handball) makeup about half of the total number of registered sports organizations on the territory of the Republic of Serbia.

VI. Professional and Other Associations in the Field of Sports

184. Sports experts, for the purpose of arranging and realizing professional sports issues of common interest, join professional sports associations (associations of coaches, sports judges, etc.).[20] Sports organizations, sports associations, sports federations and other legal individuals may, in order to achieve common goals and

20. An association in the field of sports is not considered to be an association whose basic statutory reason for establishment is not the achievement of goals in the field of sports, but the achievement of some other permissible goal, in accordance with the law governing the work of the association.

interests in the field of sports, establish other associations (organizing committees, fan associations, etc.) and federations in the field of sports.

185. The provisions of the LSRS, which refer to sports associations, shall apply accordingly to the establishment, entry in the Register and performance of sports activities, as well as to other issues related to the work of associations and federations.

186. Sports organizations and professional and other associations and federations in a particular field of sport may associate appropriate sports federations for the field of sports, in accordance with the law and sports rules of the competent national sports federation for a particular field of sport.

187. The provisions of the LSRS relating to branch sports federations shall apply accordingly to the establishment, entry in the Register and performance of sports activities and sports activities, acquisition of funds and realization of income, as well as to other issues related to the work of the sports federation not otherwise specified (*see* Articles 105–106 of the LSRS). These associations are a form of professional organization of sports workers, which aim to improve the position and working conditions of workers in sports.

VII. Sports Associations

188. Sports associations are a special form of association for the purpose of arranging and achieving common goals and interests, as well as joint performance in the field of sports, to associate in sports associations.

189. The sports association is the holder of the right to a common name and common symbols unless otherwise provided by the statute of the sports association.

190. On the establishment, entry in the Register, performing sports activities and sports activities, acquiring funds and generating income, resolving disputes, liability, as well as other issues related to the work of sports associations, the provisions of the LS, which refer to sports associations, shall apply accordingly, unless otherwise provided by this Law (*see* Article 96 of the LSRS).

191. There are two well-known sports clubs in Serbia, with clubs in their composition – SD ‘Crvena Zvezda’ and SD ‘Partizan’.

VIII. Sports Economic Association

192. Sports economic associations perform economic activities in the field of sports.

193. The name of a sports economic association must not be misled as to the branch or area of sport to which the sports company belongs or the type of legal entity in question.

194. A sports economic association may be established by natural and/or legal persons, in accordance with the LSRS.

195. A sports economic association may be established as a limited liability company or a joint-stock company.

196. A sports economic association may hire or register athletes and sports experts on the basis of a concluded contract.

197. A sports economic association may perform sports activities if it meets the requirements of Article 35 of the LSRS and if those activities are performed as the predominant activity of a sports company. The fulfilment of the conditions is determined by a decision of the sports inspector within the inspection supervision. The decision of the sports inspector may be appealed to the Ministry within fifteen days from the day of delivery of the decision.

198. The net profit realized by the association in the current year must be at least 70% reinvested in the sports activities of that company.

199. The same person may not directly, indirectly or through related parties, in terms of the law governing companies, be the owner or share in more than one sports company in the same level of competition, and within the same branch of sport may have stocks or shares that account for a maximum of 5% of the share capital of a sports company only in another sports company.

200. Stocks or shares of a sports company may not, directly, indirectly or through related parties have persons whose jobs and activities may directly affect the competition in the relevant branch of sport, i.e., the level of competition (sports judges, sports mediators, athletes, coaches, etc.), as well as owners of sports bookmakers and employees of sports bookmakers.

201. If a person acquires shares, i.e., shares contrary to the provisions, he is obliged to alienate his shares, i.e., shares that he acquired without delay, even though he was not entitled to it, and until he does so, he cannot exercise the rights from acquired shares or shares into one sports organization. Until the alienation of the share, i.e., stocks, the rights from the share, i.e., shares, are exercised by the commissioner when appointed by the competent national branch sports federation.

202. A person who has shares or stocks in a sports company, and who is elected or appointed to a public office or a position in a body of a political party is obliged to transfer the management rights based on the shares to the legal or an individual who is not a person related to him, that he, in his own name, and on behalf of the official, performs them until the termination of public office, i.e., function in the body of a political party, and to inform the sports company about this transfer. Acquisition of a share, i.e., action, contrary to this law is null and void.

203. The provisions of the LS Arbitration shall apply according to the resolution of disputes arising in connection with the performance of sports activities and activities of a sports economic association with other participants in the sports system.

204. The regulations governing the protection of competition shall accordingly apply to the violation of competition in the performance of sports activities unless this is contrary to the very nature of sports activities.

205. The provisions of the law which regulates the takeover of joint-stock companies by publishing takeover bids do not apply to a sports company established in the form of a joint-stock company (*see* Article 92 of the LSRS).

206. When it comes to the organization of sports associations and sports companies, although there are many similarities because it is about sports organizations, there are still certain differences. Namely, a sports economic association may be established by a legal entity or individual with the status of a joint-stock company or a limited liability company, with the primary goal of making a profit, which is not the case with a sports association. In addition, sports companies must respect the regulations of commercial law.

IX. Entrepreneur

207. An entrepreneur is an individual who has a certain role in the sports system.

208. An entrepreneur engaged in professional work in the field of sports must have an appropriate sports title in accordance with LSRS.

209. An entrepreneur may perform sports activities if he has provided the appropriate facility, appropriate equipment, hired appropriate sports experts and if he meets the requirements in terms of safety in performing activities, including the necessary acts (rules of order, etc.) unless otherwise provided by law.

210. The Minister shall prescribe more detailed conditions. The fulfilment of the conditions is determined by a decision of the sports inspector within the inspection supervision. The decision of the sports inspector may be appealed to the Ministry within fifteen days from the day of delivery of the decision.

211. Mediation activities during the transfer of an athlete or sports expert from one sports organization to another and during the conclusion of a contract between an athlete, i.e., sports expert and sports organization, may be performed by a company or entrepreneur in the field of sports if he has a work permit issued by the competent national branch sports federation, as well as other persons in accordance with the rules of the competent international sports federation (hereinafter: sports mediation organization).

212. A sports mediation organization may perform the activity of sports mediation provided that it has an engaged sports expert with the appropriate sports title and the appropriate work permit issued by the competent national branch sports federation.

213. The competent national branch sports federation determines the conditions and procedure for obtaining a work permit. The Ministry gives its consent.

214. The competent national branch sports federation issues a work permit to the sports mediation organization and notifies the Ministry of each issuance of the licence, within fifteen days from the day of issuance.

215. The competent national branch sports federation is obliged to make a public announcement on the official website of the federation of issued work permits.

216. Appropriate personal data shall be entered into the work permit of the sports mediation organization.

217. A work permit issued to a sports mediation organization by the competent international sports federation shall be considered a valid work permit for the period for which it was issued.

218. The contract on mediation in sports, as well as all amendments to that contract, are concluded in writing and certified in accordance with the law and must contain the amount of compensation to the organization for sports mediation, the term for which it is concluded and the scope of authorization of the organization for sports mediation and the power of attorney, otherwise, it is void.

219. The contract on mediation in sports is concluded for a maximum period of two years, with the proviso that the contract on mediation may be re-concluded between the same contracting parties after the expiration of this period.

220. An agreement between an athlete or sports expert and a sports organization concluded with the mediation or representation of a sports mediation organization must contain the designation of the sports mediation organization, otherwise, it is void.

221. A sports mediation organization may protect the interests of only one party from the mediation contract, otherwise, it owes compensation to the person with whom it has concluded a mediation contract.

222. A mediation contract with an athlete who does not have full legal capacity can be validly concluded only with the prior written and certified in accordance with the law consent of both parents or guardians.

223. The provisions of the LSRS that refer to the organization for sports mediation also apply to all natural and legal persons who have concluded agreements on investment in athletes, i.e., sports experts, on the basis of which they are entitled to a part of income arising from performing their sports activities.

224. Legal and natural persons who do not participate in sports competitions that are within the competent national branch sports federation that organizes sports competitions and whose predominant activity is the provision of professional work in sports (football schools, tennis schools, camps, fitness centres, other sports centres etc.), they may perform sports activities only in the form of uneconomic association, i.e., the appropriate form of entrepreneurship, and they may not have the word 'club' or the word 'federation' or the word 'sports club' in the name of that company, i.e., the appropriate form of entrepreneurship.

225. Performing activities by a sports association contrary to the stated conditions are the basis for the termination of the sports association. The existence of conditions for the termination of a sports association is determined by the sports inspector (Articles 93–95 of the LSRS).

226. Based on the presented institutions within the governmental and non-governmental sectors in the field of sports in the Republic of Serbia, it can be concluded that the sports system in the Republic of Serbia is developing through the cooperation of state institutions, sports clubs, associations and other organizations in the field of sports.

Chapter 2. Public Regulation

227. Today, most constitutions of modern states do not contain explicit provisions that define the right to sport as a human right.[21] In the Constitution, this issue is approached indirectly.

228. The Constitution only states that everyone has the right to protection of their physical and mental health, as well as that the Republic of Serbia helps the development of health and physical culture.[22] Regarding sports, it was only mentioned that the Republic of Serbia, within its competence, regulates and provides a system in the field of sports.[23]

229. LSRS states that the right to sport is a basic human right, although there is no such provision in the Constitution.[24] This means that every person has the right to freely decide whether to engage in sports and physical activity when to do so and in what way. Freedom of choice to play sports is allowed only within the limits provided by the LSRS. The laws also list restrictions on freedom of choice. Thus, it is stated that playing sports must be humane, free, healthy, safe in accordance with the protection of the natural environment and the social environment, tolerant, fair, ethically acceptable, responsible, independent of abuses and goals contrary to the sports spirit.[25]

230. In addition to the LS as the most important legal source in the field of sports, the Law on Prevention of Doping in Sports and the Law on Prevention of Violence and Misconduct at Sports Events has been adopted in the Republic of Serbia.

231. Law on Prevention of Doping in Sports[26] regulates measures and activities to prevent doping. The constitutional framework for the enactment of this law is contained in Article 97, paragraph 10 of the Constitution of the RS, which states that the RS regulates and provides a system in the field of physical culture. The main reason for passing this Law is that doping in sports is neither a small nor a sporadic phenomenon. It is not possible to say exactly how pronounced this problem is in

21. *See*, Stefan Andonović, *Pravo na sport kao ljudsko pravo*, Strani pravni život, No. 61, Beograd, 2017, 136.
22. *See*, Art. 68, para. 1 and para. 4 of the Constitution of the Republic of Serbia, 'Official Gazette of RS', No. 98/2006.
23. *See* Art. 97, para. 1, item 10, of the Constitution of the Republic of Serbia, 'Official Gazette of RS', No. 98/2006.
24. Such a formulation can be understood in different ways. One is that the right to sports is a narrower right in relation to the right to play sports, as the right to freely choose activities and decide whether someone will play sports or not. Also, this formulation can be understood in a way that can equate the right to sports with the right to play sports. It is considered that a sign of equality should be placed between the right to sports and the right to play sports, since they cannot exist without each other, and the right to play sports may imply some additional elements. *See*, Andonović, *supra*, 138.
25. *See*, Art. 4, para. 2 of the LSRS.
26. *See*, Law on Prevention of Doping in Sports ('Official Gazette of RS', RS, Nos 111/2014 and 47/2021).

our sport because the control has been poorly done in recent years, and only recently have serious measures been taken to combat doping. Some cases of established doping of athletes at international competitions are proof that the use of illicit substances and means is present in our athletes as well. During the adoption of the LS of the Republic of Serbia, it was considered that organizations in the field of sports could fight the problem of doping, but it turned out to be an unrealistic expectation.[27] The law consists of four parts: basic provisions, anti-doping agency provisions, supervision and penal provisions.

232. Law on Prevention of Violence and Misconduct at Sports Events[28] measures for the prevention of violence and misconduct at sports events and in connection with sports events are determined, as well as the obligations of the organizers and the powers of the competent authorities in the implementation of these measures. According to the provisions of this law, sports events include sports competitions and sports events. The adoption of this Law is a key step in regulating this matter. The law consists of three parts: basic provisions, measures to prevent violence and misconduct at sports events and penal provisions.[29]

233. In addition to the Constitution and the LS, public regulations in the field of sports also include ratified international conventions. The RS Constitution contains a provision stating that ratified international agreements are part of the RS legal order, that they are directly applicable and that they must be in accordance with the Constitution, omitting legal acts, which logically says that laws must be in accordance with ratified international agreements.[30] On the basis of ratified international conventions and documents important for the field of sports in the Republic of Serbia, the Law on Ratification of the European Convention against Doping in Sport and the Law on Ratification of the European Convention for the Prevention of Violence and Misconduct at Sports Events, especially Football Matches.

234. Law on Ratification of the European Convention against Doping in Sport[31] ratified the European Convention against Doping in Sport, as amended, done at Strasbourg on 16 November 1989, in the original in the English and French languages.

235. Concerned about the violence and misconduct of spectators at sports events, especially at football matches, RS has passed the Law on Ratification of the European Convention for the Prevention of Violence and Misconduct at Sports

27. *See*, Nenad Đurđević, *Commentary on the Law on Prevention of Doping in Sports* (Kragujevac 2008), 73.
28. *See*, Law on Prevention of Violence and Misconduct at Sports Events ('Official Gazette of RS', Nos 67/2003, 101/2005 – other law, 90/2007 – other law, 111/2009, 104/2013 – other law i 87/2018).
29. *See*, Branislav Milosavljević, *Prevention of Violence at Sports Events from the Aspect of Security Services*, Archives of Legal and Social Sciences (Beograd 2013), 73.
30. *See*, Art. 16, para. 2, of the Constitution of the Republic of Serbia, 'Official Gazette of RS', No. 98/2006.
31. *See*, Law on Ratification of the European Convention against Doping in Sport ('Official Gazette of SFRJ- Međunarodni ugovori', No. 4/1991).

Events, Especially Football Matches,[32] adopted on 19 August 1985 in Strasbourg, in the original in the English and French languages.

236. In addition to the Constitution, the LS and ratified international conventions, the field of sports in the RS is legally regulated by the following laws, regulations and by-laws:

(1) Criminal Law.[33]
(2) Copyright and Related Rights Act.[34]
(3) Law on Safety and Health at Work.[35]
(4) Law on Budget System.[36]
(5) Gambling Act.[37]
(6) Law on Information and Media.[38]
(7) Law on Public Ski Resorts (LSRS).[39]
(8) Law on Public Order and Peace (LPOP).[40]
(9) Law on Ministries (LoM).[41]
(10) Law on Obligations.[42]
(11) Advertising Act.[43]
(12) Law on Geographical Indications.[44]
(13) Patent Law.[45]
(14) Law on Pension and Disability Insurance (LPDI).[46]
(15) Law on Corporate Income Tax (LCIT).[47]
(16) Law on Personal Income Tax (LPIT).[48]
(17) Property Tax Act.[49]
(18) Law on Ratification of the Nairobi Treaty on the Protection of the Olympic Symbol.[50]

32. *See*, Law on Ratification of the European Convention for the Prevention of Violence and Misconduct at Sports Events, Especially Football Matches ('Official Gazette of RS – Međunarodni ugovori', No. 9/1990).
33. *See*, Criminal Law ('Official Gazette of RS', Nos 85/2005 … 35/2019).
34. *See*, Copyright and Related Rights Act ('Official Gazette of RS', Nos 104/2009 … 66/2019).
35. *See*, Law on Safety and Health at Work ('Official Gazette of RS', Nos 101/2005 … 113/2017-other law).
36. *See*, Law on Budget System ('Official Gazette of RS', Nos 54/2009 … 113/2017).
37. *See*, Gambling Act ('Official Gazette of RS', Nos 88/2011, 93/2012).
38. *See*, Law on Information and Media ('Official Gazette of RS', Nos 83/2014 … 12/2016 – authentic interpretation).
39. *See*, Law on Public Ski Resorts ('Official Gazette of RS', No. 46/2006).
40. *See*, Law on Public Order and Peace ('Official Gazette of RS', Nos 6/2016 … 24/2018).
41. *See*, Law on Ministries ('Official Gazette of RS', Nos 44/2014 … 62/2017).
42. *See*, Law on Obligations ('Official Gazette of SFRJ', Nos 29/1978 … 'Official Gazette of SCG', No. 1/2003 – Ustavna povelja).
43. *See*, Advertising Act ('Official Gazette of RS', No. 6/2016).
44. *See*, Law on Geographical Indications ('Official Gazette of RS', No. 18/2010).
45. *See*, Patent Law ('Official Gazette of RS', Nos 99/2011, 113/2017).
46. *See*, Law on Pension and Disability Insurance ('Official Gazette of RS', Nos 34/2003 … 86/2019).
47. *See*, Law on Corporate Income Tax ('Official Gazette of RS', Nos 25/2001 … 153/2020).
48. *See*, Law on Personal Income Tax ('Official Gazette of RS', Nos 24/2001 … 44/2021).
49. *See*, Property Tax Act ('Official Gazette of RS', Nos 26/2001 … 114/2020).
50. *See*, Law on Ratification of the Nairobi Treaty on the Protection of the Olympic Symbol ('Official

(19) Law on Legal Protection of Industrial Design.[51]
(20) Misdemeanor Law.[52]
(21) Accounting law.[53]
(22) Broadcasting Act.[54]
(23) Labour Law (LL).[55]
(24) Law on Free Access to Information of Public Importance (LFAI).[56]
(25) Law on Prevention of Discrimination against Persons with Disabilities.[57]
(26) Law on Associations (LoAss).[58]
(27) Law on Determining Certain Competencies of the Autonomous Province of Vojvodina (LAPV).[59]
(28) Law on Employment and Unemployment Insurance.[60]
(29) Law on Health Insurance (LHI).[61]
(30) Law on Trademarks (LoT).[62]
(31) Code of Criminal Procedure.[63]
(32) Rulebook on more detailed criteria for determining the general interest in the field of sports.[64]
(33) Rulebook on detailed conditions and criteria for scholarships for top athletes and for financial assistance to top athletes (RTA).[65]
(34) Rulebook on detailed conditions for performing sports activities and sports activities.[66]
(35) Rulebook on doping control at sports competitions and out of competitions.[67]

Gazette of RS SRJ- Međunarodni ugovori', No. 1/1999).

51. *See*, Law on Legal Protection of Industrial Design ('Official Gazette of RS', Nos 104/2009, 45/2015).
52. *See*, Misdemeanor Law ('Official Gazette of RS', Nos 65/2013 … 98/2016).
53. *See*, Accounting law ('Official Gazette of RS', Nos 52/2013 … 73/2019 – other law).
54. *See*, Broadcasting Act ('Official Gazette of RS', Nos 42/2002 … 79/2005).
55. *See*, Labor law ('Official Gazette of RS', Nos 24/2005 … 95/2018 – authentic interpretation).
56. *See*, Law on Free Access to Information of Public Importance to Sports ('Official Gazette of RS', Nos 120/2004 … 36/2010).
57. *See*, Law on Prevention of Discrimination Against Persons with Disabilities ('Official Gazette of RS', Nos 33/2006, 13/2016).
58. *See*, Law on Associations ('Official Gazette of RS', Nos 51/2009, 99/2011).
59. *See*, Law on Determining Certain Competencies of the Autonomous Province of Vojvodina ('Official Gazette of RS', Nos 99/2009, 67/2012).
60. *See*, Law on Employment and Unemployment Insurance ('Official Gazette of RS', Nos 36/2009 … 113/2017 – other law).
61. *See*, Health Insurance Act ('Official Gazette of RS', No. 25/2019).
62. *See*, Trademark Law ('Official Gazette of RS', Nos 104/2009, 10/2013).
63. *See*, Code of Criminal Procedure ('Official Gazette of RS', Nos 72/2011 … 55/2014).
64. *See*, Rulebook on detailed criteria for determining the general interest in the field of sports ('Official Gazette of RS', No. 39/2006).
65. *See*, Rulebook on detailed conditions and criteria for scholarships for top athletes and for financial assistance to top athletes ('Official Gazette of RS', No. 124/2012).
66. *See*, Rulebook on detailed conditions for performing sports activities and sports activities ('Official Gazette of RS', No. 42/2017).
67. *See*, Rulebook on doping control at sports competitions and out of competitions ('Official Gazette of RS', No. 38/2021).

(36) Rulebook on the Use of Public Sports Facilities and the Performance of Sports Activities in Public Sports Facilities (RSF).[68]
(37) Rulebook on national categorization of sports.[69]
(38) Rulebook on compctent national sports federations for sports branches and areas of sports in the Republic of Serbia (RCNSF).[70]
(39) Rulebook on supervision of professional work in the field of sports.[71]
(40) Rulebook on the nomenclature of sports occupations and titles (PSO).[72]
(41) Rulebook on the content and manner of keeping a single record of associations, organizations and entrepreneurs in the field of sports.[73]
(42) Rulebook on the content and manner of keeping the Register of associations, societies and federations in the field of sports (RReg).[74]
(43) Rulebook on sports branches and areas of sports in the Republic of Serbia and sports disciplines within sports branches and areas of sports (RSB).[75]
(44) Rulebook on conditions for performing sports activities and activities.[76]

237. A brief overview of the most important additional sources indicates the multidimensionality, heterogeneity and importance of sports law in the legal system of the Republic of Serbia.

238. This chapter will present the public regulations of the Republic of Serbia important for engaging in sports activities with special reference to the basic rights and freedoms of citizens of the Republic of Serbia in the field of sports: freedom of association, prohibition of discrimination in sports and sports for people with disabilities. In addition, government conditions and permits, public safety, tax treatment and dispute resolution in sports will be discussed.

§1. Freedom of Association

239. Freedom of association in sports is guaranteed within the general freedom of association defined by the Constitution, in accordance with Article 55, which reads:

---

68. *See* Rulebook on the use of public sports facilities and the performance of sports activities in public sports facilities ('Official Gazette of RS', No. 55/2013).
69. *See* Rulebook on national categorization of sports ('Official Gazette of RS', No. 12/2017).
70. *See* Rulebook on competent national sports federations for sports branches and areas of sports in the Republic of Serbia ('Official Gazette of RS', Nos 95/2016, 45/2018).
71. *See* Rulebook on supervision of professional work in the field of sports ('Official Gazette of RS', No. 92/2011).
72. *See* Rulebook on the nomenclature of sports occupations and titles ('Official Gazette of RS', No. 7/2013).
73. *See* Rulebook on the content and manner of keeping unique records of associations, organizations and entrepreneurs in the field of sports ('Official Gazette of RS', No. 108/2017).
74. *See* Rulebook on the content and manner of keeping the Register of associations, societies and federations in the field of sports ('Official Gazette of RS', No. 24/2011).
75. *See* Rulebook on sports branches and areas of sports in the Republic of Serbia and sports disciplines within sports branches and areas of sports ('Official Gazette of RS', Nos 51/2016 … 44/2018).
76. *See* Rulebook on conditions for performing sports activities and activities ('Official Gazette of RS', No. 63/2013).

> Freedom of political, trade union and any other association and the right to remain outside any association are guaranteed. Associations are established without prior approval, with entry in the register kept by a state body, in accordance with the law. Secret and paramilitary associations are banned. The Constitutional Court may prohibit only an association whose activities are aimed at violently overthrowing the constitutional order, violating guaranteed human or minority rights or inciting racial, national or religious hatred.[77]

In this way, a solid legal framework has been created for the creation and operation of various sports associations and clubs in the Republic of Serbia.

In accordance with the stated Constitutional provisions, there are the following forms of sports associations:

(1) Sports organizations (sports associations and sports economic associations).
(2) Sports associations.
(3) Branch sports federations.
(4) Sports Federation of Serbia and other territorial sports federations.
(5) OKS.
(6) PKS.
(7) Professional and other associations and federations in the field of sports.
(8) Institute for Sports and Sports Medicine of the Republic of Serbia.
(9) Institutions and companies for performing sports activities.
(10) Sports endowments of the foundation and funds.

240. The conditions for the establishment, operation and termination of each of the above forms of sports association are defined by the provisions of the relevant laws and by-laws (*see* Articles 36–111 of the ZS), which were discussed in more detail in the previous chapter.

241. When it comes to freedom of association, we believe that due attention should be paid to sports for people with disabilities and their freedom of association.

I. Freedom of Association of Persons with Disabilities and Non-discrimination

242. Creating conditions for monitoring and development of sports for persons with disabilities is an obligation of the Republic of Serbia, the Autonomous Province of Vojvodina and local self-government units, and can be considered an important segment of public policy in the field of sports.

243. Playing recreational and professional sports is a basic human right, the validity of which extends to persons with disabilities. Protection of this right from

77. *See* Constitution of the Republic of Serbia ('Official Gazette of RS', No. 98/2006).

any form of discriminatory behaviour, in addition to the anti-discrimination legislation of the Republic of Serbia, is prescribed by the relevant provisions of the LSRS.

244. Legal provisions stipulate that everyone has the right to play sports. Playing sports must be humane, free and voluntary, healthy and safe, in accordance with the natural environment and social environment, fair, tolerant, ethically acceptable, responsible, independent of abuses and goals that are contrary to the sports spirit and available to all citizens under equal conditions, regardless of age, level of physical abilities, degree of possible disability, gender and other personal characteristics.

245. Any direct and indirect discrimination, including hate speech, on any grounds, by athletes, sports experts, sports organizations and other persons participating in the sports system, in an overt or covert manner, based on any actual or presumed personal characteristic, is prohibited. The provisions of the law governing the prohibition of discrimination shall apply to the prohibition of discrimination unless otherwise provided by this Law. The Republic of Serbia, the Autonomous Province, local self-government units and organizations in the field of sports will especially undertake activities to increase the participation of children, youth, women and persons with disabilities in sports activities, popularize women's sports organizations and give equal importance to women and persons with disabilities in sports. (Article 4 of the LSRS).

246. In addition to the provision of the LSRS for the prevention of discrimination in sports, the provisions of the Law on the Prevention of Discrimination against Persons with Disabilities (LDPD) are also important. In terms of the existence of discrimination in connection with the provision of services and use of public areas, it is prescribed that under facilities in public use, in terms of this law, are: facilities in the field of education, health, social protection, culture, sports, tourism or facilities used for environmental protection, protection from natural disasters etc. (*see* Article 13, paragraph 3 of LDPD).

247. Propagation or deliberate discrimination by a public authority in proceedings before that body, through the media, in political life, in the provision of public services, in the field of labour relations, education, culture, sports, etc. is considered a particularly serious form of discrimination (*see* Article 9, paragraph 1, item 2 LDPD). In connection with the prevention of discrimination against persons with disabilities, the legislator also prescribed special measures within the competence of local self-government. Local self-government units are obliged to take measures to ensure equal participation of persons with disabilities in the cultural, sports and religious life of the community (*see* Article 37 of the LDPD). What specific measures should be taken is prescribed by each local self-government in its general and special legal acts.

248. The prohibition of discrimination also includes the prohibition of discrimination against professional athletes and athletes who wish to become so in terms of employment, earnings or working conditions, except when making a difference, i.e., placing an athlete at a disadvantage compared to other athletes in the same or similar situation is based on nature or the actual and decisive conditions for performing a certain sports activity, and the goals that are intended to be achieved are justified. The provisions of the contract between the athlete, i.e., sports expert, and the organization in the field of sports that represent discrimination of the athlete, i.e., sports expert, are null and void, and the provisions of sports rules and general acts of organizations in the field of sports that represent discrimination of participants in the sports system do not apply. This provision aims to protect athletes from any form of discrimination. In the field of sports, all types of abuse, discrimination and violence against children are prohibited.

249. Apart from the prohibition of discrimination, the issue of classification of athletes with disabilities is also important. This area is not regulated directly by the LS, but since it is essential for playing sports in this category of people, we consider it necessary that these issues be analysed in the presentation of public regulations.

250. The definition of classification is: 'Classification provides a structure for competition'. Athletes in Paralympic sports have injuries that put them at a competitive disadvantage. The consequence is the need to introduce a system that minimizes the impact of these impairments on athletic performance and that ensures that an athlete's success depends on skill, fitness, strength, endurance, tactics, and mental focus. This system is called classification.

251. The classification determines who meets the conditions for competition in Paralympic sports and it groups athletes into sports categories in accordance with their restrictions in a particular sport.[78]

252. The main factors that determine a class in a functional classification are how much an athlete's disability affects his performance (skills) in a particular sport. The classification of athletes with disabilities in a particular sport provides an appropriate structure that allows for more neutral and fair competition.

253. Sports class is a category in which athletes are classified in relation to how much their disability affects their performance in a particular sport.

254. One sports class does not include only one form of disability, but it can include athletes of different forms of disability, but these forms of disability must have the same or equal effect on their sports performance.

255. Athletes are classified by trained classifiers who must be experts in relation to the type of disability or in relation to the sports discipline.

---

78. Serbian Paralympic Committee, *See also* http://www.paralympic.rs/paraolimpijski-pokret/o-klasifikaciji #дефиниција-класификације.

256. Each classified athlete receives their own classification card which represents their identification in competitions.[79]

257. Persons with disabilities have the right to engage in sports and recreation.

258. In order for a person with a disability to be able to successfully engage in a certain sport, recreationally or professionally, it is necessary to make certain adaptations in the sport itself and/or its rules.

259. From the aspect of ensuring the accessibility of sports and recreational facilities to persons with disabilities, Article 31 of the Convention on the Rights of Persons with Disabilities, stipulates that States Parties recognize the right of all persons with disabilities to participate in cultural life on an equal basis with others. In this context, States Parties shall also take appropriate measures to ensure that persons with disabilities can organize, develop and participate in sports activities specific to persons with disabilities. To this end, they have the right to receive appropriate instruction, training and resources on an equal footing with others. To enable persons with disabilities to have access to sports and facilities for recreation and tourism. To ensure that children with disabilities have equal access to participation in play, recreational, sports and leisure activities, including activities that take place within the education system;

260. There are also certain standards regarding the accessibility of sports facilities. It is extremely important to ensure that sports facilities are accessible to people with different types of disabilities. Sports facilities must be accessible to persons with disabilities, children and the elderly (*see* Article 145, paragraph 3 of the LSRS). This provision is particularly important because its consistent application allows people with disabilities to actively participate in sports activities, which further contributes to improving the quality of life of people with different types of disabilities.

261. Entrances must be accessible, with as few barriers as possible. Any major barrier should be overcome by ramps of appropriate slopes. Doors should be designed to be used with the least possible energy consumption. In case of danger, accessible exits for evacuation should be provided, which is extremely important for the safety of athletes with disabilities. Changing rooms must be accessible to persons of both sexes. Furniture in sports facilities, as well as the sports fields themselves, should be of contrasting colours, in order to facilitate its use by visually impaired people. All swimming pools where water sports are held must be accessible to all athletes with disabilities. Swimmers with disabilities are particularly vulnerable to injuries when entering and exiting the pool. Appropriate mobile platforms should be used to prevent such injuries. Sports facilities as a whole must be accessible to persons with disabilities, children and the elderly (*see* Article 145 LSRS).

---

79. *See*, Marko Aleksandrović, Bojan Jorgić, Filip Mirić, *Holistički pristup adaptivnom fizičkom vežbanju*-udžbenik za studente master akademskih studija, Fakultet sporta i fizičkog vaspitanja Univerziteta u Nišu, Niš, 2016, 125–131.

262. The rules on accessibility of sports facilities do not only apply to athletes with disabilities but also apply to spectators with disabilities. The Rulebook on Detailed Conditions for Performing Sports Activities and Sports Activities (PSA) stipulates that spectators with disabilities must be provided with:

(1) a separate entrance gate with appropriate access to the auditorium sector designated for them;
(2) places in the sector in the sports facility that have a good, unobstructed view of the field;
(3) provide accommodation for the companions of these persons;
(4) at least one place for spectators with disabilities should be provided for every 300 seats in the sports facility (*see* Article 8 PSA).[80]

263. Any unjustified discrimination between professional athletes would constitute discrimination, which should be combated and fought against.

§2. Government Conditions and Permits

264. As already stated, the freedom of association in sports is guaranteed within the general freedom of association defined by the Constitution, in accordance with Article 55 of the Constitution stipulates, *inter alia*, that the Constitutional Court may prohibit only an association whose activities are aimed at violently overthrowing the constitutional order, violating guaranteed human or minority rights or inciting racial, national or religious hatred.

265. According to the provisions of the LSRS, a work ban is also envisaged if the sports association does not meet the conditions for performing sports activities, and does not meet those conditions within the time limit set in the pronounced measure.

266. In addition, the scope of work of the Ministry of Youth and Sports of the Republic of Serbia includes keeping the Unified Records of Associations, Organizations and Entrepreneurs in the Field of Sports and Other Records in the Field of Sports, preparation and drafting of acts in proceedings on appeals registration with the Business Registers Agency of the Republic of Serbia in the second instance procedure, inspection supervision in accordance with the LS and regulations adopted on the basis of that law, preparation and drafting of acts in proceedings on appeals against reports on expert supervision in the second instance procedure, preparation and drafting of acts in proceedings on appeals against decisions of the sports inspector in the second instance procedure, as well as preparation and drafting of acts in court and other proceedings before the competent bodies and institutions within the scope of work.

80. *See* Art. 8. PSA, Branimir Nešić, *supra*, 191.

267. The Minister, among other things, determines the nomenclature of sports occupations and titles and typical jobs for established sports occupations and titles and conditions in terms of education, i.e., professional qualifications and professional experience for acquiring titles (*see* Article 26 of the LSRS).

268. The Ministry also gives consent to the sports rules (*see* Article 28 of the LSRS).

269. Higher education institutions, in accordance with the LSRS which regulates the activity of higher education, as well as institutes in charge of sports and sports medicine, in accordance with this Law, may be engaged in professional training for performing certain professional activities in sports.

270. Accredited higher education and scientific research institutions have the status of an organization in the field of sports in relation to the submission and implementation of programmes and the performance of professional training in the field of sports.

271. The procedure for issuing approvals for performing professional training activities is initiated by a request submitted to the Ministry by organizations.

272. The Ministry shall decide on the request for the issuance of approval, based on the determined fulfilment of conditions by the sports inspector, by a decision within two months from the day of submitting the request.

273. The permit is issued for five years and is revoked by a decision of the Ministry if the organization ceases to meet the conditions for issuing the permit or if it performs professional training activities in sports contrary to this Law or if it commits a misdemeanour related to professional training activities in sports, based on the report of the sports inspector.

274. An administrative dispute may be initiated against the decision of the Ministry in accordance with the law.

275. Data from the certificate on professional qualification for performing certain professional jobs in sports, i.e., on acquiring a certain sports title, are entered in the workbook.

276. The sports inspector will temporarily prohibit the organization from further work on professional training if it determines that it does not meet the prescribed conditions, or does not perform professional training according to the established plan and programme and the prescribed manner of professional training until those conditions or obligations are met.

277. The organization may perform professional training as a joint programme for acquiring a certain sports title and appropriate work permit if it is provided by the rules of the competent international sports federation. The Minister prescribes the framework plan and programme and manner of professional training and development and, in accordance with the Law, more detailed conditions, manner and procedure of issuing, renewing and revoking work permits for sports experts and organizations, number of vocational training participants who can enrol in one group the form and the content, except for personal data, certificates of completed professional training.

278. Organizations are obliged to submit to the Ministry every January a report on the completed professional training in the previous year and an action plan for the current year on the organization of professional training and to submit to the Ministry a report on the beginning of professional training, no later than seven days before enrolment.

279. Accredited higher education institution in the field of sports, as well as other organization that deals with vocational training in accordance with this law, keep: records of participants in vocational training, records of issued certificates and minutes of exams.

280. The Minister regulates in more detail the content, in addition to personal data, and the manner of keeping records.

281. Appropriate data shall be entered in the Certificate of Completed Vocational Training and in the Report to the Ministry (*see* Articles 29–30 of the LSRS).

282. The Minister shall regulate in detail the manner and procedure of performing professional supervision, measures for elimination of observed deficiencies, conditions for appointing a professional sports supervisor, the form and manner of issuing the ID of a professional sports supervisor and other issues of importance for conducting professional supervision in sports (*see* Article 32 LSRS).

283. Supervision over professional work in the field of sports, in accordance with the LS, through professional supervisors is performed by the Institute for Sports and Sports Medicine.

284. Professional supervision on the territory of the autonomous province is performed by the Provincial Institute for Sports and Sports Medicine, as an entrusted job.

285. The LSRS emphasizes that supervision is performed through prominent sports experts because practice has shown that the absence of such a norm was a serious limiting factor for the implementation of effective and competent professional control over the work of sports experts. The Minister shall regulate in detail the manner and procedure of performing professional supervision, measures for eliminating the observed shortcomings, conditions for appointing a professional sports supervisor, the form and manner of issuing the ID of a professional sports supervisor and other issues of importance for conducting professional supervision in sports.

286. The Ministry also determines the conditions under which an entrepreneur can perform sports activities (*see* Article 93 of the LSRS). In addition, it gives consent to the act of the competence of the branch sports federation on mediation during the transfer of an athlete or sports expert from one sports organization to another (*see* Article 94 LSRS).

287. Other competencies of the Ministry are diffusely regulated during the regulation of certain issues in the field of sports.

§3. Public Safety

288. The safety of sports events is extremely important for the level of overall safety in a country. At sports events of various kinds, a large number of people gather, so any threat to their safety can have unforeseeable consequences. This is recognized by the legislator who paid special attention to the issue of safety of sports events.

289. The organizer of a sports event is obliged to:

(1) ensure uninterrupted and safe holding of sports events;
(2) maintenance of sports, take measures that enable prevention of the risk of damage to athletes, spectators and other participants in sports events and third parties (warnings, prohibitions, provision of information and instructions, etc.), as well as measures that affect increased risks, safety of sports facilities, correctness and adequacy of installed and other equipment, provision of emergency medical care, holding the event in accordance with the propositions etc.);
(3) take the necessary security measures to prevent violence and misconduct at sports events and measures to prevent other negative phenomena in sports, in accordance with the law and sports rules;
(4) take the necessary measures to prevent doping at sports events, in accordance with the law and sports rules;
(5) take the necessary measures for the protection of nature and the environment, i.e., measures that will prevent, reduce and eliminate possible adverse effects on natural values and the environment;
(6) report the holding of a sports event in accordance with the regulations governing public gatherings of citizens.

290. The organizer of the sports event is responsible for the damage caused to athletes, spectators and other participants in the sports event and third parties due to non-compliance with regulations, and the general rules on liability for damage caused by non-compliance with regulations.

291. The competent national branch sports federation that has given consent or permission or ordered that a certain sporting event be held even though all the prescribed conditions have not been met, is jointly and severally liable with the organizer for damage suffered by one of the participants in the sporting event or a third party in the organization.

292. A sports event that is organized on the territory of the Republic of Serbia under the leadership of an international sports federation is organized and conducted in accordance with this law and the sports rules of that federation.

293. The competent national branch sports federation is obliged to initiate disciplinary proceedings and apply disciplinary measures determined by sports rules against its members (direct and indirect) who, as organizers, do not take measures.

294. The organizer of a sports event, i.e., an official of the competent national sports federation, is obliged, in accordance with the Law, not to allow the beginning of a sports event, i.e., to interrupt it permanently or temporarily or to order a sports event without spectators, in whole or in part, if conditions are not fulfilled.

295. Disciplinary measures must include: fines, deduction of points and return to a lower rank in the competition. LSRS prescribes misdemeanour penalties for organizers of sports events in case of security breaches.

296. In case of repeated violation of obligations during the same competition season, a disciplinary measure of deduction of points must be imposed, and in case of continuous and serious violation during the same competition season, a disciplinary measure of returning to a lower rank of competition must be imposed (*see* Article 157 LSRS).

297. It can be concluded that the legislator recognizes the organizer of sports events as the bearer of responsibility for its safety. In that sense, the sports organization, the organizer of the competition, is obliged to have an employee or engaged person with an appropriate sports title who coordinates the performance of tasks related to the safety of participants in sports competitions whose organizer, as well as a person with an appropriate sports title within the profession of sports manager for operational, i.e., executive, affairs (*see* Article 158, paragraph 4 of the LSRS).

298. The safety of sports events is also protected by the provisions of criminal legislation, first of all, through the nature of the criminal offence of violent behaviour at a sports event or public gathering under Article 344a of the KZ.

299. The criminal offence of violating public safety is committed by a person who physically attacks or physically settles accounts with participants in a sports event or public gathering, then someone who commits violence or damages property of greater value upon arrival or departure from a sports event or public gathering, or throws on the sports field illicit objects (pyrotechnic devices or other explosive, flammable or harmful substances that may cause bodily injuries or endanger the health of participants in a sports event or public gathering). The criminal offence of violating public safety is committed by a person who enters the sports field or part of the auditorium intended for opposing fans and causes violence, damages a sports facility, its equipment, devices and installations, provokes national, racial behaviour by his behaviour or slogans at a sports event or public gathering that is provoking religious or other hatred or intolerance based on some discriminatory basis resulting in violence or physical confrontation with participants.

300. The perpetrators of the criminal offence of Violations of Public Safety are sentenced to one to five years in prison and a fine.

301. If this crime is committed by a group, the perpetrator will be sentenced to two to eight years in prison. The ringleader of a group that commits an act of violating public safety will be punished by imprisonment for three to twelve years. If the commission of the offence resulted in a riot in which a person was seriously injured or property of greater value was damaged, the perpetrator shall be punished by imprisonment for a term between three and twelve years.

302. An official or responsible person who fails to take security measures when organizing a sports event or public gathering in order to prevent disorder, and as a result endangers the life or body of a large number of people or property of greater value, shall be punished by imprisonment for three months to three years and a fine. The perpetrator of an act committed at a sports event must be banned from attending certain sports events.

303. The criminal legislation of the Republic of Serbia envisages a special security measure that aims to prevent violent behaviour at sports events, with a pronounced effect of special prevention. It is a security measure prohibiting attendance at certain sports events. Namely, the court may impose a measure prohibiting the perpetrator of a criminal offence from attending certain sports events, when this is necessary for the protection of general safety.

304. The measure is executed in such a way that the perpetrator of the criminal offence is obliged to personally report to an official in the regional police administration, i.e., police station, in the area where the perpetrator was found, and to stay in their premises during the time before holding certain sports events.

305. The court shall determine the duration of the measure, which may not be shorter than one or longer than five years, counting from the day the decision becomes final, provided that the time spent serving the sentence is not included in the duration of this measure.

306. If the court pronounces a suspended sentence, the court will determine that the sentence will be revoked, if the perpetrator violates the ban on attending certain sports events, i.e., if he does not perform his duty. The law may stipulate a mandatory ban on attending certain sports events.

307. All these criminal sanctions and measures are aimed at actively contributing to increasing the level of security of all participants in sports events (athletes, spectators, sports workers, etc.). Their consistent application is a condition for gaining confidence in sports and the safety of sports events, and at the same time, contributes to the free and fearless enjoyment of sports.

§4. Tax

308. The tax system is a unique system of fiscal revenues of the state. When it comes to the fiscal obligations of sports associations, companies and athletes, the provisions of the relevant laws governing the tax area apply.

309. Sports entities are not exempted from the obligation to pay taxes on profit, property and other tax liabilities. At this point, the tax regime of sports organizations in the Republic of Serbia will be briefly explained.

310. Sports associations have specific tax treatment in the Republic of Serbia. They are subject to the obligation to pay the following income taxes:

(1) Membership income.
(2) Revenues from donations.
(3) Revenues from sponsorships.
(4) Rental income.
(5) Revenue from ticket sales.
(6) Revenues from the provision of services or sales of products on the market.

311. In the case of a sports organization that generates income only and exclusively from the membership fees of its members, no tax is paid.

312. When a sports organization receives a donation, i.e., a gift in money, equipment, etc., it is obliged to pay a gift tax of 2.5% according to the Law on Property Taxes (LPTs). In this case, a tax return for tax on gifts should be submitted to the competent Tax Administration, which will issue a decision on tax on gifts to be paid.

313. There are exceptions to the rule that a sports organization must meet the obligation to pay taxes in the case of concluding a gift contract.

314. If a donation from the same legal entity or individual in one calendar year amounts to RSD 100,000, no gift tax is paid because this giving is not considered a gift from the aspect of the LPTs.

315. Gift tax is not paid even in cases when you receive a donation from the following sources (regardless of the amount):

– fund or foundation;
– according to international agreements concluded by RS;

– from the Republic of Serbia, an autonomous province or local self-government.

316. More precisely, if the club receives a donation from these sources, the sports organization is exempt from paying taxes, with the obligation to file a tax return and state the grounds for tax exemption, after which the Tax Administration makes a decision on tax exemption as a gift.

317. Sponsorship differs from donations in that, in the case of sponsorship, the sponsor expects a certain consideration from the sports club, such as sponsor advertising, which is defined by the sponsorship agreement. For this reason, sponsorship income is treated as income generated from the provision of services in the market.

318. If a sports organization owns a certain facility (sports hall, gym, etc.) and issues appointments in that facility to third parties, then it generates rental income. Rent income is subject to real estate income tax, in accordance with the LPIT, in the amount of 20% of the amount of rent (less standard costs in the amount of 25%). This income, at the end of the year, is included in the calculation of the income tax base. If for sports matches, events, etc., the sports organization collects tickets from third parties, this income is considered income from the provision of services on the market and is included in the calculation of the profit tax base. There is also revenue from sponsorships and revenue from ticket sales. These revenues are treated from the tax aspect as revenues from the provision of services. Any services provided to third parties as a sports organization, even if it is a non-profit organization, are treated as income from the provision of services. This income is included in the calculation of the income tax base. If a sports organization sells some products (e.g., T-shirts with the logo of the sports association), it represents income from the sale of products on the market.

319. A non-profit organization (and therefore a sports organization) pays income tax on the profits it has made on the market. That is, on the basis of providing services or selling products on the market. Profit tax is calculated and paid on the basis of the LCIT. Profit is the difference between income and expenses that a sports organization realizes during the year. If the profit made at the end of the year is less than RSD 400,000, can be exempted from paying income tax, if the conditions provided by the provision of Article 44 of the LCIT are met:

(1) the sports organization does not distribute the realized surplus to its founders, members, directors, employees or persons related to them;
(2) the annual amount of personal income paid to employees, directors and related persons does not exceed twice the amount of the average annual salary per employee in the Republic in the year for which the right to tax exemption is determined, according to the data of the republic authority responsible for statistics;
(3) does not distribute property for the benefit of its founders, members, directors, employees or persons related to them;
(4) that it does not have a monopolistic or dominant position on the market in terms of the law governing the protection of competition.

320. These conditions must be met cumulatively in order to be entitled to a tax exemption.

321. Finally, it is important to note that even in the case of the existence of grounds for exercising the right to exemption, a tax return should be submitted to the competent Tax Administration, which is an obligation of the sports organization as a taxpayer (Aritonović, 2017).

322. It is quite clear that sports organizations have rights and obligations in the tax system of the Republic of Serbia in accordance with the positive legal regulations in this area. There will be more talk about the tax obligations of athletes in the part that refers to the status of athletes.

§5. DISPUTE SETTLEMENT

323. Numerous disputes can arise in and about sports. Disputes may arise from non-performance of contracts concluded between sports organizations and sports workers or between sports organizations.

324. Disputes in the field of sports can be resolved in court or out of court.

325. The resolution of judicial disputes occurs within the framework of the judicial system of the Republic of Serbia. In the initial stage, the appropriate lower or higher courts are not authorized, depending on the nature of the disputes. However, during the second instance procedure, functioning as appellate courts, the competent authorities are geographically situated in Serbia's four largest cities: Belgrade, Novi Sad, Niš, and Kragujevac.

326. The decisions of the appellate courts are, as a rule, final. Exceptionally, the Supreme Court of Cassation, as the highest court in the Republic of Serbia, with its seat in Belgrade, decides on the submitted legal remedies.

327. In an out-of-court settlement of disputes, the dispute is decided either by out-of-court settlement or by bringing the dispute before one of the sports arbitrations. The advantage of this way of resolving disputes is that the parties to the dispute choose the arbitrator who will resolve the dispute. Decisions made in this way are final, and in that way, great savings are realized in the name of court costs. This leads to the conclusion that out-of-court dispute resolution has its advantages over judicial dispute resolution.

328. With its provisions, the LSRS in principle, regulates the work of sports arbitrations in the Republic of Serbia.

329. Members of a sports association and a sports association may agree to resolve disputes over their free rights, except for disputes for which the court has exclusive jurisdiction – entrust to an ad hoc sports arbitration court or a Permanent

Sports Arbitration (PSA) Court at the Serbian Olympic Committee – for Olympic sports, PSA Court at the Sports Federation of Serbia – for non-Olympic sports and the PSA Court at the PKS – for Paralympic Sports, and when it comes to disputes related to termination, annulment or fulfilment of the contract between the athlete and the PSA court at the competent national branch sports federation.

330. It is considered that the contract on sports arbitration is concluded even if the prosecutor files a lawsuit or an appeal to the sports arbitration, and the defendant does not object to the jurisdiction of the arbitration until the dispute is discussed.

331. The provisions on arbitration of the law governing the procedure before arbitration shall apply accordingly to sports arbitration unless otherwise determined by the LSRS.

332. The dispute may also be the subject of international sports arbitration in cases determined by the sports rules of the competent international sports federation.

333. The PSA Court may also be competent to resolve disputes arising between members of a sports association and a sports association regarding the exercise of membership rights and obligations determined by general acts of a sports association and sports rules, provided that the jurisdiction of the permanent sports court is determined in the statute of sports association or the statute of the competent national sports federation unless otherwise provided by this law. The obligation of arbitration may not be prescribed by a general act of a sports association unless otherwise prescribed by the sports rules of the competent international sports federation. The OKS, the PKS and the Sports Federation of Serbia may mutually establish a single PSA Court for the arbitral settlement of disputes in sports (*see* Article 53 of the LSRS).

334. The dispute before the sports arbitration is urgent.

335. The statute of a sports association may also provide for an attempt to resolve disputes peacefully within a sports association through mediation.

336. Only a law graduate may be appointed as an arbitrator. A person who is the owner, member of a body or employee of sports organizations in the same branch of sport, a person who participated in the decision-making in a previous case, a person who is a member of a body, official or employee of a competent sports federation may not be appointed an arbitrator, nor a person in respect of whom there are other reasons which call into question his impartiality.

337. Competences, composition and organization of PSA, conditions and manner of selection and dismissal of arbitrators, arbitration costs and procedure in matters within its jurisdiction are regulated by general acts of the OKS, PKS, Sports Federation of Serbia and competent national branch sports federation.

338. The acts and number of arbitrators on the list of arbitrators must ensure the independence, impartiality, autonomy and competence of sports arbitration in deciding and protecting the rights of participants in the proceedings, including the right of the party to the dispute to have legal representation. The Ministry gives its consent to these acts (*see* Article 54 of the LSRS).

339. In the Republic of Serbia, there is a PSA at the OKS. The PSA of the OKS consists of arbitrators, of which: up to thirty arbitrators are appointed by the competent body of the OKS, and each member of the OKS can appoint one arbitrator.

340. Disputes worth up to EUR 5,000.00 are resolved by a single arbitrator when the parties jointly appoint from the list of arbitrators of the PSA of the OKS. In case the consensus of the parties on the appointment of an individual arbitrator is not possible, he is appointed by the President of the PSA of the OKS from the list of arbitrators.

341. Disputes of a higher value are resolved by a three-member Arbitration Council, in which each party appoints one arbitrator from the list of arbitrators of the PSA of the OKS, and they jointly appoint a third arbitrator, who is also the President of the Arbitration Council. In the event that there is no possibility of joint appointment of a third member of the Arbitration Council, he shall be appointed by the President of the PSA of the OKS from the list of arbitrators.[81]

342. The procedure for resolving arbitration disputes is initiated by a lawsuit. It is considered that the arbitration procedure started on the day when the PSA of the OKS received the lawsuit. Counterclaim is not allowed.

343. The mediation procedure begins with the submission of a written proposal for initiating a mediation procedure which can be submitted by one party or both parties together.

344. The procedure for giving a non-binding legal opinion on any activity related to sports begins with the submission of a written request that may be submitted by a member of the OKS or the PSA of the OKS.

345. The PSA of the OKS makes decisions on the basis of which it resolves disputes that are brought before it:

- Laws and general acts of the Republic of Serbia.
- General acts and acts of national and international sports federations that apply to the subject matter of the dispute.
- On the basis of justice and fairness (*ex aequo et bono*), if the parties have expressly agreed.

81. Organization and composition of the Permanent Sports Arbitration OKS, *See also* https://oks.org.rs/stalna-sportska-arbitraza/organizacija-i-sastav-stalne-sportske-arbitraze/, accessed 24 Aug. 2021.

346. The arbitral award resolving the dispute shall have the force of a final court decision and shall be executed in accordance with the provisions of the Law on Enforcement Procedure. A party who is dissatisfied with the arbitral award has the right to appeal only to the Sports Arbitration Court in Lausanne, Switzerland, which will, as a last resort, finally resolve the dispute in accordance with the Sports Arbitration Code. The deadline for filing an appeal is twenty-one days from the date of receipt of the decision.[82]

347. From the aspect of legal security, the authorization of the PSA of the OKS to give opinions is especially important. These opinions are of a principled nature and help to harmonize legal practice in the field of sports. In relation to the judicial system, in their character, they are most similar to the opinions of the Supreme Court of Cassation.

348. Disputes in the field of sports can also be resolved through mediation. Unlike arbitration, where the parties independently choose an arbitrator for their case, who resolves the dispute, in the case of mediation in sports, the parties to the dispute themselves choose a mediator who will help them jointly, and amicably resolve the dispute. It is important to point out that a mediator never makes a decision that resolves a dispute. The advantages of such dispute resolution are numerous. The costs of mediation proceedings are incomparably lower than the costs of court proceedings. In this way, in addition to resolving a specific dispute, future disputes can be prevented because mutual trust between the parties is strengthened. This is especially important for the development of the sports system as a whole. Unfortunately, mediation, as a model for resolving disputes, is not sufficiently developed in the Republic of Serbia, regardless of all its benefits. With the development of mediation in Serbia, mediation related to disputes in sports will also develop.

349. In the Republic of Serbia, there is also a Permanent Court of Arbitration at the Sports Federation of Serbia.

350. In the sports system of the Republic of Serbia, the Permanent Court of Arbitration of the OKS is in charge of sports arbitration for Olympic sports, while the Permanent Court of Arbitration of the Sports Federation of Serbia is responsible for arbitration of non-Olympic sports.

351. Based on the LS and the Statute of the Sports Federation of Serbia, the Management Board of the Sports Federation of Serbia adopted the Rulebook on the Permanent Court of Arbitration at the Sports Federation of Serbia as a permanent arbitration institution at the Sports Federation of Serbia, which is responsible for resolving disputes about the rights of the federation and its members. in accordance with the law, the Statute of the Association and other general acts of the Association.

82. Procedure and applicable law before the Permanent Sports Arbitration of the OKS, *See also* https://oks.org.rs/stalna-sportska-arbitraza/pravila-postupka-i-merodavno-pravo/, accessed 24 Aug. 2021.

352. The Arbitration Court in its work and decision-making is independent and has its own seal containing the name and seat of the Arbitration Court and the symbol of the Association, with the fact that it can also use the seal of the Association in its work.

353. The funds for the functioning of the Arbitration Court are provided by the Sports Federation of Serbia, but at the same time, it supervises the administrative and material operations of the Arbitration Court.

354. Members of the Alliance and other persons under the jurisdiction of the Alliance are obliged to submit the information and documents at their disposal at the request of the Arbitration Court, to respond to the invitation of the Arbitration Court to participate in the proceedings within fifteen days of being notified of the initiation of the dispute, to respect and execute the decisions of the Arbitration Court. In addition, the rulebook stipulates that members of the association may not disparage the Arbitration Court or its decisions in public.

355. Any violation of any of these obligations is subject to disciplinary responsibility, which, depending on the severity, can be in the form of a warning, public warning, ban on sports activities, or duty in the association for up to three months.

356. The decision of the Arbitration Court is final and binding for the parties to the dispute. A member of the Alliance who does not implement the final decision of the Arbitration Court has his membership in the Alliance suspended on the day the deadline for fulfilling the decision expires, until the decision of the Arbitration Court is implemented.

357. In addition, a member of the Alliance shall cease to be a member of the Alliance on the day of expiry of the double deadline for fulfilling the decision of the Arbitration Court.

358. In terms of organization, the Arbitration Court consists of the President, Deputy President and Secretary of the Arbitration Court, who are appointed by the Management Board of the Association by a majority of the total number of members, and arbitrators from the List of Arbitrators.

359. The List of Arbitrators is formed so that each member of the Alliance can appoint one arbitrator, while the Management Board of the Alliance appoints an additional ten arbitrators.

360. The possibility of forming a special list of arbitrators for resolving disputes from a certain branch of sport is also foreseen, by agreement between the Association and the competent national branch sports association. The list of arbitrators is formed by the competent national sports association appointing fifteen arbitrators, and the Management Board of the association appointing five arbitrators.

361. The Arbitration Court performs its function through the President, Deputy President and Secretary of the Arbitration Court, arbitration panels and individual arbitrators. The President and Deputy President of the Court of Arbitration are appointed and dismissed by the Management Board of the Association, from the ranks of graduated lawyers who deal with problems in the field of sports.

362. Only a law graduate can be appointed as an arbitrator, but the arbitrator must be impartial and independent in relation to the parties and the subject of the dispute. The mandate of arbitrators lasts for five years, with the fact that they can be reappointed.

363. Competent national and territorial sports associations, members of the Association, are obliged to appoint arbitrators to the list of arbitrators, in accordance with this rulebook, within thirty days from the day of receiving the invitation from the Association and to submit the decision on the appointment of arbitrators to the Association.

364. The arbitrator in a specific case can only be a person who has declared in writing that he accepts the duties of an arbitrator and his independence.

365. The parties appoint arbitrators to resolve a specific dispute in accordance with this rulebook. The parties may agree that the arbitration shall be conducted by an arbitration panel or a sole arbitrator.

366. If the parties have not previously agreed on the number of arbitrators, the arbitration shall be conducted by a panel of three arbitrators, except when, in accordance with these regulations, the arbitration shall be conducted by a single arbitrator. Arbitration of appeals and claims for the annulment of an individual act is always conducted by a panel of three arbitrators, unless the parties expressly agree otherwise.

367. Arbitration proceedings in disputes whose value does not exceed EUR 50,000 in dinar equivalents, at the middle exchange rate of the National Bank of Serbia, are conducted by a sole arbitrator. If the dispute is to be resolved by a sole arbitrator, he shall be appointed by agreement of the parties within fifteen days from the date of notification of the defendant on the filing of the lawsuit, and if there is no such agreement, the appointment shall be made by the president of the Arbitration Court within a further period of five days.

368. The arbitration court resolves disputes:

- as a first instance and final instance for the arbitration settlement of disputes eligible for arbitration – disputes about rights freely available to the parties (persons under the jurisdiction of the Association);
- as a first instance and final instance for arbitration settlement of disputes between the Association and the members of the Association and mutual disputes between

the members of the Association regarding the realization of member's rights and obligations determined by the Statute and general acts of the Association;
- as a first instance and final instance for the arbitration settlement of disputes with a member of the Alliance determined by the Statute or general act of the member of the Alliance;
- as a second instance final appeal instance regarding the first-instance decisions of the Union bodies;
- as a second instance final appeal instance regarding the first-instance decisions of the bodies of members of the Alliance, in cases determined by the statute or general act of the member of the Alliance;
- as a final instance for determining the nullity of legally binding decisions of the Association or members of the Association, in certain cases;
- as a first instance and final instance for determining the nullity of a provision of the statute or other general act of a member of the Association due to inconsistency with the Statute or another general act of the Association.

369. The dispute may also be the subject of international sports arbitration in cases determined by the sports rules of the competent international sports federation.

370. Competent national branch sports associations, members of the Association can resolve disputes regarding the termination, annulment or determination of nullity or fulfillment of contracts between athletes, i.e., sports experts and sports organizations, i.e., branch associations through their PSAs in accordance with the LS.

371. According to the Rulebook, with the Arbitration Agreement, the parties entrust the Arbitration Court with the resolution of their future disputes or disputes arising from a certain legal relationship. The jurisdiction of the Arbitration Court can be contracted by anyone who, in accordance with the provisions of the law governing civil proceedings, has the capacity to be a party to the proceedings.

372. The arbitration agreement is void if:

- the type of dispute to which it refers is not amenable to arbitration;
- not concluded in writing;
- the parties did not have the necessary characteristics and ability to conclude it;
- if it was concluded under the influence of coercion, threat, fraud or delusion.

373. In the case of disputes arising in connection with this contract and on the occasion of it, the contracting parties exclude the possibility of litigation and agree to the jurisdiction of the PSA Court at the Sports Federation of Serbia in Belgrade, which will definitively resolve the dispute.

374. There is no suspension of proceedings in the proceedings before the Arbitration Court. Proceedings before the Arbitration Court are confidential and not public, unless the parties agree otherwise, or if this does not contradict the applicable enforcement regulations or the guarantee to protect one's own rights.

375. The deadlines set by this Rulebook are exclusive and cannot be extended. An extension may be allowed only in exceptional and justified cases by the President of the Arbitration Court, at the proposal of the President of the Chamber or by mutual agreement of the parties. The deadlines for appointing members of the Council cannot be extended. In extremely urgent cases, the President of the Arbitration Court can decide, that is, allow the deadlines established by this rulebook to be appropriately shortened.

376. Against the decision made in the first instance by the first instance competent authority, an official or body of the Association or a member of the Association, an appeal may be filed with the Arbitration Court, in accordance with this rulebook. The appeal is submitted within twenty-one days from the date of delivery of the first-instance decision, if no other deadline is set by the general act of the Association or a member of the Association.

377. In appellate disputes, the decision can be challenged due to:

- incorrectly or incompletely established factual situations;
- significant violations of procedural provisions;
- incorrect application of substantive law from laws and general acts of the Association or members of the Association;
- decisions on sanctions (penalties).

378. Ruling on the appeal, the Chamber can reject the appeal, reject it as unfounded and confirm the first-instance decision, adopt the appeal, and amend or cancel the first-instance decision.

379. In all cases in which the Arbitration Court may be competent to resolve disputes, each party, regardless of whether the jurisdiction of the Arbitration Court is determined by contract or by a general act of the Alliance or a member of the Alliance, may turn to the Arbitration Court for the purpose of mediation, i.e., conciliation in a specific dispute. Mediation, or conciliation, cannot be conducted if the dispute, by its nature, cannot be settled by an out-of-court settlement. The request for initiation of the mediation procedure is submitted to the Arbitration Court, which will ask the other party to declare this request within fifteen days from delivery. If the opposite party opposes the mediation procedure or does not declare it within a certain period, it is considered that the mediation procedure has failed. If the opposite party agrees with the proposal for conducting the mediation procedure, the President of the Arbitration Court will invite the parties to sign an agreement on the jurisdiction of the Arbitration Court within the deadline he will provide. If the parties have concluded an agreement on mediation, the President of the Arbitration

Court appoints one of the arbitrators of the Arbitration Court or, in particularly justified cases, another suitable person as a mediator. The mediator examines the statements and proposals of the parties, and if necessary collects certain information and hears the partics. After examining the case to a sufficient extent, the mediator draws up a written settlement proposal and submits it to the parties. The parties do not have to accept the arbitrator's settlement proposal. A settlement reached in mediation has the force of a settlement reached out of court. If the parties conclude a settlement, its content is recorded in the minutes signed by the parties and the mediator.

380. The decision on costs in proceedings before the Court of Arbitration, with the Tariff of Costs of the Court of Arbitration, is made by the Board of Directors of the Association by a majority of the total number of votes, on the proposal of the President of the Court of Arbitration. The arbitration court decides on the costs of the arbitration depending on the value, type and complexity of the dispute. The arbitral tribunal shall decide on the costs of the arbitration in the final arbitral award and, if it deems it expedient, in any other award. The costs of the arbitration include: compensation for the work of the arbitrator (according to the tariff), reasonable travel and other expenses of the arbitrator, reasonable costs of expert testimony and other evidentiary actions ordered by the Arbitration Court, reasonable travel and other expenses of witnesses, to the extent approved by the Arbitration Court, representation costs and other costs incurred by the parties in connection with the arbitration, to the extent that the Arbitral Court judges that their amount is reasonable, as well as the administrative costs of the Arbitral Court.

381. When submitting a claim, counterclaim, appeal, request for mediation and request for a legal opinion, the applicant is obliged to deposit in advance to the account of the Federation, i.e., the Arbitration Court, an advance payment of the arbitration costs determined by the President of the Arbitration Court within the limits prescribed by the Tariff and the registration fee in the amount specified Tariff.

382. The consent to the Rulebook is given by the Minister of Sports.

383. In the Republic of Serbia, there is also a Permanent Court of Arbitration at the Sports Federation of Serbia.

384. In the sports system of the Republic of Serbia, the Permanent Court of Arbitration of the OKS is in charge of sports arbitration for Olympic sports, while the Permanent Court of Arbitration of the Sports Federation of Serbia is responsible for arbitration of non-Olympic sports.

385. Based on the LS and the Statute of the Sports Federation of Serbia, the Management Board of the Sports Federation of Serbia adopted the Rulebook on the Permanent Court of Arbitration at the Sports Federation of Serbia as a permanent arbitration institution at the Sports Federation of Serbia, which is responsible for resolving disputes about the rights of the federation and its members. in accordance with the law, the Statute of the Association and other general acts of the Association.

386. The Arbitration Court in its work and decision-making is independent and independent and has its own seal containing the name and seat of the Arbitration Court and the symbol of the Association, with the fact that it can also use the seal of the Association in its work.

387. The funds for the functioning of the Arbitration Court are provided by the Sports Federation of Serbia, but at the same time, it supervises the administrative and material operations of the Arbitration Court.

388. Members of the Alliance and other persons under the jurisdiction of the Alliance are obliged to submit the information and documents at their disposal at the request of the Arbitration Court, to respond to the invitation of the Arbitration Court to participate in the proceedings within fifteen days of being notified of the initiation of the dispute, to respect and execute the decisions Arbitration Court. In addition, the rulebook stipulates that members of the association may not disparage the Arbitration Court or its decisions in public.

389. Any violation of any of these obligations is subject to disciplinary responsibility, which, depending on the severity, can be in the form of a warning, public warning, ban on sports activities, or duty in the association for up to three months.

390. The decision of the Arbitration Court is final and binding for the parties to the dispute. A member of the Alliance who does not implement the final decision of the Arbitration Court has his membership in the Alliance suspended on the day the deadline for fulfilling the decision expires, until the decision of the Arbitration Court is implemented.

391. In addition, a member of the Alliance shall cease to be a member of the Alliance on the day of expiry of the double deadline for fulfilling the decision of the Arbitration Court.

392. In terms of organization, the Arbitration Court consists of the President, Deputy President and Secretary of the Arbitration Court, who are appointed by the Management Board of the Association by a majority of the total number of members, and arbitrators from the List of Arbitrators.

393. The list of arbitrators is formed so that each member of the Alliance can appoint one arbitrator, while the Management Board of the Alliance appoints an additional ten arbitrators.

394. The possibility of forming a special list of arbitrators for resolving disputes from a certain branch of sport is also foreseen, by agreement between the Association and the competent national branch sports association. The list of arbitrators is formed by the competent national sports association appointing fifteen arbitrators, and the Management Board of the association appointing five arbitrators.

395. The Arbitration Court performs its function through the President, Deputy President and Secretary of the Arbitration Court, arbitration panels and individual arbitrators. The President and Deputy President of the Court of Arbitration are appointed and dismissed by the Management Board of the Association, from the ranks of graduated lawyers who deal with problems in the field of sports.

396. Only a law graduate can be appointed as an arbitrator, but the arbitrator must be impartial and independent in relation to the parties and the subject of the dispute. The mandate of arbitrators lasts for five years, with the fact that they can be reappointed.

397. Competent national and territorial sports associations, members of the Association, are obliged to appoint arbitrators to the list of arbitrators, in accordance with this rulebook, within thirty days from the day of receiving the invitation from the Association and to submit the decision on the appointment of arbitrators to the Association.

398. The arbitrator in a specific case can only be a person who has declared in writing that he accepts the duties of an arbitrator and his independence.

399. The parties appoint arbitrators to resolve a specific dispute in accordance with this rulebook. The parties may agree that the arbitration shall be conducted by an arbitration panel or a sole arbitrator.

400. If the parties have not previously agreed on the number of arbitrators, the arbitration shall be conducted by a panel of three arbitrators, except when, in accordance with these regulations, the arbitration shall be conducted by a single arbitrator. Arbitration of appeals and claims for the annulment of an individual act is always conducted by a panel of three arbitrators, unless the parties expressly agree otherwise.

401. Arbitration proceedings in disputes whose value does not exceed EUR 50,000 in dinar equivalents, at the middle exchange rate of the National Bank of Serbia, are conducted by a sole arbitrator. If the dispute is to be resolved by a sole arbitrator, he shall be appointed by agreement of the parties within fifteen days from the date of notification of the defendant on the filing of the lawsuit, and if there is no such agreement, the appointment shall be made by the president of the Arbitration Court within a further period of five days.

402. The arbitration court resolves disputes:

– as a first instance and final instance for the arbitration settlement of disputes eligible for arbitration – disputes about rights freely available to the parties (persons under the jurisdiction of the Association);

- as the first instance and final instance for arbitration settlement of disputes between the Association and the members of the Association and mutual disputes between the members of the Association regarding the realization of member's rights and obligations determined by the Statute and general acts of the Association;
- as a first instance and final instance for the arbitration settlement of disputes with a member of the Alliance determined by the Statute or general act of the member of the Alliance;
- as a second-instance final appeal instance regarding the first-instance decisions of the Union bodies;
- as a second-instance final appeal instance regarding the first-instance decisions of the bodies of members of the Alliance, in cases determined by the statute or general act of the member of the Alliance;
- as a final instance for determining the nullity of legally binding decisions of the Association or members of the Association, in certain cases;
- as a first instance and final instance for determining the nullity of a provision of the statute or other general act of a member of the Association due to inconsistency with the Statute or another general act of the Association.

403. The dispute may also be the subject of international sports arbitration in cases determined by the sports rules of the competent international sports federation.

404. Competent national branch sports associations, members of the Association can resolve disputes regarding the termination, annulment or determination of nullity or fulfillment of contracts between athletes, i.e., sports experts and sports organizations, i.e., branch associations through their PSAs in accordance with the LS.

405. According to the Rulebook, with the Arbitration Agreement, the parties entrust the Arbitration Court with the resolution of their future disputes or disputes arising from a certain legal relationship. The jurisdiction of the Arbitration Court can be contracted by anyone who, in accordance with the provisions of the law governing civil proceedings, has the capacity to be a party to the proceedings.

406. The arbitration agreement is void if:

- the type of dispute to which it refers is not amenable to arbitration;
- not concluded in writing;
- the parties did not have the necessary characteristics and ability to conclude it;
- if it was concluded under the influence of coercion, threat, fraud or delusion.

407. In the case of disputes arising in connection with this contract and on the occasion of it, the contracting parties exclude the possibility of litigation and agree to the jurisdiction of the PSA Court at the Sports Federation of Serbia in Belgrade, which will definitively resolve the dispute.

408. There is no suspension of proceedings in the proceedings before the Arbitration Court. Proceedings before the Arbitration Court are confidential and not public, unless the parties agree otherwise, or if this does not contradict the applicable enforcement regulations or the guarantee to protect one's own rights.

409. The deadlines set by this Rulebook are exclusive and cannot be extended. An extension may be allowed only in exceptional and justified cases by the President of the Arbitration Court, at the proposal of the President of the Chamber or by mutual agreement of the parties. The deadlines for appointing members of the Council cannot be extended. In extremely urgent cases, the president of the Arbitration Court can decide, that is, allow the deadlines established by this rulebook to be appropriately shortened.

410. Against the decision made in the first instance by the first-instance competent authority, an official or body of the Association or a member of the Association, an appeal may be filed with the Arbitration Court, in accordance with this rulebook. The appeal is submitted within twenty-one days from the date of delivery of the first-instance decision, if no other deadline is set by the general act of the Association or a member of the Association.

411. In appellate disputes, the decision can be challenged due to:

- incorrectly or incompletely established factual situations;
- significant violations of procedural provisions;
- incorrect application of substantive law from laws and general acts of the Association or members of the Association;
- decisions on sanctions (penalties).

412. Ruling on the appeal, the Chamber can reject the appeal, reject it as unfounded and confirm the first-instance decision, adopt the appeal, and amend or cancel the first-instance decision. In all cases in which the Arbitration Court may be competent to resolve disputes, each party, regardless of whether the jurisdiction of the Arbitration Court is determined by contract or by a general act of the Alliance or a member of the Alliance, may turn to the Arbitration Court for the purpose of mediation, i.e., conciliation in a specific dispute. Mediation, or conciliation, cannot be conducted if the dispute, by its nature, cannot be settled by an out-of-court settlement. The request for initiation of the mediation procedure is submitted to the Arbitration Court, which will ask the other party to declare this request within 15 days from delivery. If the opposite party opposes the mediation procedure, or does not declare it within a certain period, it is considered that the mediation procedure has failed. If the opposite party agrees with the proposal for conducting the mediation procedure, the President of the Arbitration Court will invite the parties to sign an agreement on the jurisdiction of the Arbitration Court within the deadline he will provide. If the parties have concluded an agreement on mediation, the President of the Arbitration Court appoints one of the arbitrators of the Arbitration Court or, in particularly justified cases, another suitable person as mediator. The mediator examines the statements and proposals of the parties, and if necessary collects certain information and hears the parties. After examining the case to a sufficient extent, the mediator draws up a written settlement proposal and submits it to the parties. The parties do not have to accept the arbitrator's settlement proposal. A settlement reached in mediation has the force of a settlement reached out of court. If the parties conclude a settlement, its content is recorded in the minutes signed by the parties and the mediator.

413. The determination of costs in proceedings before the Court of Arbitration, outlined in the Tariff of Costs of the Court of Arbitration, is carried out through a majority vote by the Board of Directors of the Association. This decision is based on the proposal put forth by the President of the Court of Arbitration. The costs associated with the arbitration process are determined by the arbitration court, taking into consideration factors like the dispute's value, type, and complexity. The costs encompass various elements, including payment for the arbitrator's services (in accordance with the tariff), reasonable expenses related to the arbitrator's travel and other activities, justifiable expenses for expert testimonies and other evidentiary procedures mandated by the Arbitration Court, appropriate travel and other expenses for witnesses (subject to the Arbitration Court's approval), reasonable representation expenses, and other costs incurred by the involved parties in relation to the arbitration. The Arbitration Court assesses the reasonableness of these costs. Additionally, the administrative costs of the Arbitral Court are also included in the overall costs. The arbitral tribunal is responsible for deciding on the arbitration costs in the final arbitral award, and if deemed suitable, in any other award issued during the process.

414. Saglasnik na Pravilnik daje Ministar sporta.

415. The consent to the Rulebook is given by the Minister of Sports.

§6. Internal Audit in the Ministry of Youth and Sports

416. In the public sector of the Republic of Serbia, as part of the comprehensive system of Internal Financial Control, Internal Audit is foreseen.

417. Based on Article 82 of the Budget System Law and in accordance with Article 17, Paragraph 1, Item 1) and Article 2, Paragraph 1. point 22) of the Rulebook on common criteria for organizing and standards and methodological instructions for the conduct and reporting of internal audit in the public sector, as well as international standards for the professional practice of internal audit of the Institute of Internal Auditors, upon the proposal of the internal auditor, the Minister of Youth and Sports approves the Charter of Internal Audit Ministry of Youth and Sports.

418. It is an internal act that states the position of internal audit in the existing organizational structure of the Ministry, gives powers and determines the responsibility of the internal auditor towards the minister. The internal auditor has unhindered access to documentation, employees and assets necessary for the performance of audit tasks. Within the framework of the internal act, the scope itself is defined – the scope of work of the internal audit, in accordance with the International Standards of the professional practice of internal auditing.

419. The method of internal audit itself is described in more detail in the Internal Audit Manual of the Republic of Serbia.

420. Internal audit is an activity that provides an independent objective assessment, but at the same time an advisory activity, with the purpose of contributing to the improvement of the organization's operations. It helps the organization achieve its goals by systematically assessing and evaluating risk management, control and governance in general.

421. The internal auditor is functionally and organizationally independent in relation to other organizational units of the ministries. He reports directly to the minister about his work.

422. The internal auditor is obliged to apply the principles of objectivity, competence, confidentiality and integrity in his work.

423. The internal auditor is obliged to submit to the minister an annual report on the work of the internal audit, as well as a report on the results of each individual audit and all important findings, recommendations made, as well as actions taken to improve the operations of the audited entity.

424. The internal auditor is obliged to submit to the minister an annual report on the work of the internal audit, as well as a report on the results of each individual audit and all important findings, recommendations made, as well as actions taken to improve the operations of the audited entity.

425. The internal auditor also establishes cooperation with the State Audit Institution and other institutions, in order to improve the work and professional development of the internal audit.

Chapter 3. Private Regulation

426. A sports inspector is a person authorized to carry out inspection supervision, i.e., to examine the implementation of the LS and the regulations adopted on the basis of this law by direct insight into the business operations and actions of natural persons and organizations in the field of sports, the fulfillment of the conditions for the performance of sports activities and activities and the fulfillment of the conditions for carrying out professional training for sports professions, that is, professions.

427. In the Ministry of Youth and Sports of the Republic of Serbia, the Department for Inspection Affairs in Sports is responsible for inspection work, according to the internal organization and systematization of workplaces.

428. The scope of work of the Department for Inspection Affairs in Sports refers to: inspection supervision, i.e., the implementation of the LS and regulations adopted on the basis of this Law, the conduct of natural persons and organizations in the field of sports, determining the fulfilment of the conditions for performing sports activities and activities and determining the fulfilment of the conditions for carrying out professional training for sports professions, i.e., titles, monitoring the situation and preparing analyses, information and notices from the scope of the Department and other tasks from the scope of the Department.

429. A sports inspector must have a completed law faculty or a faculty in the field of sports, passed the state professional exam and have at least three years of work experience in the profession.

430. Sports inspectors, in addition to the ministry in charge of sports, are also stationed in local governments.

For example, in the City of Niš, in the City Administration for Social Activities, there are three positions in the position of adviser in the position of Sports Inspector. The job description stipulates that the sports inspector performs inspection supervision as an entrusted job on the territory of the local self-government unit, over legal and physical persons who perform sports activities and sports activities in accordance with the LS and the law regulating inspection supervision. The sports inspector submits to the competent judicial authority a criminal report, a report for an economic offence or a request to initiate misdemeanour proceedings, i.e., issues a misdemeanour order, in accordance with the law, if an illegality punishable by law or another regulation is discovered in the supervised entity. The sports inspector possesses the authority to impose a temporary ban on various activities that violate the law or regulations. This includes prohibiting the engagement in sports activities and other actions until the identified shortcomings are resolved. In the case of individuals who lack the prescribed qualifications or proper work permits for professional sports work, the sports inspector can temporarily suspend their involvement in such work until the necessary conditions are met.

Furthermore, the sports inspector is empowered to recommend to the relevant sports organization's governing body the initiation of proceedings for addressing breaches of work obligations, disciplinary matters, or other actions necessary to rectify identified legal or procedural irregularities within the sports sector. They can also issue directives to national sports associations to adopt required sports regulations mandated by law and instruct them to accept eligible membership applications from qualified organizations.

In instances where the rights of a member or employee of a sports organization have been violated, the sports inspector can, upon request, temporarily halt actions that contravene these rights while legal or arbitration proceedings are underway. Additionally, the inspector can compel the rectification of sports facilities that no longer serve their designated purpose and require the owners or users of these facilities to cover the related expenses. This is particularly applicable if a sports facility's usage contradicts established regulations.

The sports inspector is also authorized to temporarily suspend the operation of sports associations that have not adjusted their status in line with the law, forbid the organization of sports events that deviate from legal or regulatory requirements, and prevent individuals from participating in such events if they fail to meet legally established criteria. Approvals for programmes addressing general sports needs or citizens' interests can also be temporarily halted if they are granted in violation of the law. The inspector can request the cessation of work within the sports system until proper inspection and oversight can be conducted, and can even suggest the revocation of approvals for professional training activities due to non-compliance with legal standards.

Moreover, the sports inspector holds the authority to prohibit engagement in work for sports associations, societies, or federations that do not adhere to the legal requirements specified in their statutes and sports regulations. They can also take other measures and actions as permitted by law, and undertake additional tasks as directed by their immediate supervisor.

431. For example, in the City of Niš, in the City Administration for Social Activities, there are 3 positions in the position of adviser in the position of Sports Inspector. The job description stipulates that the sports inspector performs inspection supervision as a entrusted job on the territory of the local self-government unit, over legal and physical persons who perform sports activities and sports activities in accordance with the Law on Sports and the law regulating inspection supervision. The sports inspector submits to the competent judicial authority a criminal report, a report for an economic offense or a request to initiate misdemeanor proceedings, i.e., issues a misdemeanor order, in accordance with the law, if an illegality punishable by law or another regulation is discovered in the supervised entity.

432. There is a potential inconsistency arising from the situation where sports inspectors are placed within the Department for Educational and Sports Inspection, a unit overseen by a manager who isn't mandated to possess legal qualifications or an athletic background, despite the criteria specifying the required qualifications for that role. This criteria outlines the need for an individual to hold an advanced degree in the second-degree studies (master's academic studies, master's vocational studies, or specialist academic studies), possess a minimum of five years of professional experience, have successfully completed the state vocational and inspector exams.

433. Private regulations in the field of sports in the Republic of Serbia include various agreements that regulate relations in the field of sports (agreements on the engagement of athletes, sports workers, sponsorship agreements, etc.). The rules of the law of obligations and sports law apply in principle to these contracts.

434. In addition to the above, private regulations may also include certain provisions of the LSRS relating to the internal legal acts of sports organizations. In this way, organizations are free to regulate their relations themselves, within the limits prescribed by law.

435. The general acts of a sports association are: the statute, the rulebook and the decision which regulates certain issues in a general way.

436. The statute is the basic general act of a sports association.

437. It is obligatorily regulated by the statute:

(1) name and seat of the sports association;
(2) goals, content of activities and determination of sports branch and sports discipline, i.e., area of sports, in which sports goals are achieved;
(3) bodies, their powers, the manner of election and dismissal, the duration of the mandate and the manner of decision-making;
(4) the procedure of adoption, i.e., amendments to the statute, and other general acts of the sports association;
(5) representation of a sports association;
(6) making the work public;
(7) conditions and manner of membership and termination of membership, determining the amount of membership fees, rights, obligations and responsibilities of members, especially minors;
(8) the manner of acquiring funds for achieving sports goals and disposing of funds;
(9) way of deciding on status changes;
(10) dealing with the property of the sports association in case of termination of the association;
(11) the procedure for adopting financial and other reports;
(12) the form and content of the seal;
(13) economic and other activities that the sports association directly performs;
(14) other issues of importance for the sports association, as well as other issues determined by law.

438. Every member of a sports association has the right to receive a copy of the statute of the sports association.

439. The statute and other general acts of the sports association must be in accordance with the sports rules and this law.

440. Individual acts adopted by bodies and authorized persons in a sports association must be in accordance with the general acts of the sports association, sports rules and the law.

441. The statute of the sports association is registered and published on the website of the Business Registers Agency, in accordance with the law governing the registration procedure in the Agency.

442. The provisions of the general act of the sports association are subject to the assessment of constitutionality and legality in accordance with the Constitution and the law.

443. The sports association is obliged to make a new general act, i.e., a decision on appropriate amendments to the general act, within thirty days from the day of delivery of the final decision on annulment, and to submit an application for entry in the Register within the legal deadline.

444. If the statute of the sports association, i.e., certain provisions of the statute, is annulled, and the sports association does not make a new statute, i.e., the decision on appropriate changes to the statute – the sports association ceases to exist and is deleted from the Register. The same rules apply accordingly in the case when, in accordance with the Constitution and the law, the unconstitutionality or illegality of the provision of the general act of the sports association has been established.

445. Any member of a sports association may initiate proceedings before the locally competent basic court to determine the nullity of the general act of the sports association that was passed contrary to the statute of the sports association or sports rules, in accordance with the law governing the association.

446. In the Republic of Serbia, public and private regulations in sports are part of a single legal system, which can be assessed as positive. Private initiative in sports should be strengthened, within the limits set by law, which is a proposal *de lege ferenda*, which will contribute to the development of sports.

§1. Program Financing

447. On the basis of the LS and the Law on the Government, the Minister of Youth and Sports adopts the Rulebook on the approval and financing of programmes that realize the general interest in the field of sports.

448. This rulebook prescribes the criteria and method of approving programmes, i.e., projects that realize the general interest in the field of sports and the allocation of funds, the appearance and content of the programme proposal, i.e., the project and the documentation submitted with the proposal, the content and appearance of the report on the realization of the programme and the manner and procedure for controlling the implementation of approved programmes, that is, projects.

449. The legislator has foreseen that the general interest in the field of sports is achieved through financing or co-financing of programmes and projects from the budget of the Republic of Serbia, as well as from the funds that are generated in the budget of the Republic of Serbia by organizing games of chance.

450. Programmes that realize general interest in the field of sports can be approved if they meet the criteria in terms of:

- programme proponent;
- programme holder;
- content and quality of the programme;
- programme financing.

451. The programme proposer can be:

- Olympic Committee of Serbia – (proposal of its annual and special programme, as well as proposals of annual and special programmes of competent national branch sports federations of Olympic sports of its members);
- Paralympic Committee of Serbia – (proposal of its annual and special programme, as well as proposals of annual and special programmes of competent national branch sports federations of Paralympic sports of its members);
- Sports Federation of Serbia – (proposal of its annual and special program, as well as annual and special proposals of competent national branch sports federations of non-Olympic sports and competent national sports federations for the field of sports, special programs of territorial sports federations and other members);
- the competent national branch sports association through which the general interest in the field of sports is achieved – proposal of its annual programme for the organization of camps for promising athletes;
- the owner, that is, the user of the land or sports facility – the proposal of his annual programme (project) for the construction, equipping and maintenance of the sports facility;
- organizations in the field of sports – proposal of their special programme;
- accredited higher education institutions and scientific research institutions – proposal of their special programme.

452. The Rulebook stipulates that the holder of the programme must meet a number of conditions, i.e., be registered in accordance with the Law, be entered in the national records in accordance with the law, exclusively or predominantly operate on a non-profit basis, unless otherwise specified by law, have headquarters in the Republic of Serbia, that he is directly responsible for the preparation and execution of the programme, that he has previously performed the activity for at least one year, that he meets, in accordance with the Law, the prescribed conditions for performing sports activities and activities, that he has successfully implemented the approved programme, if was the holder of the programme in previous years, as well as having the capacity to implement the programme.

453. It is foreseen who cannot be the host of the programme. First of all, the holder of the programme cannot be in the process of liquidation, bankruptcy and under a temporary ban on activities, have a business account blocked at the time of the conclusion of the contract on the implementation of the programme and the transfer (payment) of budget funds to the business account, tax debts or debts to organizations of social security, to be punished by a final decision in the last two years for a misdemeanour or economic offence related to his financial operations, use of property, work with children and prevention of negative phenomena in sports.

454. The Rulebook regulates the case if there are several national branch sports associations.

455. In cases where multiple national branch sports federations or national sports federations are registered within a significant sports category for the Republic of Serbia, such as a specific sports discipline or the overall realm of sports, only the program of the appropriate governing national branch sports federation or national sports federation for that particular category receives financial support to serve the collective interest effectively.

456. When it comes to the programs themselves, they must meet certain criteria. According to the rulebook, it is necessary that the program:

- contributes to the realization of the general interest in the field of sports established by the Law;
- that it is in accordance with the Law and the National Strategy for the Development of Sports in the Republic of Serbia;
- that it is in accordance with the four-year development programme of the competent national sports federation;
- that it is in accordance with the sports rules of the competent national sports federation;
- that it is in accordance with the conditions, criteria and goals specified in the public call for special programmes;
- to be implemented in the Republic of Serbia, except for the programme of preparation and participation in international sports competitions;
- that it is in accordance with the principles established in the documents of international organizations of which the Republic of Serbia is a member;
- to have a significant and long-lasting impact on the development of sports in the Republic of Serbia;
- that it will be realized in the current year, if the regulations do not specify otherwise;
- that it foresees the engagement of the appropriate number of participants in the programme and the necessary resources for the implementation of the programme and that there is no doubt about the possibility of implementing the programme;
- that, as a rule, phased financing of the programme is foreseen.

457. In addition, the branch of sport within which the programme is implemented should be of special importance for the Republic of Serbia.

458. Athletes, sports experts and other persons engaged in the implementation of the programme must meet the conditions for performing sports activities and sports activities established by the Law, and their engagement must be carried out in accordance with the Law.

459. Athletes, sports experts and other persons engaged in the implementation of the programme must meet the conditions for performing sports activities and sports activities established by the Law, and their engagement must be carried out in accordance with the Law.

460. Proposals for annual and special programmes are submitted separately for each programme holder and for each area of general interest. The programme proposal contains detailed information about the programme holder, areas of general interest, participants in the implementation of the programme and the capacity in which they are engaged, goals and expected results, including which problems the programme will solve and which population groups and how the programme will be used, type and content activities and the time and place of the implementation of the programme, i.e., the performance of the activities, how the evaluation of the success of the programme will be carried out, the budget of the programme, as well as the dynamic plan for the use of funds and the method of internal monitoring and control of the implementation of the programme and evaluation of the results.

461. Public invitations and public notices in terms of this rulebook are published on the website of the Ministry. The public call for the submission of special programmes states the essential conditions and criteria that the proposed programmes must meet, in particular: the subject of the public call, the amount of funds available for the subject of the public call, the deadline by which the received funds must be used, the deadline when the programme proposals must be submitted, the date of notification of the programme holder about the approved programmes, as well as the place, time and person where the documentation regarding the public call can be obtained.

462. The Ministry's decision can determine the maximum allowed amounts per programme for certain areas of general interest in the field of sports. If such a decision is made, the maximum allowed amount is specified in the public invitation and public notice.

463. The OKS, the PKS and the Sports Federation of Serbia determine the deadline by which the competent national sports federations and territorial sports federations, their members, submit their proposals for annual and special programmes of which they are, in accordance with the Law, authorized proponents to the Ministry and about this, they notify in writing. If the competent national or territorial sports federation does not submit its proposal within the set deadline, it will be given a subsequent deadline of up to ten days to submit the proposal in justified cases, and if the proposal is not submitted even then, it will be considered that that federation has given up proposing its programmes in the current year.

464. For the assessment of annual and special programmes, the minister responsible for sports, in accordance with the Law, forms an expert commission in which, in addition to representatives of the Ministry, representatives of the OKS, the PKS, the Sports Federation of Serbia and the Institute for Sports and Sports Medicine of the Republic of Serbia participate.

465. The commission has a president and six members.

466. The assessment of the quality of annual and special programmes, including the financial plan of the programme, is carried out in accordance with the criteria established by this rulebook. Programme quality assessment includes two types of evaluation criteria: selection criteria and funding allocation criteria. The programme selection criteria include elements used to evaluate the financial and operational capabilities of the programme applicant in order to ensure that he has the necessary funds for his own work during the entire period of programme implementation and that he possesses the professional skills, expertise and experience necessary for the successful implementation of the complete programme, including partners in the implementation of the programme. The criteria for the selection of annual programmes include the evaluation of the capacity of the competent national sports association of the programme holder for the long-term achievement of general interest in the field of sports and the implementation of the proposed programme.

467. The evaluation of the quality of the annual programmes of the OKS, the Sports Federation of Serbia, the PKS and the competent national federations for the field of sports and special programmes of organizations in the field of sports is carried out according to the criteria from the Table of evaluation of the quality of special programmes, which forms an integral part of the Rulebook, according to the criteria that are divided into sections and subsections, with each subsection having a grade (points) from 1 to 5, namely: 1 – very bad; 2 – bad; 3 – appropriate; 4 – good; 5 – very good.

468. Evaluation of the quality of the programme is done by the Commission evaluating the submitted programmes according to the evaluation tables, and the total number of points is determined based on the average grades within individual sections unless otherwise specified by this regulation.

469. The proposal to not accept the programme and not to approve funds is given by the Commission if the programme is not relevant enough from the point of view of achieving the goals set by the National Strategy for the Development of Sports or the development programme of the competent national sports federation, if other programmes are more prioritized, if the financial and operational capabilities of the programme applicant are not sufficient, if the programme is of lower quality, i.e., it received a lower number of points during the evaluation of the quality of the programme proposals compared to the selected programme proposals.

470. At the Commission's proposal, the Ministry makes a preliminary decision on the allocation of funds for the next budget year for the implementation of annual programmes that realize general interest in the field of sports by 15 July of the current year. By 15 December of the current year, the Ministry revises the preliminary decision on the allocation of funds to a specific annual programme, harmonizing it with the funds determined in the budget of the Republic of Serbia for the following year.

471. By 30 December of the current year, the Ministry makes a decision on the approval of annual programmes, and informs the holders of the programmes about the amount of approved funds per programme.

472. Decisions of the Ministry on the approval of the annual and special programmes are final and an administrative dispute can be filed against them. The subject of an administrative dispute cannot be, in accordance with the Law, the amount of funds obtained on the basis of annual and special programmes.

473. In accordance with the Law, the Ministry concludes a contract on the implementation of the programme with the holder of the approved programme.

474. If the holder of the programme for the implementation of the approved programme has been allocated less funds than the funds specified in the financial plan of the programme, the holder of the programme is obliged to submit to the Ministry, before concluding the contract on the implementation of the programme, an amendment to the proposed programme in accordance with the amount of approved funds (revised programme proposal) on the appropriate the form established by this rulebook, otherwise it will be considered that he has given up on concluding the contract.

475. Holders of approved programmes are obliged to submit to the Ministry, at its request, as well as within the time limit provided by this rulebook and the contract on the implementation of the programme, and at least once a year, a report with the necessary documentation on the implementation of the programme or parts of the programme and the use of funds from the budget of the Republic of Serbia. The periodic report is submitted within fifteen days after the end of each quarter during the implementation of the programme, on a special form that is an integral part of the Rulebook.

476. The holder of the programme is obliged to submit to the Ministry within fifteen days from the end of the implementation of the programme the final (final) report on the implementation of the programme, with photocopies of the complete documentation on the expenditure of funds, marked in a way that brings it in connection with a certain type of expenses from the financial plan of the programme, certified with their own seal, and with the auditor's report (audit of fulfillment of contractual obligations).

477. The Ministry analyses the realizations and achieved effects after the completion of the programme and the submission of the report, and no later than the end of the current year for the previous year, with the aim of determining: whether the justified funds were realized in accordance with the purpose and goals of the programme and the conditions prescribed by law and this rulebook, that whether the programme was implemented efficiently and effectively in relation to the set indicators, whether the set goals were relevant, whether the expected results were achieved, whether the expected impact was achieved, whether the impacts were achieved in accordance with the expenditure of funds and whether it was ensured sustainability.

Part II. Sport and Status

Chapter 1. General Points

478. The issue of the legal status of athletes is one of the very important issues in the field of sports law. The significance of the issue is reflected in the fact that the legality of the work of all participants, subjects of sports law and the regularity of sports competitions depend on the precise definition and legal regulation of the rights, obligations and responsibilities of all participants in sports activities.

479. To better define the legal status of athletes in the Republic of Serbia, the monograph will pay special attention to the qualification of athletes, their rights and obligations arising from the statutory qualification, the relationship between labour and sports law, the employment status of athletes, social, health and pension insurance and the tax treatment of athletes.

Chapter 2. Public Regulation

480. In the Republic of Serbia, the rights, obligations and responsibilities of athletes are regulated in detail by LSRS. In addition to LSRS, this issue is specifically regulated by the following laws and by-laws:[83]

(1) Labour Law (LL).[84]
(2) Law on Employment and Unemployment Insurance.[85]
(3) LHI.[86]
(4) LPDI.[87]
(5) Law on Occupational Safety and Health.[88]
(6) LPIT.[89]
(7) Budget law.[90]
(8) Law of contract and torts (LCT).[91]
(9) Law on copyright and related rights (LCRR).[92]
(10) Law on public Information and media.[93]
(11) LPOP.[94]
(12) Law on advertising (LoA).[95]
(13) Law on Patents (LoP).[96]

83. For the sake of clarity, certain legal sources of sports law are listed again.
84. *See* 'Official Gazette of RS', Nos 24/2005, 61/2005, 54/2009, 32/2013, 75/2014, 13/2017 – Decision of the CC, 113/2017 and 95/2018 – authentic interpretation).
85. *See* 'Official Gazette of RS', Nos 36/2009, 88/2010, 38/2015, 113/2017, 113/2017 – other law and 49/2021.
86. *See* 'Official Gazette of RS', No. 25/2019.
87. *See* 'Official Gazette of RS', Nos 34/2003, 64/2004 – Decision of the CC, 84/2004 – other law, 85/2005, 101/2005 – other law, 63/2006 – Decision of the CC, 5/2009, 107/2009, 101/2010, 93/2012, 62/2013, 108/2013, 75/2014, 142/2014, 73/2018, 46/2019 – Decision of the CC, 86/2019 and 62&2021).
88. *See* 'Official Gazette of RS', Nos 101/2005, 91/2015 and 113/2017 – other law).
89. *See* 'Official Gazette of RS', Nos 24/2001, 80/2002, 80/2002 – other law, 135/2004, 62/2006, 65/2006 – corrigendum, 31/2009, 44/2009, 18/2010, 50/2011, 91/2011 – Decision of CC, 7/2012 – adjusted din. amount, 93/2012, 114/2012 – Decision of CC, 8/2013 – adjusted din. amount., 47/2013, 48/2013 – ispr., 108/2013, 6/2014 – adjusted din. amount, 57/2014, 68/2014 – dr. law, 5/2015 – adjusted din. amount, 112/2015, 5/2016 – adjusted din. amount, 7/2017 – adjusted din. amount, 113/2017, 7/2018 – adjusted din. amount, 95/2018, 4/2019 – adjusted din. amount, 86/2019, 5/2020 – adjusted din. amount, 153/2020, 156/2020 – adjusted din. amount, 6/2021 – adjusted din. amount and 44/2021.
90. *See* 'Official Gazette of RS', Nos 149/2020 and 40/2021.
91. *See* 'Official Gazette of SFRY', Nos 29/78, 39/85, 45/89 – Decision of CCY and 57/89, 'Official Gazette of FRY', No. 31/93, 'Official Gazette of Serbia and Montenegro', No. 1/2003 – Constitutional Charter and 'Official Gazette of RS', No. 18/2020.
92. *See* 'Official Gazette of RS', Nos 104/2009, 99/2011, 119/2012, 29/2016 – Decision of CC and 66/2019.
93. *See* 'Official Gazette of RS', Nos 83/2014, 58/2015 and 12/2016 – authentic interpretation.
94. *See* 'Official Gazette of RS', Nos 6/2016 and 24/2018.
95. *See* 'Official Gazette of RS', Nos 6/2016 and 52/2019 – other law.
96. *See* 'Official Gazette of RS', Nos 99/2011, 113/2017 – other law, 95/2018 and 66/2019.

(14) LPT.[97]
(15) Law on Misdemeanours (LoMis).[98]
(16) Law on accounting.[99]
(17) Law on the Ratification of the European Convention against Doping in Sport (LRECDS).[100]
(18) Law on the Ratification of the European Convention for the prevention of Violence and misconduct at Sports events, especially football matches (LRECVS).[101]
(19) LFAI.[102]
(20) ZDOSI.[103]
(21) Law on the Prevention of Doping in Sports (LPDS).[104]
(22) Law on the Prevention of Violence and Misconduct at Sports Events (LPVMS).[105]
(23) LoAss.[106]
(24) LAPV.[107]
(25) Code of Criminal Procedure.[108]
(26) RTA.[109]
(27) Rulebook on detailed conditions for performing sports activities and sports occupations (RSA).[110]
(28) Rulebook on doping control in sports competitions and out of competitions.[111]
(29) RSF.[112]
(30) Rulebook on the National Categorisation of Sports (RNCS).[113]
(31) Rulebook on the Supervision of Professional Work in the Field of Sports (RPW).[114]

---

97. *See* 'Official Gazette of RS', No. 26/2001, 'Official Gazette of FRY', No. 42/2002 – Decision of SCC and 'Official Gazette of RS', Nos 80/2002, – other law, 135/2004, 61/2007, 5/2009, 101/2010, 24/2011, 78/2011, 57/2012 – Decision of CC, 47/2013, 68/2014 – other law, 95/2018, 99/2018 – Decision of CC, 86/2019 and 144/2020.
98. *See* 'Official Gazette of RS', Nos 65/2013, 13/2016, 98/2016 – Decision of CC, 91/2019 and 91/2019 – other law.
99. *See* 'Official Gazette of RS', Nos 73/2019 and 44/2021 – other law.
100. *See* 'Official Gazette of SFRY – International Agreements', No. 4/91.
101. *See* 'Official Gazette of RS', Nos 67/2003, 101/2005 – other law, 90/2007, 72/2009 – other law, 111/2009, 104/2013 – other law and 87/2018).
102. *See* 'Official Gazette of RS', Nos 120/2004, 54/2007, 104/2009 and 36/2010.
103. *See* 'Official Gazette of RS', Nos 33/2006 and 13/2016.
104. *See* 'Official Gazette of RS', Nos 111/2014 and 47/2021.
105. *See* 'Official Gazette of RS', Nos 67/2003, 101/2005 – other law, 90/2007, 72/2009 – other law, 111/2009, 104/2013 – other law and 87/2018.
106. *See* 'Official Gazette of RS', Nos 51/2009, 99/2011 – other laws and 44/2018 – other law.
107. *See* 'Official Gazette of RS', Nos 99/2009, 67/2012 – Decision of CC and 18/2020 – other law.
108. *See* 'Official Gazette of RS', Nos 72/2011, 101/2011, 121/2012, 32/2013, 45/2013, 55/2014, 35/2019, 27/2021 – Decision of CC 62/2021 – Decision of CC.
109. *See* 'Official Gazette of RS', No. 124/2012.
110. *See* 'Official Gazette of RS', No. 42/2017.
111. *See* 'Official Bulletin of ADAS', No. 38/2021.
112. *See* 'Official Gazette of RS', No. 55/2013.
113. *See* 'Official Gazette of RS', No. 12/2017.
114. *See* 'Official Gazette of RS', No. 92/2011.

(32) PSO.[115]
(33) Rulebook on the categorisation of top athletes.[116]
(34) Rulebook on the content and manner of keeping a single record of associations, organizations and entrepreneurs in the field of sports (Rrec).[117]
(35) RSB.[118]
(36) Rulebook on the work permit of sports experts.[119]
(37) Rulebook on professional training for performing certain professional jobs in sports.[120]
(38) Rulebook on detailed conditions and criteria for scholarships for top athletes.[121]
(39) Rulebook on detailed conditions and criteria for scholarships for top amateur athletes for sports training and for the award of financial aid to top athletes with special merits.[122]
(40) Rulebook on the professional sports exam.[123]
(41) Rulebook on the national categorisation of sports experts.[124]
(42) Rulebook on the national categorisation of top athletes.[125]
(43) Rulebook on conducting health examinations of athletes and sports experts.[126]
(44) Regulation on national sports recognition and cash prizes.[127]

481. These laws and legal acts include norms directly or indirectly regulating certain issues of importance for the legal status of an athlete, which is precisely regulated by sports rules, collective agreements in the field of professional sports and the agreement between the athlete and the sports organization regarding amateur athletes.

§1. Qualification of the Legal Status

482. In order to discuss the legal status of an athlete, the rights and obligations arising from the appropriate legal status, and the issue of defining the athlete necessarily arises as a preliminary issue.

483. Although this issue was discussed in the introductory part (athlete, amateur athlete, professional athlete, athlete competitor, top athlete, promising athlete, talented athlete, categorized athlete), as a reminder, and for reasons of integrity, or

115. *See* 'Official Gazette of RS', No. 86/2020.
116. *See* 'Official Gazette of RS', No. 123/2012.
117. *See* 'Official Gazette of RS', No. 108/2017.
118. *See* 'Official Gazette of RS', No. 44/2018.
119. *See* 'Official Gazette of RS', No. 60/2020.
120. *Ibid.*
121. *See* 'Official Gazette of RS', No. 124/2012.
122. *Ibid.*
123. *See* 'Official Gazette of RS', No. 7/2018.
124. *See* 'Official Gazette of RS', No. 25/2013.
125. *See* 'Official Gazette of RS', No. 123/2012.
126. *See* 'Official Gazette of RS', No. 88/2020.
127. *See* 'Official Gazette of RS', Nos 22/2016, 83/2017, 74/2021.

easier understanding of the rights and obligations arising from the appropriate legal status of the athlete, at this point, we will briefly look at only the most important categories of athletes.

484. According to LSRS, an athlete is any person who engages in sports activities independently or within sports organizations, as an amateur or professional.[128] His/her legal position depends on whether the athlete engages in physical activity as an amateur or professional.[129]

485. Although LSRS does not contain a precise definition of an amateur athlete, based on the provisions of the Law on professional athletes, it can be concluded that an amateur athlete is a person who does not meet the requirements of the law regarding obtaining the status of a professional athlete (negative definition). At the same time, the legislator makes a distinction between amateur athletes and amateur competing athletes, so depending on the group to which they belong, it regulates the issue of the legal status of these persons, their rights, obligations and responsibilities.

486. A professional athlete is a person who engages in sports activities in the form of an occupation. Performing sports activities professionally can be done independently or within one of the sports organizations, but under the conditions and in the manner provided for in LSRS. According to Article 13 and Article 14 of LSRS, two forms of professional sports are provided for employment and entrepreneurship (independent performance of activities). Under the professional athlete, LSRS also includes trainers, technical and sports directors and other persons whose only occupation is the physical preparation of athletes.[130]

487. In accordance with LSRS, an amateur athlete means a person whose earnings are not the goal of engaging in sports activities and does not engage in those activities in the form of an occupation.[131]

488. An athlete competitor is equally understood as an amateur athlete and a professional athlete who participates in a sports competition. In doing so, they may

128. *See* Art. 9 paras 1–2.

129. An opinion is increasingly present in the scientific public according to which an athlete-professional can be distinguished from an athlete-amateur. According to the prevailing opinion, the difference is that a professional athlete spends all his/her time and all his/her psychophysical energy in activities that become his/her main occupation in life, and an amateur can provide funds for personal nutrition and possibly for other basic life needs from his/her sports activities. Some authors, however, believe that money is the main element for distinguishing a professional athlete from an amateur athlete. According to this opinion, if money is earned by sports activity, and if it is the only source of income for life, it is a professional, but if money is only a necessary supplement to subsistence (but not essential for survival) it is an amateur.

130. They must meet the criteria of the national sports federation and perform their activities in accordance with its regulations. Respect for the regulations of the sports federation, among other things, aims to make a difference between sports activity for leisure (amateurs), from professional activity, as a work commitment from which the employee in that sphere is supported.

131. *See* Art. 3, para. 8 LSRS.

participate in the competition as members of a sports organization or independently, in accordance with the law and sports rules. For an athlete to be able to compete independently, it is necessary that the sports rules allow it in accordance with Articles 10 and 11 of LSRS.[132]

489. The Sports Federation of Serbia, as the competent body, whose competence is determined by LSRS, within its activities and on the basis of special regulations, also determines the categorization of athletes based on results, age, gender and national sports categorization.[133] According to special regulations, the Sports Federation of Serbia also regulates the manner of assigning a certain rank – sports status (status of a top athlete, status of a promising athlete, status of a talented athlete, etc.).

490. According to the National Categorization of Athletes, a top athlete is an athlete who, based on the achieved top sports results at sports competitions and other ways of achieving them, in accordance with the sports rules of the competent international sports federation, is ranked in the category of top athletes.

491. A top athlete can independently engage in sports activities in individual sports and as an independent professional athlete, or entrepreneur.[134] At the same time, the legislator provides an equal opportunity for an amateur athlete to enjoy the privileges of a top athlete, provided that he/she has achieved top results in sports competitions and that the Sports Federation of Serbia has categorized him/her as a top athlete.

492. A top athlete also enjoys certain privileges. Thus, regarding a top professional athlete, the budget of the Republic of Serbia allocates funds for scholarships for his/her further sports training, and if it is a top amateur athlete, then privileges are acquired within the right to health, social and pension insurance.[135]

---

132. As sport represents a special area of life, which takes place in special weather and space conditions, sports rules are of special importance, which each sports activity has individually. The legislator, recognizing the significance and importance of sports rules for the regulation of sports, provides an opportunity for sports organizations to independently adopt sports rules and autonomously regulate issues related to sports activities and occupations in accordance with the Law. In this context, sports rules mean statutes, regulations and decisions of sports organizations. *See* Art. 10 and Art. 11 of LSRS.
133. The National Categorization of Sports determines the ranking criteria and determines the ranking of sports branches based on the achieved sports results achieved by athletes, sports organizations and national sports teams at international sports competitions, number of registered sports organizations, athletes and sports experts, national and international traditions, national and international media representation and popularity, health, social and other influence on participants, financial significance and financial independence, advertising attractiveness, availability of certain sports branches and other important factors. The national categorization of athletes also includes the categorization of athletes with disabilities.
134. *See* Art. 14 para. 1.
135. *See* Art. 15 para. 1 and Art. 16 para. 1. When assigning the appropriate sports status, it is especially emphasized that for women athletes who are on pregnancy and maternity leave, results achieved one year before pregnancy are counted.

493. Regulations on the categorization of top athletes[136] and the Rulebook on the amendments to the Rulebook on the categorization of top athletes,[137,138] athletes are awarded the category of a top athlete and the appropriate sports status for the results achieved at senior domestic and international sports competitions, at the junior world and European championships and cadet world and European championships. Thus, in the category of top athletes, the following can be distinguished:

- Top athlete – an athlete with merits (results in the last four years are calculated, provided that in this period he remains in the competition system of the competent national branch sports federation).
- Top athlete – international rank (results in the last two years are counted, provided that in this period he/she achieves a sports result that corresponds to the sports status of the top athlete. – national rank).
- Top athlete – national rank (sports results achieved in the previous year are counted).

494. Promising sportsman/woman is a minor athlete who, on the basis of achieved sports results, is ranked, in accordance with the National Categorization of Sportsmen/women, in the category of promising sportsmen/women. Since he/she is a minor, a contract with an athlete who does not have full legal capacity can produce valid effect only with the written consent of both parents or guardians, certified in accordance with the Law, and based on previously determined medical fitness of the athlete who does not have full legal capacity. Medical fitness is determined by the competent health service or the institution responsible for sports and sports medicine. When concluding and executing an employment contract with a sports organization, a minor athlete enjoys special protection prescribed by the law which regulates the conditions for employment and work of persons under 18 years of age.[139]

495. Talented sportsman/woman is an adult athlete who, on the basis of achieved sports results, is ranked, in accordance with the National Categorization of Sportsmen/women, in the category of talented sportsmen/women.

496. According to the Rulebook on National Categorization, athletes are also categorized depending on the type of sports activity. The following athletes are distinguished:

(1) athletes of the first category (athletes in athletics, water polo, rowing, kayaking, canoeing, basketball, volleyball, swimming, handball, archery, tennis, football, wrestling, taekwondo);

---

136. *See* 'Official Gazette of RS', No. 123/2012.
137. *See* 'Official Gazette of RS', No. 159/2020.
138. The mentioned rulebooks stipulate that the ranking procedure is initiated by a request submitted by the competent national branch sports federation, with an explanation and accompanying documentation proving the fulfilment of criteria and measures.
139. *See* Art. 10 paras 4, 6.

(2) athletes of the second category (athletes in the field of cycling, boxing, aviation sports activities, gymnastics, karate, kickboxing, bowling, mountaineering, table tennis, judo, chess, athletics (Paralympic sports), table tennis (Paralympic sports) and shooting, sport for the blind and partially sighted, participants in the Special Olympics);
(3) athletes of the third category (athletes in the field of motoring, American football, badminton, bodybuilding, weightlifting, sailing, equestrian sports (Olympic and FEI disciplines), gallop sports, trotting, fencing, motorsports, savate, synchronized swimming, skiing, sport dancing, sport fishing, archery, triathlon, ice hockey, jet ski, jujitsu, fitness, sitting volleyball (Paralympic sport), Powerlifting (Paralympic sport), swimming (Paralympic sport), archery (Paralympic sport));
(4) athletes of the fourth category (athletes of aikido, baseball, boules, bridge, goa, golf, curling, kendo, kyokushinkai, skating, korfball, orienteering, darts, underwater sports, rafting, rugby, rugby 13, sambo, diving, skiing on the water, sport climbing, field hockey, Tug of War, badminton (Paralympic sport), cycling (Paralympic sport), Goalball (blind and partially sighted – Paralympic sport), canoe (Paralympic sport), wheelchair basketball Paralympic sport), skiing (Paralympic sport), taekwondo (Paralympic sport), non-Paralympic sport for persons with disabilities);
(5) athletes of the fifth category (athletes aerobics, Ashihara Kaikan, biathlon, billiards (pool), bobsleigh, bowling, Wushu kung fu, cricket, Lifesaving, flying targets, paintball, Powerlifting, practical shooting, sledging, sky ball, squash, snooker, sports speleology, softball).[140]

497. According to LSRS, sports experts are natural persons who perform professional work in accordance with the Law. Given the fact under LSRS, a professional athlete includes trainers, technical and sports directors and other persons whose only occupation is the physical preparation of the athlete for the competition, according to the PSO,[141] the following persons also fall under the category of athletes:

(1) sports trainer;
(2) sports instructor;
(3) organizer of recreation in sports;
(4) sports manager;
(5) organizer of sports business;
(6) sports mediator;
(7) sports referee;
(8) sports guide;
(9) sports lifeguard;
(10) sports archiver;
(11) sports statistician;

140. *See* Art. 2 of the Rulebook on National Categorisation of Sports 'Official Gazette of RS', No. 12/2017.
141. *See* 'Official Gazette of RS', No. 86/2020.

(12) sports journalist;
(13) sports reporter;
(14) sports advisor;
(15) sports propagandist;
(16) sports physician;
(17) sports physiotherapist;
(18) sports masseur;
(19) sports psychologist;
(20) sports nutritionist (Article 3 RSO).

498. The National Categorization of Sports Experts determines the criteria and measures for ranking sports experts based on the quality of work, performance, level of expertise and national categorization of sports and regulates the manner of assigning the appropriate rank – sports status.

499. The Rulebook on the national categorization of sports experts[142] provides the criteria and benchmarks for ranking sports experts in individual sports:

(1) top sports trainer – trainer with merits (if within two years, he/she worked with one athlete who acquired the sports status of a top athlete – athlete with merits);
(2) top sports trainer – international rank (if within two years, he/she has worked with two athletes who have acquired the sports status of a top athlete – international rank at least, or if he/she has worked with one athlete who has within a period of two years acquired the sports status of a top athlete – international rank or with five athletes who have acquired the sports status of top athletes – national rank, at least);
(3) top sports trainer – national rank (if in the past two years, he/she has worked with five athletes who have acquired the sports status of top athletes – national rank at least, or if he/she works, or has worked in the past two years with two athletes who have acquired the sports status of a top athlete – national rank or with five athletes who have acquired the sports status of promising athletes, at least).

500. The appropriate sports status is awarded to sports experts who lead national sports teams and to club sports trainers.[143]

501. Criteria and benchmarks for ranking sports experts in team sports are:

(1) top sports trainer – trainer with merits (if in the past two years, he/she has worked with a team whose members have acquired the sports status of a top athlete – athlete with merits);

142. *See* 'Official Gazette of RS', No. 25/2013.
143. A club sports trainer can achieve the appropriate sports status provided that at least 20% of the athletes from the coaching club participate in the national sports team.

(2) top sports trainer – international rank (if he/she has worked in the past two years with one team whose athletes have acquired the sports status of top athletes – international rank);
(3) top sports trainer – national rank (if in the past two years, he/she has worked with one team whose athletes have acquired the sports status of top athletes – national rank at least).

502. Only the most general classifications of athletes are presented here, while they are elaborated in detail in the appropriate regulations issued by the Minister responsible for youth and sports.

§2. Fundamental Rights and Obligations

503. LSRS prescribes in detail the rights and obligations of athletes, stating that they are regulated by sports rules, a collective agreement in the field of professional sports and an agreement between the athlete and the sports organization.[144]

504. Sports rules cannot determine the lesser rights of athletes or more unfavourable conditions for performing sports activities than those provided by law. Sports rules must be in accordance with the Law, the collective agreement must be in accordance with the Law, individual agreements as well, as well as in accordance with sports rules and the collective agreement. It is important to note that with each lower act, athletes can be given greater rights, even rights that are not provided by the higher act unless it is contrary to the Law.

505. All sports organizations, regardless of the status of the athlete, conclude a contract with the athlete which regulates mutual rights, obligations and responsibilities. A contract with an athlete who does not have full legal capacity may be validly concluded only with the written consent of both parents or guardians, certified in accordance with the Law, and on the basis of previously determined medical fitness of the athlete who does not have full legal capacity by the competent health service or institute competent for sports and sports medicine.[145]

506. The legal nature of the contract varies depending on whether the contract is concluded with a professional athlete or an amateur athlete.

507. The sports organization concludes an employment contract with the professional athlete, while it concludes a contract agreement with the amateur athlete, as a rule, a temporary service contract. It is important to point out that the contract cannot provide for lesser rights for the athlete, than those provided by the Law, which is not the case when it comes to contracting greater rights.

144. *See* Art. 9 of LSRS.
145. *See* Art. 10 para. 6 of LSRS.

508. The rights, obligations and responsibilities of amateur athletes are regulated by the Law, sports rules of the competent national sports federation and general acts of the sports organization, while the rights, obligations and responsibilities of amateur athletes who are provided with monetary compensation for sports are regulated by the agreement between the athlete and the sports organization (contract on scholarship of a minor athlete for sports training or contract on performing sports activities) in addition to the cited acts.[146] An amateur athlete who engages in sports activities as a member of a sports association, without a contract, has the rights established by the sports rules and the general act of the sports organization.[147]

509. According to the contract on performing sports activities, the amateur competitor and the sports organization determine, in accordance with the sports rules, in particular: monetary compensation for sports activities, monetary and other prizes for achieved sports results, accommodation and food costs during sports preparations and sports competition, compensation for concluding a contract and compensation for the use of the athlete's image.[148]

510. In sports practice, it is no longer considered that the basic characteristic of an amateur athlete is that he/she does not receive financial compensation for engaging in sports activities. In order to remove all doubts about the legal admissibility of contracting cash benefits for amateur athletes, the legislator just wants to remove any dilemma stipulating that the contract that provides financial compensation for amateur athletes, as well as the contract on the compensation for concluding a contract on performing sports activities of the amateur athlete, produce a valid legal effect.[149]

511. LSRS and the Rulebook on detailed conditions and criteria for scholarships for top amateur athletes for sports training and for the award of financial aid to top athletes with special merits regulate the payment of sports scholarships.[150]

512. According to the Law on Budget, funds are planned on an annual level for the payment of sports scholarships.

513. A top amateur athlete can receive a scholarship for sports training if the following conditions are met:

- in the current year he/she is categorized as a top athlete by the valid National Categorization of Athletes;

146. *See* Art. 10 para. 1 of LSRS.
147. *See* Art. 17 para. 1 of LSRS.
148. *See* Art. 17 para. 2 of LSRS.
149. These are contracts that athletes sign when transferring from club to club.
150. The Regulation on National Sports Recognitions and Cash Prizes determines more detailed conditions, manner of payment and the amount of national sports recognitions and monetary awards for a special contribution to the development and affirmation of sport. *See* 'Official Gazette of RS', Nos 22/16, 83/17 and 65/19.

- he/she does not have the status of a professional athlete in accordance with the LS;
- he/she is a member of the competent national branch sports federation whose programmes achieve the general interest in the field of sports, i.e., organizations in the field of sports that are members of that branch federation;
- he/she has been proposed by the competent national branch sports federation in the annual programme for obtaining scholarships for sports training of top amateur athletes within the number of scholarships to which that branch sports federation is entitled in accordance with the said Rulebook;
- he/she actively engages in sports activities in the organization in the field of sports in the Republic of Serbia in the current year;
- in the last five years, he/she has played for at least one year for a domestic organization in the field of sports;
- he/she fulfils obligations towards the national sports team;
- in terms of age, namely: is between 15 to 26 years – top athletes – national rank, and up to 30 years – athletes in Paralympic sports; he/she has not reached the age of 30 – top athlete – international rank, and up to the age of 40 – athlete in Paralympic sports;
- he/she has not turned 45 – top athlete – athlete with merits;
- he/she the status of a student in the current year and achieved an overall 'very good' school performance in the previous school year – for athletes aged 15 to 19;
- his/her medical fitness to perform sports activities has been determined, in accordance with the law;
- he/she respects the anti-doping rules prescribed by the LPDS.[151]

514. The right to a scholarship ceases for athletes by gaining national recognition for special contributions to the development and affirmation of sports in accordance with the LS or the cessation of fulfilling the conditions for receiving a scholarship.

515. A national sports recognition is awarded to athletes, citizens of the Republic of Serbia, who as members of the national sports team of the Republic of Serbia win a medal at the Olympic Games, Paralympic Games, Chess Olympics, world and European championships in Olympic and Paralympic sports, or have been or will be world record holders in Olympic and Paralympic sports, or become finalists of the DAVIS Cup or the FED Cup of the International Tennis Federation.

516. Financial aid can be received by a top athlete with special merits for the development of sports who is ranked as an athlete with merits through the categorization of athletes, in accordance with this Law.

517. Financial assistance may be used to cover expenses that the sportsman/woman has personally incurred in preparing for or participating in competitions or for the treatment caused by an injury sustained in the competition, or to cover other

151. *See* 'Official Gazette of RS', No. 101/05.

particularly eligible costs, provided that these costs are not already covered by expenses of organizations in the field of sports, sponsors or donors, i.e., that the costs of treatment are not covered by health insurance, in accordance with the Law.

518. It is forbidden to expose an athlete to sports activities that may endanger or worsen his/her health condition. Doping of athletes is prohibited, in accordance with the Law. It is forbidden to expose children to sports activities and physical exercises that may endanger or worsen their health condition or negatively affect psychosocial and motor development or schooling.[152]

519. An athlete who is physically injured by another competitor during the competition has the right to compensation for damage if the injury was caused by negligent or gross violation of sports rules.

520. The general rules on liability for damage, provided by the Law of Contracts and Torts, apply to the liability for damage suffered by an athlete and a sports expert when engaging in sports activities.[153]

521. According to Article 155 of the Law of Contracts and Torts,[154] damage is the diminution of one's property (ordinary damage) and the prevention of its increase (lost benefit), as well as the infliction of physical or mental pain or fear on another (intangible damage).

522. From the aspect of compensation for damage that threatens athletes during sports activities, the provision of Article 195 of LoCT is particularly interesting, according to which if someone inflicts bodily injury or impairs the health of the other person, he/she is obliged to reimburse him/her for the costs of treatment and other necessary costs in this regard, as well as the revenue lost due to incapacity for work during treatment.

523. If the injured person loses his/her earnings due to a complete or partial incapacity for work, or his/her needs are permanently increased, or the possibilities of his/her further development and advancement are destroyed or reduced, the perpetrator is obliged to pay the injured party a certain rent as compensation for the damage. This provision refers to cases of severe and especially severe bodily injuries, which, in terms of their intensity and scope, exceed the usual injuries that can occur when engaging in various sports activities.

524. Hence, LSRS regulates only those cases of damage that occur as a result of a serious bodily injury that one competitor inflicts on another during the competition and in connection with the competition. According to the LSRS, damage does

152. *See* Art. 22 of LSRS.
153. *See* Art. 23 of LSRS.
154. Hereinafter referred to as: LCT.

not mean damage which, in accordance with sports rules, is the result of common threats and risks of engaging in certain sports activities, i.e., performing certain professional work in sports.[155]

525. The issue of property liability of an athlete for bodily injuries inflicted on another competitor during the competition is one of the most complex issues not only in domestic but also in the wider world literature and court practice. The first reason for such a thing is the fact that the deprivation of rights consists of a bodily injury, and second in the circumstance that the general legal rules on liability for damage do not provide for damage caused during the performance of sports activities.

526. The bodily injury in the sense of civil law means the violation of physical or mental integrity. Injuries caused during sports activities must be of certain severity to be considered bodily injuries. Small scratches, bruises and slight muscle strains are not assessed as bodily injuries.[156]

527. Damage to the opponent, as a rule, occurs due to a forbidden or risky game. There is an exception to this rule when the injury occurred due to behaviour that is conditionally allowed (sliding tackle in football). Depending on the type of sport, bodily injuries also differ. At the same time, the division into martial and non-martial arts is very important as the basis for the classification of bodily injuries. The use of illicit/illegal sports equipment (leg guards with sharp edges, pointed swords, narrow crampons on the football boots) is also the basis of the mentioned classification. From the mentioned injuries, one should distinguish those that are a consequence of 'violence' that does not fall under bodily injury/sports damage and to which other rules apply.[157] To be considered a bodily injury from the aspect of law, it is necessary that it is related to the typical risks of a specific sports activity within the competition.

528. The basis of liability for the caused damage is the fault of the athlete. An athlete acts wrongly if his/her behaviour was contrary to the sports rules, if he/she was aware of it and if he/she could have avoided the behaviour he/she should have avoided, but did not. This is why intent represents the most severe type of guilt, which exists in an athlete who knowingly and willingly causes harm to another.[158]

---

155. *See* Art. 23 para. 1 of LSRS.
156. In the foreign legal literature, the position has long been held that injuries in sports are not real bodily injuries, and that they should be equated with procedures performed by a physician in the physical integrity of the patient. The main argument for this was the fact that sport serves health and body maintenance. However, in the recent legal literature, this position has been completely rejected. *See*: Nenad Đurđević, *Commentary on the Law on Sports*, Belgrade, 1997, 31.
157. Violence, as a rule, consists of hitting, trampling, and similar actions.
158. The athlete's intent is very difficult to prove. It is necessary to prove that the athlete had a lot of time to think about his/her action. As conscious and willing movements are difficult to prove in sports and differ from reflexes, precisely due to the game that takes place quickly, it is difficult to prove the athlete's intent.

Otherwise, if the damage occurred as a consequence of an action that cannot be attributed to the athlete's fault, the injured party, as a rule, is not entitled to compensation for the damage.

529. Unlike intent as a severe form of guilt, negligence, which is reflected in the neglect of attention required of people in sports, is a milder form of guilt. The cause of the damage must be visible, and the illegality of the action must be known for the damage to be considered to have occurred. Therefore, the actions of the athlete are not illegal if they are in accordance with the sports rules. This further means that the athlete is liable for damage caused to others only if it is the result of violating sports rules. The athlete shall be liable for damage caused to another competitor due to a violation of the sports rules and if it was caused intentionally or due to gross negligence.

530. In property liability, individual attention is not explored. Objective attention is a criterion for determining property liability. Therefore, for each specific case, the existence or non-existence of certain standards is examined, i.e., adherence to certain rules of conduct. Everyone who participates in a certain type of sports competition must adhere to the rules that apply to the area, and especially the degree of attention which is then expected. Therefore, it is considered that every athlete acted carelessly and did not have the attention expected from a cautious and alert athlete. Due to the different types of risks that accompany different sports activities, all actions of athletes must be observed and assessed depending on the specific case, type of sports activities and the amount of the risks that accompany the activity.

§3. Employment Regulations

531. Employing sports experts is another very important legal issue as important as employing athletes since without adequate professional work and training process, it is not possible to achieve top sports results, as required of every professional athlete. Adequate professional staff (sports referees, trainers, health professionals) are also important for the development of recreational and school sports.

532. The rights, obligations and responsibilities of athletes are regulated by law, sports rules of the competent national branch sports federation, collective agreement, rulebook (when no collective agreement has been concluded with the employer) and the agreement between the athlete and the sports organization. A special collective agreement is concluded by the representative trade union and the corresponding representative association in sports, in accordance with the law.

533. It is generally accepted that the relationship between a professional athlete and a sports organization is a relationship that contains all the characteristics of an employment relationship. This further means that a professional athlete has all the rights, obligations and responsibilities arising from the LL unless otherwise provided by the LS or sports rules.

534. Article 13 of LSRS stipulates that a professional athlete establishes an employment relationship with a sports organization by concluding an employment contract, for a definite period of time, for a maximum of five years. At the end of this period, the professional athlete may re-enter into a contract with the same or another sports organization. Interruptions of work shorter than thirty days do not affect the duration of employment. A professional athlete has all the rights, obligations and responsibilities from the employment relationship in accordance with the law governing labour unless otherwise provided by this Law or the sports rules of the competent international sports federation.

535. With the employment contract, professional athletes and the sports organization determine the salary and other income in accordance with this Law and the Law regulating labour. Other income of a professional athlete determined in accordance with this Law does not have the character of the salary. Appropriate taxes and contributions on the salary, i.e., on the income of citizens, are paid on the salary and other income of a professional athlete, in accordance with the Law.

536. If the athlete is engaged in a sports organization outside his/her place of residence, the sports organization may provide the athlete with free accommodation on the territory of the local self-government unit in which the seat of the sports organization is located, in which case it is not considered other income of the athlete.

537. Remunerations can also be determined by general acts of the sports organization. Working hours, vacations, absences and other rights and obligations of a professional athlete towards the sports organization are adjusted to the regime of sports preparations, i.e., competitions. A professional athlete may be temporarily referred to another sports organization on the basis of a written agreement between the sports organization to which he/she is referred and the sports organization with which he/she is employed, with the consent of the professional athlete, in accordance with this law.

538. A top athlete can independently engage in sports activities in individual sports and as an independent professional athlete, i.e., entrepreneur. No special space, equipment or staff are required to perform the activity.

539. When concluding and executing an employment contract with a sports organization, a minor athlete enjoys special protection prescribed by the law which regulates the conditions for employment and work of persons under 18 years of age. The sports organization and the athlete are obliged to adhere to the rights and obligations determined by the acts. A contract with an athlete who does not have full legal capacity may be validly concluded only with the written consent of both parents or guardians, certified in accordance with the Law, and on the basis of previously determined medical fitness of the athlete who does not have full legal capacity by the competent health service or institute competent for sports and sports medicine. Before the conclusion of the contract, the sports organization shall inform the athlete of the rights, obligations and responsibilities.

540. Engaging in sports activities in accordance with the contract on performing sports activities is considered work outside employment, in accordance with the Law. An athlete and a sports organization may conclude only one contract for the athlete to engage in sports activities in a sports organization, in accordance with this Law. A contract between a sports organization and an athlete that is concluded contrary to the provisions of this Law is void. Athletes who do not have a validly concluded contract with a certain sports organization may not be denied the right to conclude a contract with another sports organization, i.e., transferring to another sports organization and registering and performing for it at sports competitions as an athlete, unless otherwise provided by this Law.

541. In case of the termination or annulment of the contract between the athlete and the sports organization, the dispute between the sports organization which he/she leaves and the sports organization to which he transfers on the amount and payment of the agreed transfer fee, or fees for development, i.e., training of the athlete determined by sports rules may not influence the sports activities of the athlete and the right to perform for the sports organization to which he/she has transferred.

542. The athlete is entitled to compensation for the damage he/she suffers from acts of discrimination of the organization in the field of sports. Compensation for the development, i.e., training of the athlete is calculated when concluding the first professional contract in accordance with the sports rules of the competent national branch and international sports federation, based on investments, i.e., actual costs of the sports organization/organizations that contributed to the athlete's development, whereby the last year of training can be counted as the year in which the athlete turned 21. The sports organization which the athlete leaves cannot claim compensation for the development or training of the athlete if the athlete or his/her parent or guardian paid the membership fee or compensation for sports activities, sports equipment and sports preparations, i.e., the fee must be proportionally reduced. Compensation cannot be claimed if the athlete's contract with the sports organization is terminated due to the fault of the sports organization, as well as after the cessation of the athlete's development or training.

543. The contract and all amendments to the contract, including the agreed termination of the contract between the athlete and the sports organization shall be concluded in writing and certified in accordance with the law, otherwise, it is void. The contract between the athlete and the sports organization is signed by the athlete and the person authorized to represent the sports organization, and in case the athlete is a person without full legal capacity, the contract is signed accordingly. In case of concluding a contract and determining nullity, annulment, agreed termination of the contract or termination of the contract between the sports organization and the athlete due to non-fulfilment of contractual obligations, the sports organization is obliged to inform the competent national branch sports federation without delay.

544. An amateur athlete who engages in sports activities as a member of a sports association, without a contract, has the rights established by the sports rules and the general act of the sports organization. According to the contract on performing sports activities, the amateur competitor and the sports organization determine, in accordance with the sports rules, in particular: monetary compensation for sports activities, monetary and other prizes for achieved sports results, accommodation and food costs during sports preparations and sports competition, compensation for concluding a contract and compensation for the use of the athlete's image. The contract on scholarships for a minor athlete for sports training determines, in accordance with the sports rules, in particular, financial scholarship and reimbursement of accommodation and food costs during sports preparations and sports competitions. The scholarship agreement is to be concluded no later than the athlete reaches the age of maturity. The general acts of the sports organization may determine a special compensation in the name of financial assistance to top athletes with special merits.

545. A promising athlete is entitled to a scholarship for sports training, in accordance with the sports rules of the competent national branch sports federation. National sports federations establish special programmes for the care of promising athletes.

546. A sports expert may establish an employment relationship with an organization in the field of sports by concluding an employment contract, in accordance with the Law, or concluding a contract on professional engagement. A sports expert establishes an employment relationship with an organization in the field of sports by concluding an employment contract, for an indefinite period of time or for a definite period of time, up to a maximum of five years. The provisions of this Law on the conclusion of a contract between an athlete and a sports organization shall apply accordingly to the conclusion of a contract between a sports expert and an organization in the field of sports. Engaging in professional work in accordance with the contract of professional engagement is considered work outside the employment relationship, in accordance with the Law. In the event that a sports expert engages in professional work in a sports organization as a member of a sports association without a contract, the sports organization decides to appoint a sports expert to perform a certain sports profession in the sports organization, in accordance with the Law and sports rules. A sports expert, i.e., a sports expert who engages in professional work as a member of a sports association without a contract and without compensation, has the rights determined by the sports rules and general acts of the sports association. A foreign citizen who performs professional work in sports in the Republic of Serbia, in addition to the conditions prescribed by this Law, must also meet other conditions determined by the regulations governing the field of employment of foreign citizens in the Republic of Serbia. The employment contract of a sports expert and an organization in the field of sports determines the salary and other income in accordance with this law and the law governing labour, and the contract of professional engagement determines the remuneration for performing professional work in the organization in the field of sports and other income of a sports expert in accordance with this law.

547. Other income of a sports expert is cash and other rewards for achieved sports results, compensation for accommodation, food and travel during sports preparations and sports competitions, cash and other compensation for concluding a contract, compensation for using the image of a sports expert and other similar income.

548. Remuneration for performing professional work and other remuneration of a sports expert determined in accordance with this Law shall not have the character of a salary.

549. Appropriate taxes and contributions on the salary, i.e., on the income of citizens, are paid on the salary and other income of a sports expert, in accordance with the Law. The income of a member can be determined by general acts of the organization in the field of sports. A sports expert has all rights, obligations and responsibilities from employment in accordance with the law governing labour unless otherwise provided by this Law or sports rules of the competent international sports federation.

550. Working hours, vacations, absences and other rights and obligations of a sports expert towards the organization in the field of sports are adjusted to the regime of sports preparations, i.e., competitions (Article 19 of LSRS).

551. In relation to other labour relations, the provisions of labour and social law apply. In this sense, the provision of Article 88 LL is particularly interesting, according to which overtime work and redistribution of working hours of an employee who is younger than 18 years of age is prohibited. An employee under the age of 18 may not work at night, except: (1) if he/she performs work in the field of culture, sports, art and advertising; (2) when it is necessary to continue work interrupted due to force majeure, provided that such work lasts a certain time and must be completed without delay, and the employer does not have a sufficient number of other adult employees available. The working hours' regime of athletes defined in this manner is in accordance with Article 19 of LSRS.

552. Based on the above, it is concluded that although LSRS in Article 13 provides that a professional athlete establishes an employment relationship with a sports organization by concluding an employment contract, the employment relationship arising from such a contract has a number of specifics.[159]

553. The first specificity is reflected in the fact that the LS does not recognize indefinite term employment, which is the basis of employment. According to the LL, employment for an indefinite period of time is the rule, while employment for a definite period of time is an exception to the rule. In sports law, definite term employment is the rule, and employment for an indefinite period is an exception,

159. *See* Art. 13 of LSRS.

which is in line with the nature of sports law, because the athlete constantly strives to improve, advance in his/her career and increase his/her career prospects.[160]

554. Another specificity comes to the fore in the unilateral termination of the employment contract of a professional athlete. While the general rules on the unilateral termination of the contract stipulate that an employee may unilaterally terminate the contract without additional explanation, a professional athlete cannot do this unless there are justified reasons for doing so. In other words, he/she cannot leave the club on his/her own initiative by unilateral dismissal without this leading to sports sanctions against him/her.[161]

555. The third specificity derives from Article 19 of LSRS and the right to rest, leave and other rights and obligations of a professional athlete that he/she must adjust to the sports organization, in terms of adjusting the regime of sports preparations, i.e., competitions. This means that the rights of eight-hour working hours, overtime work, work during holidays, etc. cannot be applied to a professional athlete.

556. Despite the above specifics of sports law in the field of labour relations, which make it special in the sense that classical institutes of the LL cannot be applied to it, there are a large number of institutes of the individual and collective LL applied in sports.[162]

§4. Labour Market Regulation

557. A professional athlete can do sports at the top level for a certain number of years. Therefore, the time after the end of the sports career should be planned timely, which can be a special challenge for many professional athletes.

558. Recognizing this problem, OKS started the implementation of the *Career After Sports Project. Career After Sports Project* was created with the aim of providing athletes with advice and assistance on how to achieve good results in other spheres of life in addition to sports and how to achieve a successful transition from sports to business.

559. *Career After Sports* is a programme established by the IOC and is implemented in cooperation with the Adecco Group, the world's leading company in the field of human resources.

---

160. Such an exception to the rule is not the only case in the legal system of Serbia, since the Law on Higher Education in Art. 75 stipulates that a person with the title of an assistant professor and associate professor establishes employment for a definite period of time, while a person with the title of a full professor establishes employment for an indefinite period of time.
161. *See* Labour law with elements of social security, Official Gazette, Belgrade, 2020, 32.
162. For example, a professional athlete has the right to an adequate salary, occupational safety and health, etc.

560. Athletes throughout their careers invest exceptional efforts and show great dedication, energy and with their success enjoy the support of clubs, federations and the public. At the end of their career, the interest of the public decreases, and they slowly move to a 'normal life', where additional knowledge and skills are usually needed.

561. Vast research has shown that a number of athletes face a big problem and questions about what to do and how to proceed. This programme has the following goals: planning and preparation for life after a sports career; providing support to athletes and achieving a sense of security for former athletes.[163] Most athletes, after completing their sports careers, remain in the world of sports by coaching or leading various sports federations.

562. Therefore, we believe that in terms of resolving this issue, the role of the labour market is very important, which should design a programme that will ensure that athletes continue their activities, primarily in the direction of transferring knowledge, skills and experience to young athletes.

§5. Social Security

563. With regards to the rights in the field of pension and disability insurance of athletes, the general provisions of the LPDI apply[164] unless they are contrary to the provisions of LSRS.

564. Thus, an injury at a sports competition is also considered an occupational injury.[165]

565. Similarly, legal norms in the case of disability and bodily injury stipulate that this right is exercised by persons who suffer an injury by participating in sports competitions.[166]

566. In this manner, the rights of athletes are protected and regulated by the general provisions of the law regulating labour relations and rights in the field of pension and disability insurance. The general provisions of labour legislation and legislation on pension and disability insurance also apply to athletes provided they are not contrary to the provisions of sports law.[167]

163. Career after sports – Olympic Committee of Serbia, https://oks.org.rs/karijera-posle-sporta/, accessed on 30 Aug. 2021.
164. Hereinafter referred to as: LPDI.
165. *See* Art. 22 of LPDI.
166. *See* Art. 254 of LPDI.
167. The provisions of LSRS have the force of *lex specialis* effect in relation to the general provisions of labour legislation and legislation on pension and disability insurance.

567. The sports organization is obliged to conclude a contract on the insurance of its top athletes and top sports experts from the consequences of an accident during sports activities, i.e., professional work in sports, based on the established ranking of athletes and sports experts.

568. To an athlete who independently engages in sports activities as the only and basic occupation, the legislator determines this property in order to exercise the rights and obligations under social security, established by law.[168]

569. The insured amount for which compulsory insurance must be agreed per athlete, i.e., sports expert, may not be lower than: EUR 10,000 in RSD equivalent in case of the death of the athlete, i.e., sports expert; EUR 20,000 in RSD equivalent in case of the permanent loss of the general working ability of the athlete, i.e., sports expert or ability to engage in sports activities and sports activities; EUR 5,000 in RSD equivalent in case of a temporary inability to engage in sports activities and sports activities, in the name of compensation for the loss of income and actual costs of treatment of the athlete, i.e., sports expert.

570. The competent national branch sports federation is obliged to insure the athlete, i.e., sports expert who performs for the national sports team, from the consequences of an accident during the performance for the national sports team, if the athlete or sports expert is not covered by insurance. If the sports organization or the competent national branch sports federation does not conclude the contract, they are obliged to compensate the damage suffered by the athlete, i.e., the sports expert who is not insured.

571. The competent national branch sports federation may determine the obligation of sports organizations within the competence of the Federation to ensure athletes and sports experts through the Federation, by bearing the costs of the insurance. In this case, along with the athlete's application, he/she is obliged to submit a certificate from the Sports Federation of Serbia which determines the status of the athlete.

572. If the athlete performs independently, the legislator envisages the possibility of providing funds for health and pension and disability insurance on the basis

168. Determining the status of an independent entrepreneur for the purpose of exercising the right to health and pension insurance is not an exception within the framework of sports law. Just as the Law on Performing Artistic or Other Activities in the Field of Culture provides an opportunity for persons who independently perform a certain activity in the field of culture to determine the ability to perform independent activity in order to exercise the right to health and pension insurance, such an opportunity is provided to athletes independently performing sports activity as the only and basic occupation. With this solution, the legislator wanted to enable athletes to socially insure themselves while doing sports, without having to create some other organizational establishment (e.g., to register a shop). Determining the status of an athlete who independently engages in sports activity as the only and basic occupation, determining the criteria on the basis of which the athlete is determined such a characteristic, and determining the time of beginning and cessation of sports as the only and basic occupation is entrusted to the Sports Federation of Serbia. *See* Art. 15 and Art. 21 of LSRS.

of contributions paid by the athlete himself/herself. Instead of the athlete, funds for pension and disability insurance and health insurance can be provided by sports organizations, sports federations and other legal entities in whole or in part.

573. The rights from pension and disability insurance are exercised by an independent athlete with the retirement and disability insurance organization with which he/she is insured. His/her rights are personal and non-transferable and are acquired and exercised depending on the length and volume of investment. The procedure for determining the length of service for retirement is initiated at the request of the insured athlete, and the procedure for exercising the rights based on disability is initiated by the Republic Pension and Disability Insurance Fund, and at the request of the athlete.

574. The rights from the health insurance of an athlete who independently performs sports activity are exercised in the organizational unit of the Republic Institute for Health Insurance according to the place of performance of the activity. Health insurance rights are provided to family members of the insured athlete.

575. It should be emphasized here that the legislator does not exclude the possibility for an independent athlete to be able to establish some organizational form of private entrepreneurship. But in this case, the athlete enjoys the stated privilege as long as he/she performs sports activities in the form of non-profit activities (while he/she does sports for physical maintenance or competes independently with other athletes for the purpose of sports competition). In other words, the athlete enjoys the privilege as long as he/she does not provide services to others, i.e., until he/she enters the sphere of activities provided by the Law on Enterprises and the Law on Private Entrepreneurship.

576. While a professional athlete is covered by social insurance, either on the basis of an employment contract or him/her performing an activity independently, this is not the case with an amateur athlete.

577. Article 15 of LSRS states: 'Amateur athletes who are not compulsorily insured in terms of the law governing pension and disability insurance may be included in compulsory insurance under the conditions, to the extent and in the manner provided by that law.

Funds for pension and disability insurance of athletes referred to in paragraph 1 of this Article may be provided by sports organizations and other legal entities, in part or in full'.[169]

578. However, in the practice of amateur athletes, it usually falls under some type of compulsory health insurance. As it is in principle, possible for an athlete to do sports even though he/she is not insured, the legislator envisages the possibility for uninsured athletes to be insured due to frequent bodily injuries within sports activities.

169. *See* Art. 15 of LSRS.

579. Funds for health insurance are provided from the contributions paid by the athlete. Instead of the athlete, the obligations based on health insurance can be taken over by a sports organization or another legal entity. Most often in practice, this is a club or a sponsor. Considering that the amateur athlete also signs a contract with the sports organization in which mutual rights and obligations are regulated, the provisions on additional health insurance for the athlete can also be an integral part of this contract.[170]

580. The stated provisions of sports law in the Republic of Serbia clearly show that the overall legal status of athletes in the field of social insurance is clearly and precisely determined, which can be assessed as positive.

§6. Scholarships for Top Amateur Athletes

581. Scholarships for top amateur athletes are regulated by the Rulebook on scholarships for top amateur athletes for sports training and the award of financial aid to top athletes with special merits.

582. This Rulebook is issued by the relevant minister, and it determines the detailed conditions and criteria, the method and procedure for the approval of scholarships for top amateur athletes for sports training and for the award of financial aid to top athletes with special merits, as well as the criteria for determining the amount of the monthly scholarship amount and the amount of cash help.

583. A top amateur athlete can receive a scholarship for sports training if the following conditions are met:

- that in the current year, the athlete is categorized as a top athlete by the valid National Categorization;
- that he does not have the status of a professional athlete in accordance with the LS;
- that he is a member of the competent national branch sports association whose programmes realize the general interest in the field of sports, i.e., the organization in the field of sports is a member of that branch association;
- that the competent national branch sports association proposes it in the annual programme for receiving scholarships for the sports training of top amateur athletes within the number of scholarships to which that branch sports association is entitled in accordance with this rulebook;
- that in the current year, he is actively engaged in sports activities in the organization in field of sports in the Republic of Serbia;
- that in the last five years, he has performed at least one year for a domestic organization in the field of sports;
- to fulfil obligations towards the national sports team;

170. The exception to this rule is a top athlete because his/her health insurance is provided through funds from the budget of the Republic of Serbia.

- that it meets the requirements regarding age;
- that he has the status of a student in the current year and that he achieved at least very good success in the previous school year – for athletes aged 15 to 19;
- that he is medically fit to perform sports activities, in accordance with the Law;
- to comply with the anti-doping rules prescribed by the LPDS.

584. The right to a scholarship for sports training ends for an athlete upon obtaining national recognition for a special contribution to the development and affirmation of sports in accordance with the Law.

585. The number of scholarships that can be received by top amateur athletes for sports training of the same competent national branch sports federation is determined according to the rank of the sport determined by the National Sports Categorization and the rank of the competent national branch sports federation determined by the National Categorization of National Branch Sports Federations.

586. For team sports, the first and second categories of sports branches and competent national sports federations, a quota is determined by selections, at the proposal of the competent national sports federation, in accordance with the budget and achieved results.

587. In the fourth category of sports branches and competent national sports federations, only a top amateur athlete who is categorized as a top athlete – meritorious athlete or top athlete – international rank can receive a scholarship.

588. The amount of monthly scholarships for the sports training of top amateur athletes is determined according to the following criteria:

- top athlete – meritorious athlete – one and a half average net earnings in the Republic of Serbia for the month of December of the previous year, according to the data of the authority responsible for statistics;
- top athlete – international rank – one average net salary in the Republic of Serbia for the month of December of the previous year, according to the data of the authority responsible for statistics;
- top athlete – national rank – 70% of the average net salary in the Republic of Serbia for the month of December of the previous year, according to the data of the authority responsible for statistics.

589. The scholarship for the sports training of top amateur athletes is determined for a period of one year and is paid in accordance with the contract.

590. A top athlete with special merits for the development of sports in the Republic of Serbia, who is ranked as a top athlete by the National Classification of Athletes – a deserving athlete can receive financial assistance, if the following conditions are met:

- that in previous years, he achieved sports results intended for categorization in the rank of a top athlete – meritorious athlete;
- that he does not have the status of a professional athlete;
- that he is a member of the competent national branch sports association whose programs achieve general interest in the field of sports, i.e., the organization in the field of sports is a member of that competent national branch sports association;
- to cover the expenses that the athlete personally incurred for preparations or participation in the competition or for treatment caused by an injury caused during the competition, or other specially justified expenses;
- to fulfil obligations towards the national sports team;
- to comply with the anti-doping rules prescribed by the LPDS;
- that the competent national branch sports federation has determined that there is a justified need for financial assistance to a top athlete;
- that the treatment costs are not covered by health insurance, in accordance with the law;
- to be proposed by the competent national branch sports federation in the annual programme for awarding financial aid to top athletes with special merits.

591. Exceptionally, a top athlete who is a member of the national sports team, and who is permanently prevented from engaging in sports activities due to an accident, can receive financial assistance.

592. A top athlete who was a medal winner at the Olympic Games, World or European Championships can receive financial assistance even if these conditions are not met, if in the last six months, he has earned an average monthly income below the average net salary in the Republic of Serbia, or there is some other particularly justified reason for giving help (treatment, etc.).

593. The Rulebook stipulates the amount of financial aid as follows:

- to cover the costs of preparation and participation in the competition – up to five average net earnings in the Republic of Serbia for the month of December of the previous year, according to the data of the authority responsible for statistics, depending on the actual needs of the top athlete, the category of the sport and the assessment to what extent the giving will affect his future sports results and the development of sports in the Republic of Serbia;
- to cover the costs of treatment – up to ten average net earnings in the Republic of Serbia for the month of December of the previous year, according to the data of the authority responsible for statistics, depending on the actual needs of the top athlete, the category of the sport and the assessment of the extent to which the compensation will affect his future sports results and development of sports in the Republic of Serbia;
- to cover other particularly justified expenses – up to three average net earnings in the Republic of Serbia for the month of December of the previous year, according to the data of the authority responsible for statistics, depending on the actual needs of the top athlete, the category of the sports branch and the assessment of

the extent to which the compensation will affect on his future sports results and the development of sports in the Republic of Serbia.

594. Financial assistance to top athletes of this rulebook is determined according to the following criteria:

- if the athlete does not generate income – one average net salary in the Republic of Serbia for the month of December of the previous year, according to the data of the authority responsible for statistics;
- if the athlete earns less than half of the average net salary in the Republic of Serbia – the amount up to the average net salary in the Republic of Serbia for the month of December of the previous year, according to the data of the authority responsible for statistics, depending on the actual needs of the top athlete, the rank within the sports status of top athletes and sports categories;
- for medical expenses and other specifically justified expenses – up to five average net earnings in the Republic of Serbia for the month of December of the previous year, according to the data of the authority responsible for statistics, depending on the actual needs of the top athlete, the rank within the sports status of the top athlete and the category of sport.

595. Financial aid to a top athlete is paid in accordance with the contract concluded by the top athlete to whom the financial aid was awarded and the ministry responsible for sports affairs, in accordance with the Law.

596. The proposal for the annual scholarship programme for the sports training of top amateur athletes and financial aid to top athletes is submitted, in accordance with the Law, by the competent national branch sports association through which the general interest in a specific branch of sport is realized.

§7. Recognitions and Awards

597. Acknowledgements and awards to athletes are awarded on the basis of the Regulation on national sports awards and monetary awards.

598. This regulation determines the detailed conditions, method of payment and amount of national sports awards and monetary awards for special contributions to the development and affirmation of sports.

599. Certain terms used in this regulation have the following meanings:

- an athlete is a citizen of the Republic of Serbia who, as a member of the senior first A selection of the national sports team of the Republic of Serbia, performed at least once in matches, i.e., individual competitions held within the framework of an international sports competition where a relevant sports result was achieved in the sense of this regulation;

- the head coach of the team is the coach of the senior first A selection of the national sports team of the Republic of Serbia in a specific collective sport, who, in his capacity as the head coach of the national sports team, prepares the team for an international sports competition, leads the team, is registered for the competition according to the sports rules of the international sports federation in which a relevant sports competition is held in his/her jurisdiction and physically attends matches, i.e., matches at that relevant sports competition;
- an athlete's coach is a coach of the senior first A selection of the national sports team of the Republic of Serbia in a specific individual sport, who, in the capacity of an individual coach of a specific athlete in the national team, prepares the athlete for an international sports competition, issues instructions to the athlete for performance in that competition, is registered for the competition by the rules of the international sports federation under whose jurisdiction the relevant sports competition is held and physically attends the matches held at that competition;
- a relevant sports result is a gold, silver or bronze medal won at the Olympic Games, Paralympic Games, Chess Olympiad, world and European championships in Olympic and Paralympic sports disciplines and a world record in Olympic and Paralympic sports disciplines, as well as participation in the DAVIS Cup final or FED Cup of the International Tennis Federation;
- the team consists of members of the national sports team of the Republic of Serbia;
- a sports organization is a sports association or a sports business company based in the territory of the Republic of Serbia, which achieves a relevant sports result within the European club championship of the highest level according to the criteria of the competent international sports federation, in sports of the first category according to the National Sports Categorization;
- Olympic and Paralympic sports disciplines are sports disciplines from Olympic and Paralympic sports that are on the programme of the summer and winter Olympic and Paralympic Games, which are determined by the IOC and the IPC for each four-year Olympic and Paralympic cycle.

600. The national sports recognition is awarded to athletes, citizens of the Republic of Serbia, who, as members of the national sports team of the Republic of Serbia, win a medal at the Olympic Games, Paralympic Games, Chess Olympiad, world and European championships in Olympic and Paralympic sports disciplines, or were, or will be, holders of the world records in Olympic and Paralympic sports disciplines, or become finalists of the DAVIS Cup or FED Cup of the International Tennis Federation.

601. The national sports award is awarded in the form of a diploma and a lifetime monthly stipend in the amount of:

- three average net earnings in the Republic of Serbia for the month of December of the previous year, according to the data of the republican body responsible for statistics – for a gold medal at the Olympic Games, Paralympic Games or Chess Olympiad;

– two and a half average net earnings in the Republic of Serbia for the month of December of the previous year, according to the data of the republican body responsible for statistics – for a silver medal at the Olympic Games, Paralympic Games, Chess Olympiad or for a gold medal at the world championship in an Olympic or Paralympic sports discipline, or for the won DAVIS Cup or FED Cup of the International Tennis Federation;
– two average net earnings in the Republic of Serbia for the month of December of the previous year, according to the data of the republican body responsible for statistics – for a bronze medal at the Olympic Games, Paralympic Games, Chess Olympiad or for a silver medal at the world championship in an Olympic or Paralympic sports discipline or for a gold medal at the European Championship in an Olympic or Paralympic sports discipline or for a world record in an Olympic or Paralympic sports discipline;
– one and a half average net earnings in the Republic of Serbia for the month of December of the previous year, according to the data of the republican authority responsible for statistics – for a bronze medal at the world championship in an Olympic or Paralympic sports discipline or for a silver medal at the European championships in an Olympic or Paralympic sports discipline;
– one average net salary in the Republic of Serbia for the month of December of the previous year, according to the data of the republican authority responsible for statistics – for a bronze medal at the European championship in an Olympic or Paralympic sports discipline.

602. In the event that an athlete who has acquired the right to national sports recognition, and after achieving a relevant sports result in the sense of this regulation, takes part in a sports competition for the representation of a foreign country, i.e., a foreign national sports association or as an individual representative of a foreign country, i.e., a foreign national sports association the amount of national sports recognition is permanently reduced by 25%.

603. In the event that an athlete during his sports career achieves several sports results that are the basis for awarding a national sports award, the best (most valuable) sports result will be taken into account as the basis for awarding that award.

604. A cash award for achieved sports results in Olympic and Paralympic sports is awarded to athletes and coaches who are citizens of the Republic of Serbia, who, as members of the national sports team of the Republic of Serbia, at the Olympic Games, Paralympic Games, Chess Olympiad and world and European championships in an Olympic or Paralympic sports discipline win one of the medals or become finalists of the Davis Cup or Fed Cup of the International Tennis Federation.

605. In the event that the athlete and his coach, at the same competition, achieve several sports results that are the basis for awarding a monetary award, they will be awarded one monetary award for the best (most valuable) sports result achieved at that competition.

606. In the event that at the same competition in an individual sport, several athletes, who have the same coach, achieve sports results that are the basis for awarding a monetary award to the coach, the athlete will be awarded one monetary award for each athlete for the best (most valuable) sports result of each individually determined athletes achieved at that competition.

607. For a medal won in team or individual sports at the Olympic Games, the Paralympic Games and the Chess Olympiad, a cash prize is awarded to each medal winner and the head coach of the team, i.e., athlete's coach in the amount of:

- EUR 70,000 in dinar equivalent, for the gold medal;
- EUR 60,000 in dinar equivalent, for the silver medal;
- EUR 50,000 in dinar equivalent, for the bronze medal.

608. Cash prizes are paid in dinar equivalents at the middle exchange rate of the National Bank of Serbia valid on the day of payment.

609. For a medal won at the world championship in team or individual sports in an Olympic or Paralympic sports discipline, or for participation in the finals of the DAVIS Cup or FED Cup of the International Tennis Federation, a cash prize is awarded for each medal winner and the head coach of the team, i.e., athlete's coach in the amount of:

- EUR 30,000 in dinar equivalent, for the gold medal;
- EUR 25,000 in dinar equivalent, for the silver medal;
- EUR 20,000 in dinar equivalent, for the bronze medal.

610. For a medal won at the European Championship in team or individual sports in an Olympic or Paralympic sports discipline, a cash prize is awarded to each medal winner and the head coach of the team, i.e., athlete's coach in the amount of:

- EUR 20,000 in dinar equivalent, for the gold medal;
- EUR 15,000 in dinar equivalent, for the silver medal;
- EUR 10,000 in dinar equivalent, for the bronze medal.

611. For winning the European club championship of the highest level according to the criteria of the competent international sports federation, in sports of the first category according to the National categorization of sports, a monetary award is awarded to the sports organization in the amount determined by the Government in a special decision.

612. The national sports award and monetary award for a medal won at the world or European championship in an Olympic or Paralympic sports discipline are awarded only for the results achieved in the first A national senior sports team of the Republic of Serbia.

613. The government, on the proposal of the ministry responsible for sports, adopts a decision on the awarding of a national sports award, i.e., a monetary award.

614. The right to national sports recognition is exercised by the athlete from the day of the decision on the awarding of that recognition, with the lifelong monthly monetary income being paid to the athlete after the athlete reaches 40 years of age.

615. The national sports recognition can be awarded to the same athlete only once.

616. On the basis of the Government's decision on the awarding of a national sports award, that is, a monetary award, the Ministry concludes with the athlete, coach, or sports organization that has achieved a relevant sports result in an agreement on the payment of a lifetime monthly monetary income, that is, a monetary award.

617. Lifetime monthly stipends, as well as monetary awards, are paid from the funds of the budget of the Republic of Serbia determined by the Ministry.

618. The request for awarding a national sports award, i.e., a monetary award, is submitted to the Ministry in writing within thirty days from the day of the end of the international sports competition in which the relevant sports result was achieved, i.e., within thirty days from the day of the official recognition of the achieved world record by a competent international sports federation.

619. The request must contain information on:

- the first and last name and unique identification number of the athlete, that is, the coach who submits the request;
- the name and headquarters of the sports organization that submits the request, and the name and surname and unique registration number of the representative of the sports organization;
- the competent national sports association in whose national sports team the athlete or coach achieved a relevant sports result, or in which the sports organization is a member;
- the name, time and venue of the sports competition where the relevant sports result was achieved;
- frequency of sports competition (every year, every second year, every fourth year);
- the name of the competent international sports federation or other organization responsible for holding the sports competition where the relevant sports result was achieved;
- the number and type of medals won;
- the number of the current account to which the payment of the national sports award, i.e., the monetary award, should be made.

620. The following evidence shall be submitted with the request:

- documents certifying by the competent national sports federation or the competent international sports federation that the athlete or coach, i.e., the sports organization participated in the appropriate international sports competition in accordance with the sports rules of the competent national and international sports federation and that he achieved a relevant sporting achievement result;
- certificate of citizenship of the Republic of Serbia of the athlete, that is, the coach at the time of submission of the request;
- the authorization of the athlete, i.e., the coach, that the competent national sports federation can submit a request for the awarding of a national sports award, i.e., a monetary award, on his behalf and on his behalf.

621. Exceptionally, in the case when, in accordance with the act regulating sports branches and areas of sports and sports disciplines within sports branches and areas of sports in the Republic of Serbia, the Olympic sports discipline includes all competitive categories, with the request, in addition to evidence, a document is also submitted by which the competent international sports federation confirms that the world or European championship at which the athlete or coach achieved a relevant sports result was held in an Olympic discipline as part of the qualifying Olympic cycle for participation in the Olympic or Paralympic Games.

622. The request from paragraph 1 of this article is submitted by an athlete, coach, or representative of a sports organization who has achieved a relevant sports result, or upon authorization of the athlete, or coach, by the competent national sports association of which the athlete or coach is a member.

623. Within thirty days from the date of submission of the proper request, the Ministry submits to the Government a proposal for awarding a national sports award, i.e., a monetary award.

624. If the holder of a national sports award damages the reputation of sports, and thus, the reputation of the Republic of Serbia, by his behaviour or participation in activities that are not in accordance with the law, sports rules or other general acts of organizations in the field of sports, the Government may, on the proposal of the Ministry, decide by decision not to award, that is, to cancel the national sports award.

625. An administrative dispute can be filed against this decision of the Government.

626. Athletes and coaches who acquired the right to national sports recognition according to the regulations that were in force until the date of entry into force of this regulation, continue to exercise that right in accordance with the regulation according to which they acquired it, while athletes who achieved a relevant sports result after the entry into force of the Decree on National Awards and Prizes for Special Contribution to the Development and Affirmation of Sports and the Decree on

National Sports Awards and Cash Prizes, the right to national recognition is exercised in the amount and under the conditions established by those decrees, and lifetime monthly cash income is paid to the athlete after reaching the age of 40 years of the athlete's life and in the amount determined by the regulation that was in force at the time of achieving the relevant sports result.

627. Athletes and coaches who have achieved a relevant sports result by the date of entry into force of the Regulation on National Recognitions and Awards for Special Contribution to the Development and Affirmation of Sports and who have reported that result to the Ministry by the deadline prescribed by that Regulation, exercise the right to national recognition in the amount and under the conditions established according to the regulation that was in force until the entry into force of that regulation and lifetime monthly cash income is paid to the athlete or coach after the athlete or coach reaches 35 years of age and in the amount determined by the regulation that was in force at the time of achieving the relevant sports result.

628. Athletes who, after the entry into force of this regulation, achieve a more valuable result in relation to the result on the basis of which they gained the right to a national sports recognition, may submit a request for adjustment of that right.

§8. Tax

629. Like other citizens, athletes are also taxpayers if they reside in the territory of the Republic of Serbia.

630. The income of athletes and sports experts includes income earned by professional athletes, amateur athletes, sports experts and experts in sports, from sports organizations, i.e., organizations for performing sports activities, sports associations and federations, which do not have the character of a salary in terms of regulations governing sports.

631. Income is considered earnings based on:

(1) fees for concluding the contract (transfer, etc.);
(2) fees for the use of the athlete's image;
(3) financial aid to top athletes with special merits;
(4) scholarships for top athletes for sports training;
(5) cash and other prizes;
(6) national recognition and awards for special contributions to the development and affirmation of sports;
(7) fees and rewards for the work of sports experts, i.e., experts in sports (trainers, referees, delegates, etc.);
(8) other types of income except for the stated income.

632. Taxable income for earnings is gross income less standard costs of 50%. The annual personal income tax is paid on the basis of the following rates:

– on the amount of up to six times the average annual salary – 10%;
– on the amount over six times the average annual salary – 10% for the amount up to six times the average annual salary + 15% for the amount over six times the average annual salary.

633. A taxpayer who invests in an alternative investment fund, i.e., in the purchase of an investment unit of an alternative investment fund, is recognized the right to a tax credit on account of the annual personal income tax up to 50% of the investment made in the calendar year for which the annual personal income tax is determined.

634. The right to a tax credit can be exercised only on the basis of fully paid cash deposits by which shares or stakes in an alternative investment fund, i.e., investment units of an alternative investment fund are acquired. The tax credit cannot exceed 50% of the determined tax liability based on the annual personal income tax.[171]

635. Athletes, depending on their annual net income, may also be subject to a special personal income tax.

636. As can be seen, athletes who earn income from sports activities and other activities are taxpayers in the Republic of Serbia. In this manner, significant revenues of the budget of the Republic of Serbia are provided. Many athletes/taxpayers become residents of other countries due to the existence of lower tax rates. Such cases, to a lesser extent, exist in our country.

§9. Settlement of Disputes

637. The manner of resolving disputes in the field of sports was discussed in several previous chapters. The procedure for resolving disputes from the aspect of judicial and out-of-court protection of individual and collective rights of athletes will be briefly repeated here.

638. Athletes enjoy judicial protection of their rights before the courts of the Republic of Serbia, as do all other legal entities. Any different behaviour would constitute discrimination.

639. Disputes can arise from various relationships related to sports (labour, property, proceedings for the compensation of tangible and intangible damage).

640. For the protection of individual rights, the possibility of out-of-court settlement of disputes is especially important. With its provisions, LSRS in principle, regulates the work of sports arbitrations in the Republic of Serbia. Members of a sports association and a sports association may agree to entrust the resolution of a

171. *See* Arts 89 and 89a of LoC.

dispute on the rights at their disposal, except for disputes for which the exclusive jurisdiction of the court has been determined, ad hoc to the Sports Arbitration Court or PSA Court with the OKS – for Olympic sports, PSA Court with the Sports Federation of Serbia – for non-Olympic sports and PSA Court with the PKS – for Paralympic sports, and when it comes to sports regarding the termination, annulment or determination of nullity or fulfilment of the contract between the athlete, i.e., the sports expert and the sports organization – and to the PSA court at the competent national branch sports federation. It is considered that the contract on sports arbitration is concluded even if the claimant files a lawsuit or an appeal to the sports arbitration, and the defendant does not object to the jurisdiction of the arbitration until the subject of the dispute is discussed. The provisions on arbitration of the law governing the proceedings before arbitration shall apply to the arbitration unless otherwise provided by this Law.

641. The dispute may also be the subject of international sports arbitration in cases determined by the sports rules of the competent international sports federation. The PSA Court may also be competent to resolve disputes arising between members of the sports association and the sports association regarding the exercise of membership rights and obligations determined by general acts of the sports association and sports rules, provided that the jurisdiction of the permanent sports court is determined in the statute of the sports association or the statute of the competent national sports federation unless otherwise provided by this Law.

642. The obligation of arbitration may not be prescribed by a general act of a sports association unless otherwise prescribed by the sports rules of the competent international sports federation. The OKS, the PKS and the Sports Federation of Serbia may mutually establish a single PSA court for the arbitral settlement of disputes in sports.[172]

643. The dispute before the sports arbitration is urgent. The statute of a sports association may also provide for an attempt to resolve disputes peacefully within a sports association through mediation.

644. Only a Bachelor of Law may be appointed as an arbitrator. A person who is the owner, member of the body or employee of sports organizations in the same branch of sport, a person who participated in the decision-making in the previous proceedings, a person who is a member of the body, official or employee of the competent sports federation may not be appointed arbitrator, nor a person in respect of whom there are other reasons which call into question his/her impartiality.

645. Competencies, composition and organization of PSA, conditions and manner of selection and dismissal of arbitrators, arbitration costs and proceedings in matters within its competence are regulated by general acts of the OKS, PKS, Sports Federation of Serbia and competent national branch sports federation.

172. *See* Art. 53 of LSRS.

646. Acts and arbitrators must ensure the independence, impartiality, autonomy and competence of sports arbitration in deciding and protecting the rights of participants in the proceedings, including the right of the party to the dispute to have a legal representative. The Ministry gives its consent to these acts.[173]

647. In the Republic of Serbia, there is a PSA with the OKS. The PSA of OKS consists of arbitrators, of which up to thirty arbitrators are appointed by the competent body of OKS, and each member of OKS can appoint one arbitrator.

648. Disputes worth up to EUR 5,000.00 are resolved by a single arbitrator, jointly appointed by the parties from the list of arbitrators of the PSA of OKS. In case the consensus of the parties on the appointment of an individual arbitrator is not possible, he/she is appointed by the President of the PSA of OKS from the list of arbitrators.

649. Disputes of higher value are resolved by a three-member Arbitration Council, in which each party appoints one arbitrator from the list of arbitrators of the PSA of OKS, and they jointly appoint a third arbitrator, who is also the President of the Arbitration Council. In the event that there is no possibility of joint appointment of a third member of the Arbitration Council, he/she shall be appointed by the President of the PSA of OKS from the list of arbitrators.[174]

650. The proceedings for resolving the disputes are initiated by a lawsuit. It is considered that the arbitration proceeding started on the day when the PSA of OKS received the lawsuit. Counterclaim is not allowed.

651. The mediation procedure begins with the submission of a written proposal for initiating a mediation procedure, which can be submitted by one party or both parties together.

652. The procedure for giving a non-binding legal opinion on any activity related to sports begins with the submission of a written request that may be submitted by a member of OKS or the PSA of OKS.

653. PSA makes decisions on the basis of the Law and general acts of the Republic of Serbia, general acts and acts of national and international sports federations that apply to the subject matter of the dispute, and on the basis of justice and fairness (*ex aequo et bono*) if the parties have expressly agreed to do so.

654. The arbitral award resolving the dispute has the force of a final court decision and is enforced in accordance with the provisions of the Law on Enforcement Procedure. The party dissatisfied with the arbitral award has the right to lodge an appeal exclusively to the Court of Arbitration for Sport in Lausanne, Switzerland,

173. *See* Art. 54 of LSRS.
174. Organization and composition of the Permanent Sports Arbitration of OCS, https://oks.org.rs/stalna-sportska-arbitraza/organizacija-i-sastav-stalne-sportske-arbitraze/, accessed on 24 Aug. 2021.

which will, as the last instance, finally resolve the dispute in accordance with the Sports Arbitration Code. The deadline for filing an appeal is twenty-one days from the date of receipt of the award.[175]

655. The work of the PSA of OKS is regulated by the Rulebook on the PSA of OKS.

656. The PSA is a permanent and independent body within the OKS established as a permanent arbitral tribunal for the purpose of independent, impartial, autonomous and competent arbitration of disputes in sports. This Rulebook ensures the independence, impartiality, autonomy and competence of the PSA in decision-making and ensures the protection of the rights of participants in proceedings before the Stalna sportska arbitraža (SAA).

657. The basic mission of PSA is to facilitate the resolution of disputes and disputed relations related to sports through:

- mediation between the parties to the dispute and promoting mediation as a means of resolving disputes;
- arbitration in disputes;
- giving non-binding recommendations and opinions at the request of OKS, OKS members, athletes, sports experts and sports associations from Olympic sports. PSA is independent and autonomous in decision-making, and in its work makes decisions on the basis of the Law, general acts and acts of national and international sports associations applying to the subject matter of the dispute. In its work, PSA is obliged to respect and promote the basic principles of the Olympic Movement, the Olympic Charter of IOC and the Statute of OC.[176]

658. From the aspect of legal certainty, the authorization of the PSA of OKS to give opinions is especially important.

659. Disputes in the field of sports can also be resolved through mediation. Unlike arbitration, where the parties independently choose an arbitrator for their case, who resolves the dispute, in the case of mediation in sports, the parties to the dispute themselves choose a mediator who will help them resolve the dispute together.

660. It is important to point out that a mediator never makes a decision that resolves the dispute. The advantages of such dispute resolution are numerous. The costs of mediation proceedings are incomparably lower than the costs of court proceedings. Unfortunately, mediation in sports is still insufficiently applied in the Republic of Serbia.

---

175. Procedure and applicable law before the Permanent Sports Arbitration OCS, https://oks.org.rs/stalna-sportska-arbitraza/pravila-postupka-i-merodavno-pravo/, accessed on 24 Aug. 2021.
176. Rulebook on Permanent Sports Arbitration of OCS, https://oks.org.rs/akti-oks/pravilnik-o-stalnoj-sportskoj-arbitrazi-oks/, accessed on 29 Aug. 2021.

Chapter 3. Private Regulation

661. In the Republic of Serbia, freedom of contract is guaranteed, in accordance with positive legal regulations. There are numerous contracts for sports activities, contracts in the field of media rights, etc. The general rules of the Law of Contracts and Torts apply to this area.

662. Athlete transfers take place according to special legal norms and have a great impact on the labour market in the field of sports.

663. A transfer contract is, written and certified in accordance with the law, a contract between a sports organization with which the athlete has a valid contract in accordance with this Law and the sports organization to which the athlete transfers, based on which the sports organization with which the athlete has a valid contract agrees to terminate the contract with the athlete by mutual agreement for a certain fee in order to transfer to the sports organization with which the transfer contract is concluded.[177]

664. The assignment agreement is, written and certified in accordance with the law, a contract between a sports organization with which the athlete has a valid contract in accordance with this Law and a sports organization to which the athlete temporarily transfers on the basis of which the sports organization with which the athlete has a valid contract agrees to temporarily transfer the athlete to the sports organization with which the transfer agreement is concluded.[178]

665. This contract can be validly concluded only with the written and in accordance with the law-certified consent of the athlete. International transfer, i.e., transfer of a minor athlete to a foreign sports organization is not allowed, except in special cases determined by the sports rules of the competent international sports federation.[179]

666. National transfer, i.e., transfer of a minor athlete to a domestic sports organization outside the place of residence of the minor athlete is not allowed, unless the transfer is approved by the competent national branch sports federation in accordance with the criteria and in the procedure established by sports rules. The criteria must be in accordance with this Law and the sports rules of the competent international sports federation for the relevant branch of sport and they cannot restrict the right of a minor athlete to transfer to another sports organization that is not related to sports activities (education, family ties, etc.).

667. The competent national branch sports federation keeps records of transfers, i.e., transfers of minor athletes and notifies the Ministry within fifteen days of each transfer, i.e., registered transfer of a minor athlete. Appropriate personal data are

177. *See* Art. 18 of LSRS.
178. *See* Art. 18 para. 2 of LSRS.
179. *See* Art. 18 para. 4 of LSRS.

kept in the records of transfers, i.e., transfers of minor athletes to another sports organization. Contracts on the basis of which third parties acquire exclusive rights over the future economic rights of the sports organization in future transfers of the athlete are void.[180]

668. Full legal regulation of the labour market in the field of sports is necessary also for the reason that sports transfers provide a flow of significant financial resources, both at the national and international levels. This is especially true of transfers in sports that are very popular (football, basketball, etc.).

669. Expensive transfers of football players have always attracted the attention of the public, especially if criminal acts were committed during them. Currently, in the Republic of Serbia, the prosecution of the perpetrators of these crimes is within the competence of the Prosecutor's Office for Organized Crime. We believe that the introduction of special prosecutor's offices would contribute to better criminal protection from illegal activities in the labour market in the field of sports.

670. Finally, it should be noted that private regulation must be in accordance with the laws and by-laws of the Republic of Serbia. This creates a unique and efficient legal system in the field of sports, as a precondition for its prosperity.

180. In this manner, the economic position of the athlete is protected, especially when it comes to minors. *See* Art. 18 para. 10 of LSRS.

Part III. Doping and Sports

Chapter 1. General Issues

671. The essential value of sports is the sports spirit, which is the basis of Olympism, and it is characterized, above all, by ethics, honesty, respect for rules and laws, respect for oneself and other participants in sports. Sport as a sublime activity, aimed at building the mind and the body, must be available to all under equal conditions. All participants in sports are expected to have a minimum of ethical behaviour to preserve physical and mental health and the fair play relationship.

672. Unfortunately, abuses have been present since the beginning of sport. The use of doping is contrary to the stated basic values of modern sport and represents its gross abuse. Doping is harmful in many ways for athletes and sports in general. It destroys the health of athletes, leads to unrealistic results and irregularities of competition, and destroys the reputation of sports and sports organizations.

673. International organizations and all international and national sports federations put the fight against doping in the foreground and state it as a primary task. In the fight against doping, they see the basis for the protection of the health of athletes, preservation of the equality of chances (competition) and the maintenance of the credibility of the sports branch. The adoption of the World Anti-Doping Code and the European Convention against Doping in Sports clearly defines the role of all factors in the fight against doping.

674. In the Republic of Serbia, where sport is defined as an activity of special importance (Article 2 LS of RS), a very restrictive anti-doping legislation is in force. In addition to LS of RS, as the highest legal act regulating the field of sports, the European Convention against Doping in Sports was ratified, so a special Law on Doping is in force.[181] Its consistent application aims to ensure the protection of the health of athletes, the regularity of sports competitions and results, as well as the preservation of the reputation of sports in society.

181. *See* 'Official Gazette of RS', No. 111/2014.

Chapter 2. Public Regulation

675. In the Republic of Serbia, public regulations regarding doping in sports are based on both LS of RS and the Law on Prevention of Doping in Sports. The constitutional framework for the enactment of this Law is contained in Article 97, item 10 of the Constitution of 2006, according to which the Republic of Serbia regulates and provides the system in the field of sports.

676. According to LS of RS, as a general act, it is prohibited that athletes be exposed to sports activities that may endanger or worsen their health condition (Article 22). In terms of the prohibition of abuse in the field of sports, the Law explicitly states doping as a strictly prohibited activity (Article 22, paragraph 2). In this sense, a sports organization, like all other participants in sports, is obliged to engage in the fight against doping in sports during the performance of sports activities. That the fight against doping in sports is one of the primary goals in the Republic of Serbia is confirmed by Article 112, paragraph 10 of the Law, in which the fight against doping is explicitly stated as a general interest in the field of sports. The fight against doping in sports is also envisaged by the 2014–2018 Strategy for the Development of Sports in the Republic of Serbia.[182]

677. Doping in sports in the Republic of Serbia is regulated by the following laws and regulations:[183]

- LRECDS.[184]
- Law on the Ratification of the International Convention against doping in sport.[185]
- LS.[186]
- LPDS.[187]
- Law on animal welfare.[188]
- Law on medicines and medical devices.[189]
- Rulebook on the harmonization of ADAS anti-doping rules with the World Anti-Doping Code.
- Rulebook on determining the responsibility of a person who has committed an anti-doping rule violation.[190]

---

182. *See* 'Official Gazette of RS', No. 1/2015, whereby the 2018–2028 Strategy for the Development of Sports in the Republic of Serbia has not been adopted yet, although the Law on Sports stipulates that the National Strategy for the Development of Sports will be adopted by the end of 2018 at the latest.
183. Cited laws available at http://www.parlament.gov.rs, and Rulebooks at http://www.adas.org.rs/informacije/dokumenti-preuzimanje/.
184. *See* 'Official Gazette of SFRY – International Agreements', No. 4/91.
185. *See* 'Official Gazette of RS – International agreements', No. 38/2009.
186. *See* 'Official Gazette of RS', No. 10/2016.
187. *See* 'Official Gazette of RS', Nos 111/2014 and 47/2021.
188. *See* 'Official Gazette of RS', No. 41/2009.
189. *See* 'Official Gazette of RS', Nos 30/2010, 107/2012, 113/2017 – other law and 105/2017 – other law.
190. *See* 'Official Bulletin of ADAS', No. 38 of 12 Mar. 2021.

- Rulebook on disciplinary measures and the procedure for their imposition in cases of established violation of anti-doping rules.
- Rulebook on the Doping control at sports competitions and out of Competitions (RDC).[191]
- Rulebook on the list of prohibited doping substances.[192]
- Rulebook on granting exemptions for therapeutic use.[193]
- Rulebook on the list of prohibited doping agents for horses.[194]
- Rulebook on determining the appearance of the label with the 'DOPING FREE' sign and the procedure for issuing the label.[195]
- Statute of the ADAS.[196]

678. The LRECDS[197] ratifies the European Convention against doping in sport, as amended, done at Strasbourg on 16 November 1989, in the English and French languages.

679. The Law on the Ratification of the International Convention against Doping in Sport[198] acknowledges the International Convention against Doping in Sport, adopted on 19 October 2005 in Paris, in the Arabic, Chinese, English, French, Russian and Spanish languages.

680. The LS[199] envisages that organizations in the field of sports achieve their goals and perform sports activities and sports occupations in accordance with the Law, sports rules, ratified conventions in the field of sports and principles established in the documents of international organizations of which the Republic of Serbia is a member.

681. To harmonize activities on the prevention of negative phenomena in sports, including doping, LS of RS envisages that the Government of the Republic of Serbia establishes a National Council for the Prevention of Negative Manifestations in Sports.[200]

682. The National Council consists of the representatives of the Ministry in Charge of Interior Affairs, the Ministry in Charge of Justice, the Ministry in Charge of Education and the Ministry of Youth and Sports.[201] By position, the members of

---

191. *Ibid.*
192. *See* 'Official Gazette of RS', No. 156/2020.
193. *See* 'Official Bulletin of ADAS', No. 38 of 12 Mar. 2021.
194. *See* 'Official Gazette of RS', No. 23/2021.
195. *See* 'Official Gazette of RS', No. 139/2014.
196. *Ibid.*
197. *See* 'Official Gazette of SFRY – International Agreements', No. 4/91.
198. *See* 'Official Gazette of RS – International Agreements', No. 38/2009.
199. *See* 'Official Gazette of RS', No. 10/2016.
200. *See* The National Council for the Prevention of Negative Manifestations in Sports was formed on the basis of Art. 167 para. 1 of the Law on Sports ('Official Gazette of RS', No. 10/16) and Art. 43 para. 1 of the Law on the Government ('Official Gazette of RS', Nos 55/05, 71/05 – correction, 101/07, 65/08, 16/11, 68/12 – CC, 72/12 and 7/14 – CC).
201. *See* https://www.mos.gov.rs/.

the Council are the Republic Public Prosecutor, the President of the OKS, the President of the PKS, the President of the Sports Federation of Serbia, the President of the Association of Sports Journalists of Serbia, the Director of the ADAS and the presidents of the major branch sports federations – football, basketball, volleyball, handball and water polo federation.

683. The task of the Council is to coordinate activities on the prevention of violence and misconduct of spectators at sports events, doping in sports, fixing matches/games and other negative manifestations in sports, as well as the fulfilment of international obligations in these areas. In carrying out its tasks, the Council initiates or proposes measures and activities of state administration bodies and competent national sports federations to meet international obligations, which include, *inter alia*, the European Convention against Doping in Sport and the International Convention against Doping in Sport.

684. On the basis of the ratified European Convention against doping in sport in the Republic of Serbia, the Law on the prevention of doping in sport was adopted[202] strictly prohibiting the doping of athletes and regulating measures and activities for the prevention of doping in sports (Articles 1 and 2).

685. In terms of the LPDS of RS, doping in sports is considered to be the existence of one or more violations of anti-doping rules (Article 2, paragraph 2).

686. In Article 3, the Law exhaustively lists cases that are considered violations of anti-doping rules:

(1) the presence of a prohibited substance or its metabolites or markers in the body sample of an athlete;
(2) use or attempt to use (application, introduction, injection or consumption in any way) a prohibited substance or a prohibited method (hereinafter: doping agents);
(3) refusal, or omission without convincing justification, of giving a sample after the notification of the doping control or avoiding giving a sample in another way;
(4) any combination of three missed doping tests and/or failure in completing the Athlete Location Form, in accordance with international performance management standards approved by the World Anti-Doping Agency (WADA), within a period of twelve months, by the athlete included in the registered test group;
(5) interfering with or attempting to interfere with any part of the doping control;
(6) illegal possession of doping agents by the athlete or persons assisting the athlete;

202. *See* 'Official Gazette of RS', Nos 111/2014 and 47/2021). Hereinafter: LPDS of RS.

(7) unauthorized sale, transport, shipment, delivery or distribution of a prohibited doping substance or prohibited doping method (either physically, electronically or otherwise) by the athlete, persons assisting the athlete or through a third party, to any person under the jurisdiction of any sports organizations, or an attempt to do so;
(8) giving or attempting to give or administering or attempting to administer any doping agent to the athlete in competition, or giving or attempting to give or administer or attempting to administer to any athlete out of competition any doping agent prohibited out of competition;
(9) assisting, inciting, aiding, supporting, concealing, creating conditions or any other form of intentional complicity or attempted complicity in violation or attempted violation of anti-doping rules or in violation of a measure imposed due to the violation of anti-doping rules;
(10) association, in a professional or sport-related capacity, of an athlete or another person under the jurisdiction of the authorized anti-doping organization with a person assisting the athlete who is subject to a measure imposed for violating anti-doping rules or has been sentenced in criminal, misdemeanour or other proceedings for an act in violation of the anti-doping rules within the meaning of this Law, if the sentence is still in force or less than six years have passed since the imposition of such a sentence, or with a person who is a mediator or a representative of such a person;
(11) actions of an athlete or another person who poses a threat or serves to intimidate another person with the intention of discouraging him/her from disclosing information related to doping and non-compliance with anti-doping rules or aims to put the person, who provided evidence or information in good faith related to doping and non-compliance with anti-doping rules, into an unfavourable position, to an authorized anti-doping organization or a competent state authority.

687. From the point of view of doping control, the athlete under the World Anti-Doping Code[203] is any person who participates in sport at the international level (as defined by each international sports federation) or at the national level (as defined by each national anti-doping organization), and any other person who participates in sport at a lower level. At the national level, anti-doping rules are mandatory for all athletes in national teams and for all athletes who have the right to compete in any national championship in any sport. This does not mean that all these persons must be included in the registered test group of the national anti-doping organization. The national anti-doping organization may include athletes in competitions at lower levels than the national ones in the anti-doping programme.

688. From the point of view of the European Sports Charter,[204] an athlete is a person who engages in a certain form of physical activity which, through

203. *See* Anti-Doping Convention – Strasbourg, 16.XI.1989 – Coehttps://rm.coe.int Hereinafter: the Code.
204. *See* European Sports Charter, https://www.cok.me.

unorganized or organized participation, aims to express or improve physical fitness and mental well-being, create social relationships or achieve results in competitions.

689. LPDS of RS uses the generic term '*athlete*', so it is clear that the provisions of the Law apply to all persons who are considered athletes (sportsmen/women), and which are clearly defined in LPDS. In accordance with LPDS, an athlete is any person who engages in some physical exercise, recreationally or training in a club, independently or organized, at sports events or out of them, (Article 9, paragraph 1 of LPDS). Bearing in mind that LPDS of RS uses the generic term 'athlete' and that LPDS is a 'more general' law, it is clear that the provisions of LPDS of RS apply to all persons considered athletes (sportsmen/women) under Article 9 of LPDS.

690. It is clearly defined that it is not necessary that there should be an intent, negligence, failure or conscious use of a doping agent in the athlete's conduct in order for an anti-doping rule violation to be considered existent.

691. It is the obligation of every athlete to ensure that no prohibited substances enter his/her body. In this context, he/she is obliged to personally make sure that any medicine or preparation he/she uses does not contain a prohibited substance.[205] Lists of prohibited doping agents are published in the 'Official Gazette of the Republic of Serbia' (Article 22 of LPDS).

692. The Anti-doping Agency, as an authorized anti-doping organization in terms of LPDS of RS (Article 4), may conduct the doping control of both amateur and professional athletes, as well as recreational athletes, and may organize control in competition and out of competition (Article 7, paragraph 5 of LPDS of RS). It is clear that, in most cases, the doping control is focused on athletes competing, and that special attention is paid to top athletes, as well as to those athletes who want to continue their careers after the expiration of the ban on participation due to doping.

693. Anti-doping rules are not violated in cases of approved exemptions for therapeutic use and other exemptions established by the World Anti-Doping Code (Article 3, paragraph 3 of LPDS of RS).

694. The central institution for combating doping in sport is the WADA. The activities of the Anti-Doping Agency of Serbia, which is a member of WADA, are especially important for the prevention of doping in sports.

205. The task and the responsibility of the sportsman/woman is also to know the current doping list. It is always available on the World Anti-Doping Agency website: www.wada-ama.org. According to Art. 4.2 of the World Anti-Doping Code, there should be only one list of prohibited substances, the one established by the World Anti-Doping Agency. In any case, you should know the anti-doping rules of your sports federation as well as of the national sports federation.

695. The Anti-Doping Agency regulates, determines, organizes and conducts doping controls at sports competitions and out of sports competitions, except for the one conducted by another authorized anti-doping organization in accordance with the World Anti-Doping Code. Article 21 of LPDS of RS stipulates that the anti-doping agency performs sports activities/occupations related to the prevention of doping in sports and in particular:

(1) takes measures to reduce doping in sports and its long-term elimination;
(2) explains what is meant by a certain term related to the problem of doping in sports;
(3) takes care of providing the necessary equipment for the analysis of doping samples and the necessary means for doping control;
(4) gains insight into the organization and implementation of doping control at international competitions organized in the Republic of Serbia;
(5) determines the annual plan of the doping control which it conducts;
(6) issues an official newsletter;
(7) achieves international professional cooperation on issues related to the prevention of doping in sports and concludes testing agreements;
(8) establishes cooperation with interested competent state bodies and organizations in the field of sports in connection with the prevention of doping in sports and damage to the health of athletes through the use of doping;
(9) organizes educational and other campaigns against doping in sports;
(10) informs the public about the activities undertaken against doping in sports, including the organization of an internet presentation (website) on which general acts and decisions of the bodies of the Anti-Doping Agency are published;
(11) give recommendations and advice for undertaking measures by state bodies and organizations in the field of sports in order to prevent doping in sports;
(12) organizes research, conferences, seminars, round tables and issues publications on issues related to the fight against doping in sports;
(13) monitors and collects information related to legal and other measures taken in other countries and international organizations in the fight against doping in sports;
(14) monitors and collects information on measures taken by state bodies and organizations in the field of sports in the fight against doping in sports;
(15) determines the appearance of the label with the 'DOPING FREE' sign which is placed on the tested products containing food supplements and the procedure for issuing the label, as an entrusted task;
(16) performs other tasks and takes other measures related to the prevention of doping in sports, which are in accordance with the World Anti-Doping Code within the competence of the national anti-doping organization.

696. The doping control is a procedure which includes planning test schedules, selecting athletes for testing, determining a registered test group, collecting and handling samples, laboratory analysis, managing results, searches and appeals (Article 7, paragraph 3 of LPDS of RS). Doping control shall be organized and carried out in such a manner that any possibility of a sample replacement or manipulation of any kind is excluded (Article 7, paragraph 4 LPDS of RS). Doping control can be organized both in competitions and out of competition, announced and unannounced (Article 7, paragraph 5 of LPDS of RS). Doping control shall be carried out by taking urine and blood samples or using other authorized techniques for the detection of prohibited substances and methods (Article 7, paragraph 6 of LPDS of RS). Doping control or analysis of doping samples and related analytical data or information collected at the doping control may be undertaken by an authorized organization for any legitimate anti-doping purposes.

697. The Anti-Doping Agency may collect samples, at any time and in any place, from any athlete or recreational athlete over which it has jurisdiction in accordance with this Law and the World Anti-Doping Code, including athletes who are subject to a ban on competition, in accordance with international standards approved by the WADA.

698. Doping control can be carried out only by authorized and qualified controllers, i.e., by persons who have an ID issued by the Anti-Doping Agency or which the agency has recognized as an equivalent agency (Article 8 of LPDS of RS).

699. The Anti-Doping Agency determines the organization in which the analysis of doping samples of athletes, i.e., animals participating in competitions, will be performed. The organization in which the doping analysis is conducted must have a valid homologation issued by an authorized international body or organization (WADA), and in the doping control procedure, the samples taken must be stored, handled and analysed in accordance with the provisions of this Law and relevant international standards approved by the WADA. The selection of the organization is done in accordance with the law governing public procurement (Article 9 of LPDS of RS).

700. The procurement of goods for doping control is carried out in accordance with the law governing public procurement. For public doping control services, conducting the procedure of determining responsibility for the violation of anti-doping rules and issuing a label with the ‘DOPING FREE’ sign, the service user pays a fee to the Anti-Doping Agency, in accordance with the law. Sports activities referred to in paragraph 1 of this Article are performed in accordance with the World Anti-Doping Code.

701. The doping control itself is regulated in more detail by the Rulebook on doping control at sports competitions and out of competitions.[206]

702. The Rulebook regulates the procedure of doping control conducted at sports competitions and out of sports competitions, determines the national registered test group of athletes and regulates the obligations of athletes included in

206. *See* ‘Official Bulletin of ADAS’, No. 38 of 12 Mar. 2021.

the national registered test group, and determines the appearance of the ID document of the doping controller of the ADAS.[207]

703. Article 2 of the Rulebook defines doping control, in accordance with LPDS of RS and the Code, includes all steps and phases, starting from risk assessment and planning of testing schedules to the final decision on any appeal and application of the imposed measures.

704. The OKS, Sports Federation of Serbia and other competent national sports federations are responsible to coordinate and supervise the implementation of measures to prevent doping within the federation and to cooperate with the Anti-Doping Agency of Serbia in conducting the doping control and submitting prescribed acts and data, which are obliged to determine the responsible person, with the appropriate title in sports (Article 4).

705. The obligations determined by LPDS of RS and the Rulebook regarding the doping control are applied as follows:

(1) to all organizations in the field of sports that have their headquarters in the territory of the Republic of Serbia or engage in sports activities and occupations in the territory of the Republic of Serbia;
(2) to all athletes, recreational athletes and competitors, who participate in the performance of sports activities in the territory of the Republic of Serbia, regardless of their citizenship, unless otherwise provided by the LPDS and this Rulebook;
(3) to all other participants (especially persons assisting athletes), in performing sports activities and occupations in the territory of the Republic of Serbia, regardless of their citizenship, unless otherwise provided by the LPDS and this Rulebook.

706. The Rulebook on doping control at sports competitions and out of competitions prescribes how the ID document looks like and how the controllers identify themselves, and the person who holds the issued doping controller ID document is obliged to use it exclusively for the purpose for which it was issued, i.e., only for monitoring the doping control implementation and taking measures to prevent doping in sports when performing sports activities and occupations in the territory of the Republic of Serbia (Article 10 and Article 11).

707. According to the Rulebook, a person with an appropriate medical education is appointed as a doping controller, who has previously completed the training for doping controllers organized by the Anti-Doping Agency of Serbia, WADA or another appropriate competent anti-doping organization. The doping controller is appointed for a period of two years and may be reappointed (Article 16).

207. *See also* http://www.adas.org.rs/.

708. ADAS conducts planning and testing in competitions and out of competitions (Article 17).

709. ADAS conducts planning and testing in competitions:

(1) on the basis of a periodic doping control plan, adopted by the ADAS Managing Board, in accordance with the requirements of the International Standard for Testing and Investigation;
(2) on the basis of the requirements arising from the technical document for specific analyses in sports;
(3) on the basis of a special decision of the ADAS Director;
(4) at the request of the Ministry in Charge of Sports Affairs;
(5) at the request of the sports inspector;
(6) upon a reasoned proposal of the competent national sports federation, organization of the league sports competition, organizer of the sports competition and sports organization, i.e., athletes participating in the sports competition, bearing the costs of the doping control, and based on the decision of the ADAS Director;
(7) in the semifinals and finals of national championships, as well as in the semifinals or finals of the playoffs of national competitions, with the costs of conducting the doping control borne by the competent national sports federation.[208]

710. ADAS conducts planning and testing out of competitions:

(1) on the basis of a periodic doping control plan, adopted by the ADAS Managing Board, in accordance with the requirements of the International Standard for Testing and Investigation;
(2) on the basis of the requirements arising from the technical document for specific analyses in sports;
(3) on the basis of a special decision of the ADAS Director;
(4) at the request of the Ministry in Charge of Sports Affairs;
(5) at the request of the sports inspector;
(6) upon a reasoned proposal of the competent national sports federation, organization of the league sports competition, organizer of the sports competition and sports organization, i.e., athletes participating in the sports competition, bearing the costs of the doping control, and based on the decision of the ADAS Director;
(7) in the semifinals and finals of national championships, as well as in the semifinals or finals of the playoffs of national competitions, with the costs of conducting the doping control borne by the competent national sports federation;
(8) on the basis of coordination with other anti-doping organizations in connection with the implementation of control over the same athletes.

---

208. *See* Art. 17 of the Rulebook on doping control in sports competitions and out of competition.

711. The Rulebook stipulates that when determining sports competitions which will be subject to doping control, priority is given to professional sports competitions, national sports competitions, and qualification competitions directly leading to participation in national sports championships and competitions which directly affect participation in international sports competitions.

712. Sports federations also have a significant role to play in the prevention of doping in sports. Article 10 of LPDS of RS provides for the competence of the national sports federation.

713. The competent national sports federation is obliged to:

(1) determine disciplinary measures by sports rules and regulate the procedure of their imposition in cases of established violation of anti-doping rules, in accordance with this Law and the rules of the Anti-Doping Agency, and to ensure that in the procedure of the imposition of measures to persons responsible for doping their personality and right to appropriate legal protection are respected (respect for privacy, timely search, guarantee of the right to a legal statement, fair, professional, operationally independent and impartial search body, right to a representative at personal expense, access to files, submission of evidence, standards regarding doping, timely information, timely, written and reasoned decision, right to appeal, etc.);
(2) ensure, within the competence of the federation, that athletes, sports experts and other persons for whom responsibility for doping has been determined are imposed appropriate disciplinary measures, in accordance with this Law and the rules of the competent anti-doping organization;
(3) not to recognize the sports result in the achievement of which an athlete under doping was a participant;
(4) not to allow athletes, sports experts and other persons within the competence of the national sports federation to participate in a sports event who have been imposed a measure due to doping, or have been sentenced, in accordance with this Law, for a criminal offence or misdemeanour;
(5) adopt an anti-doping action programme and submit it to the Anti-Doping Agency within fifteen days;
(6) provide constant individual medical monitoring of categorized athletes and to this end adopt the necessary acts and take concrete measures;
(7) ensure, through sports rules and in cooperation with the anti-doping agency, that members of the federation, especially sports experts and registered athletes of all ages, are continuously, and at least once a year, informed and educated about current regulations related to doping in sports and the harmful health consequences of the use of doping substances;
(8) ensure by sports rules that any person who is a member of the federation or is otherwise within the competence of the federation to respect, apply, support

and implement measures to prevent doping in sports determined in accordance with this Law, and when it finds that a person has not met such an obligation, to take appropriate measures, which must include the possibility of exclusion from specific future sports events or all sports events taking place over a period of time;

(9) appoint a responsible person, i.e., an appropriate sports expert to supervise the implementation of measures to prevent doping;

(10) report the competition to the Anti-Doping Agency at least twenty-one days before the competition organized by it or under its control, as well as submit the competition calendar for the following year to the Anti-Doping Agency by the end of the current year at the latest;

(11) inform the Anti-Doping Agency at least once in six months about training plans and preparation of top athletes and national sports teams;

(12) completely deny funding to athletes, sports experts, sports organizations and other persons who do not comply with the applicable anti-doping rules;

(13) control the anti-doping programmes of its members, as well as the implementation of those programs;

(14) inform the Ministry in Charge of Sports and the Anti-Doping Agency at the end of the year about the measures for combating doping taken during the year;

(15) establish and implement anti-doping rules for animals participating in the sport in which animals compete, in accordance with the rules of the Anti-Doping Agency and the competent international sports federation;

(16) not to allow the performance of any sports activity and sports occupation or any position within the competence of the federation to a person who, in accordance with this Law, was imposed a measure due to the violation of anti-doping rules or criminal or misdemeanour sentence, during the imposed measure, i.e., sentence;

(17) organize doping control out of sports competitions and at sports competitions within the competence of the federation and bear the costs of its implementation, in accordance with this Law and the annual doping control plan determined by the Anti-Doping Agency;

(18) promote the strengthening of the values of sports ethics, fair play and the health of athletes;

(19) report to the Anti-Doping Agency and the competent international sports federation any information indicating a violation or in connection with the violation of anti-doping rules and cooperate with the Anti-Doping Agency and another authorized anti-doping organization in conducting the investigation;

(20) require its members to report all information indicating or relating to anti-doping rule violations and to participate in investigations conducted by the Anti-Doping Agency or any other authorized anti-doping organization competent to conduct the investigation;

(21) adopt rules for the protection of persons;

(22) inform the Anti-Doping Agency and athletes, i.e., other persons to whom the decision refers, about every decision they make in the results management process;

(23) respect and apply the measures adopted by the Anti-Doping Agency.

714. The competent national sports federation that does not respect all of the above cannot receive funds from public revenues.

715. The Anti-Doping Agency issues rules on the harmonization of the anti-doping activities of the Anti-Doping Agency and the competent national sports federations with the World Anti-Doping Code and this Law.

716. When the Anti-Doping Agency determines that the competent national sports federation or other organization in the field of sports has not harmonized its rules with the World Anti-Doping Code and this Law or has not applied them or does not comply with them, it may take measures against this organization to provide for by this Law and the World Anti-Doping Code.

717. The competent national sports federation is obliged to submit a copy of these rules to the Ministry in Charge of Sports Affairs and the Anti-Doping Agency within fifteen days from the day the sports rules come into force which determine the measures for the prevention of doping, i.e., their amendments.

718. The competent national sports federation, organization of a league sports competition, organizer of a sports competition and sports organization or a sportsman/woman participating in a sports competition may propose to the Anti-Doping Agency to conduct the doping control at specific competitions or the doping control out of the competition of specific teams, training groups or individual athletes by bearing the costs for conducting the doping control.

719. Athletes who are in the status of Olympic candidates, top and other categorized athletes, athletes of an international rank, athletes who wish to continue their sports career after the expiration of the ban on participation in competitions due to doping, as well as other categories of athletes determined by the Anti-Doping Agency (registered test group).

720. In cooperation with the competent national sports federations, ADAS establishes a national registered test group of athletes. The national registered test group may include:

(1) Athletes who have been designated as Olympic candidates by the Serbian Olympic Committee.
(2) Athletes of a national rank referred to in Article 6, paragraph 2 of this Rulebook.
(3) Athletes of an international rank, in accordance with the rules of the competent international sports federation, if they are not in the registered group of the international sports federation.
(4) Athletes who have been declared responsible for violating anti-doping rules and athletes who wish to continue their sports career after the expiration of the ban on participation in competitions due to doping.
(5) Athletes who are members of national sports teams.

(6) Athletes whose result is among the three best results in the Republic of Serbia, achieved in the previous/current year.
(7) Athletes who have seen significant and unexpected improvement in performance over the past twelve months.
(8) Athletes who are selected as targets by ADAS.

721. According to the Rulebook, but also in accordance with the International Standard for Testing and Investigation approved by the WADA, every athlete from the national registered test group is obliged to:

(1) notify ADAS and the responsible person in the competent national sports federation of his/her location every three months;
(2) update this information if necessary so that it is accurate and complete at all times;
(3) make himself/herself available for testing at the specified location.

722. ADAS informs the athlete and his/her competent national sports federation that it has included him/her in the national registered test group or excluded him/her from it, without delay. In addition, it is the duty of ADAS to inform athletes from the registered test group about the rights and obligations related to the implementation of the doping control, as well as the manner of submitting requests for granting Therapeutic Use Exemptions (TUE). The Anti-Doping Agency of Serbia has the obligation to timely and regularly (as a rule, every three months and before the start of the competition season), make a decision and update the data on the registered test group depending on the competition calendar.

723. The Rulebook on doping control at sports competitions and out of competitions also regulates how athletes are selected for testing both at competitions and out of competitions (Article 24).

724. Regarding doping controls in competitions, athletes are selected for testing as follows:

(1) in accordance with the previously established doping control plan, based on a risk assessment;
(2) random selection method;
(3) based on the achieved sports results;
(4) at the discretion of the ADAS doping controller;
(5) at the request of the sports inspector;
(6) at the proposal of authorized organizations from the Rulebook on doping control at sports competitions and out of competitions.[209]

725. As a rule, in individual competitions, three first-placed athletes and another athlete, athletes who break or equal the national, European or world record are

209. *See* Art. 24 of the Rulebook on doping control of sports competitions and out of competition.

selected, while in team competitions, two or three athletes from each team are selected by random draw or targeted selection.

726. The athletes for whom there is a suspicion of doping will also be tested by the so-called targeted testing, or according to the judgment of the doping controller. If the competitions last longer, it is not excluded that the same athlete will be tested more than once.

727. Control out of competition is performed on athletes who are in the national registered test group, athletes who have been banned from participating in competitions due to anti-doping rule violations during the ban period, and athletes for whom targeted testing has been determined.

728. Athletes are selected for testing out of the competition:

(1) in accordance with the previously established periodic control plan, based on a risk assessment;
(2) random sampling method;
(3) on the basis of a special decision of the ADAS Director;
(4) at the proposal of authorized organizations from the Rulebook on doping control at sports competitions and out of competitions;
(5) at the proposal of the competent international sports federation;
(6) at the proposal of the WADA;
(7) at the proposal of the athlete;
(8) on the basis of the request of the sports inspector or the Ministry in Charge of Sports.

729. The testing itself begins with informing the athlete that he/she should start the doping control, i.e., that he/she has been selected for the doping control. The athlete may be notified orally or in writing, provided that the oral notification must be confirmed in writing. The athlete needs to sign the notification and from this moment on, he/she is under the strict supervision of the controller until the conclusion of the doping control. The notice states the place and time of the sampling of the athlete.

730. During the doping control, the athlete may be accompanied by a person whom he/she trusts and, if necessary, an interpreter. In the case of a minor athlete, a companion is allowed at all times during doping control.

731. Athletes with disabilities are also subject to doping control, and the doping controller has the obligation to adjust the sampling process to the needs of athletes with disabilities while documenting all deviations from the standard procedure.

732. When taking a sample for doping control with persons with disabilities, the doping controller may allow the assistance of a representative or companion, if the athlete agrees.

733. The Rulebook on doping Control at sports competitions and out of competitions clearly defines the duties of doping controllers, athletes and organizers of sports competitions (Article 30).

734. The duties of the doping controller in relation to the conduct of the doping control are as follows:

- not undertake doping control if there is any conflict of interest in relation to the result of the doping control;
- inform the athlete, in person without prior notice or in exceptional cases by telephone (during the last five minutes within the mandatory period of sixty minutes), that the athlete has been selected for the doping control, and that he/she must undergo the doping control (if the athlete is orally informed, a written notice is served to him/her subsequently);
- check whether a third-party notification of the doping control is required before notifying the athlete, which will be the case in the case of a minor athlete and if the disability of the athlete requires it;
- inform the athlete about the place of the doping control;
- ensure that there is no possibility of manipulation when giving samples;
- state the name of the institution (ADAS) on whose behalf they conduct the doping control;
- acquaint the athlete with his/her rights, obligations and responsibilities, including the right to request a postponement of reporting to the doping control station for a justified reason and the obligation to respect the procedure of collecting samples;
- inform the athlete that from the moment of the notification of the doping control until the conclusion of the doping control, he/she must not move away from the field of view of the doping controller, i.e., authorized escort and from the moment of contact with the athlete until the athlete leaves, the doping control station after the sampling procedure, keep the athlete under constant supervision;
- have an appropriate ID document issued by ADAS and/or the document which it has recognized as equivalent, and it identifies athletes, and at the request of the athlete or his/her legal representative to additionally document their identity with an ID card (passport);
- before the sports competition, visit the sports facility, i.e., the organizer of the competition and inform the appropriate official (e.g., technical delegate) about the need for doping control and to make sure that the doping control point is adequately equipped;
- ensure that ADAS and/or the competent international sports federation have sent all forms and kits for the doping control and that they take care of their safety;
- provide, if necessary, companions to athletes at the place for giving the sample, who have the appropriate identification and are familiar with the competition plan and the layout of the premises in the sports facility;
- make sure that the athletes and their companions understand what type of samples will be taken, what the sampling procedure is and what conditions need to be met before collecting the sample;

- allow the athletes to adequately rehydrate or take food before giving a sample, with a warning that they are doing so at their own risk and that the intake of too much fluid may slow down the production of an appropriate sample;
- warn the athlete that the urine sample he/she gives should be the first urine of the athlete after the notification, i.e., that the athlete must not urinate under the shower or in any other way before giving the sample to the doping controller;
- allow the athlete to independently choose a sample container and a kit;
- allow the athlete to take with them one companion and, if necessary, an interpreter;
- enable, at the request of the minor athlete, the presence of his/her legal representative when giving the sample, whereby the legal representative will not directly supervise the giving of the urine sample unless the athlete wishes so;
- supervise sampling at the doping control station;
- accurately and completely fill in all documentation on the doping control form;
- accept and note all complaints and objections to irregularities related to the doping control procedure and report this to ADAS and/or the International Sports Association;
- confiscate all items that have been used or are suspected to have been used in an anti-doping rule violation and in another appropriate manner, ensure obtaining the evidence of the anti-doping rule violation.[210]

735. The doping controller/escort will ask the athlete to sign the appropriate form confirming that he/she has received the doping control notification. If the athlete refuses or avoids receiving or signing the doping control notification or declares that he/she will not come for the doping control, the doping controller/escort, if possible, notifies the athlete of the consequences of refusing or failing to comply with the testing obligation. The refusal of the athlete is entered in the appropriate section of the doping control form.

736. The duties of the athlete in relation to doping control are provided for in Article 31 of the Rulebook. The duties of the athlete are to:

- when notified that he/she has been selected for the doping control, sign the consent in the doping control form;
- submit to the doping controller a document for personal identification (identity card; passport; valid licence with a photo);
- follow the doping controller and/or his/her companion to the doping control point or DCS, as soon as possible;
- inform the doping controller if he/she participates in further competitions on the same day. In this case, the doping controller may order that the testing be performed later in the day, provided that the athlete is under constant escort until he or she returns to the doping control station to provide a sample;
- a urine and/or blood sample or other established sample;

210. *See* Art. 30 of the Rulebook on doping control in sports competitions and out of competition.

- leave the place for doping control, i.e., DCS only with the permission of the doping controller, and under the condition that he/she is accompanied and supervised by the doping controller or escort at all times (time of leaving and returning is entered in the doping control form);
- respect the rules for conducting the doping control determined by this Rulebook and the instructions of the doping controller;
- fully cooperates with ADAS in the investigation of anti-doping rule violations;
- disclose the identity of his/her support staff at the request of ADAS or another authorized anti-doping organization;
- behave politely towards the doping controller or another person involved in the doping control.[211]

737. The doping control can also be performed when an athlete does not have a document for personal identification if he/she is personally known to the doping controller.

738. The duties of the organizer of the sports competition at which it is determined that doping control will be carried out are as follows:

- to provide adequate premises and necessary equipment for the doping control;
- to provide financial resources for the complete implementation of the doping control: procurement of doping kits, doping controller per diems, accommodation and transportation of doping, sending samples to the laboratory, analysis of the samples sent and other costs of ADAS and/or the International Sports Federation;
- to cooperate with doping controllers and authorized ADAS officials;
- to issue the necessary accreditations for participation in the doping control and monitoring of sports competition to doping controllers and authorized ADAS officials (Director, President and Vice Presidents of the ADAS management Board, President of the TUE Board, President of the Anti-Doping Committee) appointed by ADAS.

739. The laboratory in which the doping analysis is performed must be accredited by the WADA, and the Board of ADAS determines the laboratory in which the analysis of the taken doping samples of athletes will be performed. If the laboratory is not accredited as stated, the analysis cannot be considered valid.

740. In doing so, the Rulebook on doping control at sports competitions and out of competition clearly defines the protocol for the storage and transport of samples to an accredited laboratory, as well as the management of results, notification of the analysis results and internal audit.

741. ADAS is responsible for managing the results of doping controls out of competition, while in addition to ADAS, the national sports federation, i.e., the international sports association is also responsible for competitions.

---

211. *See* Art. 31 of the Rulebook on doping control of sports competitions and out of competition.

742. In case sample A is negative, i.e., the presence of prohibited substances has not been determined, the data is entered into the ADAS database, while sample B can be stored for up to ten years, within the long-term storage of samples.

743. In case sample A is positive, it is necessary for ADAS to undertake a test to determine whether a TUE has been granted or will be granted and whether there is a deviation from international standards for testing or laboratory analysis that has caused a positive result of the laboratory analysis;

744. This test, according to the Rulebook, should be completed no later than seven after receiving the results of laboratory analyses.

745. After the first testing, ADAS, if necessary, undertakes further investigations in accordance with the list of prohibited doping substances. If during the previous testing, it has been established that neither is there an approved TUE nor will it be approved, as well as that there are no deviations which caused the positive result of the laboratory analysis, ADAS without delay notifies the athlete in writing (with a return receipt), to the last address communicated to ADAS or the competent national sports federation, or by e-mail to the address left by the athlete on the doping control form, about:

- the analytical finding deviating from the allowed (positive result of analyses);
- the anti-doping rule that has been violated;
- the right to request the analysis of sample B without delay, and at the latest within seven days, and if he/she fails to do so, he/she shall be deemed to have waived his/her right to the analysis of sample B;
- the date, time and place of the analysis of sample B, if the athlete or anti-doping organization has decided to request the analysis of sample B;
- the right for him/her and/or his/her representative to be present at the opening and analysis of sample B, within the period provided for by international standards for the laboratory analysis, if the analysis is required;
- the right of the athlete to request copies of the laboratory report on the analysis of the sample;
- the right of the athlete to submit a written statement to ADAS;
- the date and circumstances of the testing and the possible consequences of the anti-doping rule violation;
- imposing a temporary suspension, in accordance with this Rulebook and the World Anti-Doping Code.

746. In addition to the athlete, the competent national sports federation, i.e., the international sports federation, as well as the WADA will be notified of the violation of the anti-doping rules.

747. If ADAS decides not to treat the analytical finding deviating from the permitted one as an anti-doping rule violation, it notifies the athlete and the relevant anti-doping organizations, in accordance with Article 14.1.2 of the Code.

748. In all cases where the notification of violation of the anti-doping rules does not lead to the imposition of a temporary suspension in accordance with the provisions of the World Anti-Doping Code and this regulation, athletes will be offered to accept a voluntary temporary suspension until a final decision is made.

749. The Anti-Doping Agency establishes, at least once a year, the list of doping agents for athletes and the list of prohibited doping agents for animals (reference lists of prohibited pharmacological classes of doping substances and doping methods), in accordance with the European Convention on the prevention of doping in sports, international standards for the list of prohibited agents approved by the WADA and the sports rules of the competent international sports federations for sports in which animals participate.

750. Lists of prohibited doping agents are published in the 'Official Gazette of the Republic of Serbia'.

751. The Management Board of the ADAS has adopted the Rulebook on the List of prohibited doping agents,[212] which precisely regulates this area.

752. The list of prohibited doping agents is determined after the WADA publishes the List of prohibited doping substances (agents) for the next year, and Amendments to the List of prohibited substances are made if the WADA makes changes during the year.

753. By the same analogy, the Rulebook on the list of prohibited doping agents for horses was adopted.[213]

754. The Rulebook on approving exemptions for therapeutic use was adopted as a by-law.[214]

755. This Rulebook regulates the criteria and procedure for approving exemptions for therapeutic use, i.e., exempting athletes from the ban on the use of certain substances and/or methods from the list of prohibited doping agents for the purpose of treating certain diseases and medical conditions.

756. According to this Rulebook, athletes may be granted the use of prohibited substances and/or methods that are on the list of prohibited doping agents, i.e., an exemption may be granted for the therapeutic use of prohibited substances for therapeutic purposes (hereinafter: TUE), in the case when there is a clear and necessary medical need.

---

212. *See* The Rulebook was published in the 'Official Gazette of RS', No. 156/2020 of 25 Dec. 2020, and entered into force on 2 Jan. 2021.
213. *See* The Rulebook was published in the 'Official Gazette of RS', No. 23/2021 of 16 Mar. 2021, and entered into force on 24 Mar. 2021.
214. *See* 'Official Bulletin of ADAS', No. 38 of 12 Mar. 2021.

757. The presence of a prohibited substance and its metabolites and/or markers shall not be considered an anti-doping rule violation if it complies with the rules on granting exemptions for therapeutic use.

758. TUE is approved in accordance with the LPDS, this Rulebook, World Anti-Doping Code, Rulebook establishing the list of prohibited doping substances, and international standards for granting exemptions for therapeutic use approved by the WADA.

759. The athlete is required to seek and obtain TUE approval before using or possessing the substance, provided that the medical condition must be diagnosed in accordance with the existing international standards, Checklist for Therapeutic Use Exemption (TUE) Application and guides to good medical practice of the WADA available on their official website ('Medical Information to Support the Decisions of TUECs').

760. TUE is approved by the Board for granting exemptions for the therapeutic use of the Anti-Doping Agency of Serbia. The TUE approved by ADAS is valid at any national level, in any country and does not require formal recognition from any other national anti-doping organization unless the athlete becomes an international athlete or competes in an international sporting event.

761. If the athlete of an international rank or competing in an international sporting event does not already have an ADAS approved by ADAS for a particular substance or method, the athlete must apply for TUE directly to the International Federation in accordance with the procedure set out in the International Standard for TUE.

762. The role of the physician who treats the athlete in preventing doping in sports is especially important. A physician who prescribes to the athlete an agent containing prohibited doping substances for the purpose of treatment shall inform the athlete if he/she has told him/her that he/she is engaged in sports activities.

763. The Rulebook on determining the appearance of the label with the 'DOPING FREE' sign and the procedure for issuing the label[215] determine the appearance of the label which is placed on the tested products containing food supplements and the procedure for issuing the label is regulated.

764. The approval of product labelling is done in accordance with the LPDS, as well as with the Rulebook which determines the list of prohibited doping substances and this Rulebook, while the label with the 'DOPING FREE' sign is issued by the Anti-Doping Agency of Serbia.

215. *See* 'Official Gazette of RS', No. 139/2014.

765. Labelling the product may be approved when the product has been tested for the presence of prohibited doping substances by a laboratory that has the technical and other conditions for conducting such an analysis and when all other conditions prescribed by this Rulebook have been met.

766. This labelling is approved when the product is tested in a laboratory accredited by the WADA and when it is allowed for use and distribution in the territory of the Republic of Serbia in accordance with the Law;

767. The user of the services for the public service of issuing the label pays the fee to the Anti-Doping Agency, in accordance with the Law. Each label contains a unique reference number which, when entered into the database on the Anti-Doping Agency website, provides feedback on which product the label refers to and which substances the product has been tested on.

§1. Determining Responsibilities and Resolving Disputes

768. The World Anti-Doping Code and the sports rules of the competent international sports federation also determine in which cases a dispute regarding the determination of liability may be the subject of international sports arbitration.

769. In the Republic of Serbia, the OKS or the competent national branch sports federation is competent to decide in the first instance. The cited bodies are obliged to determine the measures and regulate the procedure of imposing measures, as well as to impose appropriate measures on the persons who are determined to be responsible for doping. In the event that the OKS or the competent national branch sports federation does not make a first-instance decision in a timely manner,[216] the Anti-Doping Agency, i.e., the Anti-Doping Committee, is responsible for deciding in the first instance. Also, the possibility is provided for the decision-making authority to be taken over by the Anti-Doping Agency of Serbia even before the expiration of the one-year deadline, based on an agreement with the OKS or the competent national branch sports federation. In this case, the consent of the athlete is required.

770. The deadline is exceeded when more than one year has elapsed from the day the analysis of the taken samples determined that the athlete was under doping.

771. In the competent national branch sports federations of Serbia, the most common body which in the first instance decides on the responsibility for violating the anti-doping rules is the disciplinary commission or the disciplinary board of the federation.

772. The composition of the commission/board is different and is regulated differently, from federation to federation. The composition and decision-making procedure of the disciplinary commission/board is regulated by the statute and the

216. *See* Art. 30 para. 1 item 5) of the Law on the prevention of doping in sports.

disciplinary rulebook of the federation, which is in accordance with the Rulebook on determining the responsibility of the person who violated the anti-doping rules and LPDS of RS.

773. The Anti-Doping Committee is an expert working body formed at the Anti-Doping Agency which, in an impartial and fair manner, decides on appeals against first-instance decisions of disciplinary bodies of competent national sports federations on anti-doping rule violations, as well as for first-instance decisions on anti-doping rule violations, violations of the measures imposed due to the non-compliance with the obligations established by the World Anti-Doping Code, in cases determined by LPDS of RS and the Code (Article 26). It is an independent operational body which makes decisions independently. It has a president and eight members, who are appointed for a period of four years (Article 23, paragraph 2), from the rank of prominent experts, by the OKS, the PKS and the Sports Federation of Serbia appointing three members each, of which one is a law graduate and a doctor of medicine with at least three years of relevant experience in their profession. The members of the Anti-Doping Committee elect the President of the Anti-Doping Committee from among themselves, by a majority of the total number of members of the Anti-Doping Committee.

774. The Anti-Doping Committee decides, in individual cases, through the First Instance and Appeals Chamber for anti-doping offences (Article 26, paragraph 4).

775. The members of the First Instance and Appeals Chamber for anti-doping offences are appointed by the President of the Anti-Doping Committee, of which one member must be a law graduate and one member a doctor of medicine (Article 26, paragraph 5).

776. The Chamber has three members (president and two members), and the members of the Chamber are elected from among the members of the ADAS Anti-Doping Committee. The Chamber decides by a majority vote of the total number of members of the Chamber, while the President of the Anti-Doping Committee also has certain competencies in individual cases.

777. In order for the members of the Chamber to be impartial and objective, the Rulebook on determining the liability of persons who have violated the anti-doping rules stipulates that members of the Anti-Doping Committee may not give, in writing or orally, opinions or advice, nor be proxies or advisors in disputes conducted before the Anti-Doping Committee.

778. The procedure for liability for the violation of the anti-doping rules, violation of imposed measures due to the violation of the anti-doping rules and for non-compliance with other obligations provided by LPDS of RS, is initiated by an application (Article 27, paragraph 1) or an appeal that may be filed by:

(1) the Director of the Anti-Doping Agency;
(2) the competent international sports federation;

(3) the WADA;
(4) sports organization to which the athlete or other person belongs;
(5) the organizer of the sports competition at which the doping control was performed;
(6) competent national sports federation;
(7) the owner of the animal under doping;
(8) the athlete or other person suspected of having violated the anti-doping rules, i.e., to whom the decision to which the appeal is lodged relates;
(9) the other party to the dispute in which the decision was made;
(10) the IOC or the IPC in the event that the decision may have an effect in relation to the Olympic Games or the Paralympic Games, including decisions affecting the right to participate in the Olympic Games or the Paralympic Games;
(11) the national anti-doping organization, according to the citizenship, residence, domicile or sports licence of the person.

779. The resolution of disputes in accordance with the Rulebook on determining the liability of persons who have violated the anti-doping rules is based on the following principles:

- The proceedings are conducted in accordance with LPDS, the World Anti-Doping Code, international standards for doping control and management of results approved by the WADA, this Rulebook and other ADAS rules.
- The parties are obliged to state all the facts on which they base their claims and present evidence to establish those facts, including the right to call and examine witnesses.
- The Anti-Doping Committee is authorized to establish the facts that the parties did not present if the results of the discussion and the presentation of evidence show that this is necessary to resolve the dispute.
- The Anti-Doping Committee will conscientiously and carefully evaluate each piece of evidence separately and all the evidence together.
- In proceedings before the Anti-Doping Committee, the parties are equal.
- Each party has the right to present its views and evidence, as well as to comment on the actions and proposals of the other party.
- The proceedings are conducted without delay, there is no stay of proceedings, and in certain situations by urgent procedure, respecting the principles of rationalization.
- The proceedings are conducted in the Serbian language, and if there is a need, the suspect is entitled to a certified interpreter, but at his/her own expense.
- The proceedings take place without the presence of the public and are confidential unless the parties agree otherwise.
- The appeal proceedings before the Anti-Doping Committee include all issues relevant to the subject matter and are not limited to the issues or reasons contained in the first-instance decision or the appeal filed.
- The proceedings may also be conducted if one of the parties refuses to participate in the proceedings or fails to attend the hearing after they have received, within a reasonable time, notifications on the initiation of the proceedings, i.e., holding of the hearing.

– The costs of the proceedings are borne by the person who committed the violation of the anti-doping rules, i.e., the party who initiated the proceedings in which no violation of the anti-doping rules has been established.

780. In matters not regulated by the Rulebook on determining the liability of persons who have violated the anti-doping rules, the proceedings will be conducted in accordance with the provisions of the Code of Civil Procedure, if applicable, unless the application of these provisions corresponds to the nature of the proceedings before the Anti-Doping Committee. If the application of the provisions of the Code of Civil Procedure does not correspond to the nature of the proceedings before the Anti-Doping Committee, the Chamber will only determine the proceedings which are expedient, provided that the parties are treated equally and given the opportunity to present their defence.

781. In any case, the authorized anti-doping organization must prove the violation of the anti-doping rules in a convincing manner.

782. The following rules apply to the presentation of evidence in doping cases:[217]

(A) Analytical methods or restrictions adopted by the WADA after consultation within the relevant scientific community or which have been the subject of an expert assessment are presumed to be scientifically valid. Any athlete or other person wishing to challenge the validity of such a presumption or to refute the presumption of such a scientific basis shall, as a precondition for such a challenge, notify the WADA of the challenge and the grounds for the challenge. The Chamber may, on its own initiative, also notify the WADA of such a challenge. Within ten days from the date of receipt of the notification and documentation, the WADA has the right to intervene as a party to the dispute, appear as a friend of the court (amicus curiae) or otherwise submit evidence in the proceedings.

(B) Laboratories accredited or approved by the WADA are presumed to have conducted a sample analysis and the storage procedure in accordance with International Laboratory Standards. The athlete or other person may refute this presumption by proving that there has been a deviation from the application of the International Laboratory Standards, which is reasonably suspected to have caused an unfavourable analytical finding. If the athlete or other person refutes the presumption by indicating that there has been a deviation from the application of International Standards for Laboratories, which is reasonably suspected to have caused an unfavourable analytical finding, the burden of proving that the deviation did not cause an unfavourable analytical finding is borne by the anti-doping organization.

217. *See* Art. 48 of the Rulebook on determining the liability of a person who has committed an anti-doping rule violation.

(C) Deviation from any other international standard or other anti-doping rule or procedure set forth in the Code or in the rules of the anti-doping organization will not affect the invalidity of evidence indicating a violation of the anti-doping rules or results that constitute an unfavourable analytical finding and cannot constitute a defence for the violation of the anti-doping rules, but in case, the athlete or another person proves that deviation from one of the specific provisions of the international standard mentioned in this point could reasonably have caused the anti-doping rule violation based on unfavourable analytical findings or whereabouts failure, then the anti-doping organization must prove that such deviation did not cause an unfavourable analytical finding or whereabouts failure:

(1) a deviation from the International Standard for Testing and Investigation relating to the collection or handling of samples, which could reasonably cause an anti-doping rule violation based on an unfavourable analytical finding, in which case the authorized anti-doping organization bears the burden of determining that such deviation did not cause unfavourable analytical findings;

(2) deviation from the International Standard for Results Management or the International Standard for Testing and Investigation in relation to the finding of an unfavourable finding in the biological passport that could reasonably cause an anti-doping rule violation, in which case the authorized anti-doping organization will bear the burden to establish that such deviation did not cause the anti-doping rule violation;

(3) deviation from the International Standard for Results Management regarding the requirement to notify the athlete of the opening of Sample B, which could reasonably result in an anti-doping rule violation based on an unfavourable analytical finding, in which case the authorized anti-doping organization will have the burden of determining that such deviation did not cause the unfavourable analytical finding;

(4) deviation from the International Standard for Results Management in relation to informing the athlete that could reasonably cause an anti-doping rule violation based on whereabouts failure, in which case the authorized anti-doping organization bears the burden of determining that such deviation did not cause the whereabouts failure;

(5) facts established by a decision of a court or other authorized disciplinary body, which is not subject to appeal, are accepted as irrefutable evidence against the athlete or other person to whom these facts relate unless the athlete or other person proves that the decision is contrary to the principles of natural law;

(6) the Chamber has the right to establish that an athlete or other person suspected of violating the rules has committed the violation, if the athlete or other person refuses, and is notified in advance of the search within a reasonable time, to participate in the hearing (either in person, by telephone, as determined by the prosecuting authority) and to answer questions from the Chamber or ADAS regarding the anti-doping rule violation for which they are charged;

(7) it is the duty of athletes to ensure that no prohibited substances enter their bodies. Athletes are responsible for the presence of any prohibited substance or its metabolites or markers in their body samples. Accordingly, in order to establish a violation of the anti-doping rules of the LPDS, it is not necessary that there is intent, failure, negligence or conscious use in the conduct of the athlete. Sufficient evidence of a violation of the anti-doping rule of LPDS of RS exists when any of the following is established:
   - the presence of a prohibited substance or its metabolite or marker in sample A, and the athlete does not require the analysis of sample B and sample B is not analysed, or sample B is analysed and it also confirmed the presence of a prohibited substance or its metabolites or markers found in sample A;
   - or when sample A or B is divided into two parts and when the analysis of the part of the sample left for the purpose of confirming the findings confirms the presence of the prohibited substance or its metabolites or markers found in the first part of the sample or the athlete does not require the analysis of the part of the sample left for purposes of confirming the findings.

783. The proceedings end with a decision and can be terminated if:

- the applicant withdraws the application;
- the parties agree to terminate the proceedings;
- in case of death of the person against whom the proceedings are conducted or similar circumstances, so the proceedings become impossible;
- in other cases provided by the Rulebook on determining the responsibility of a person who has committed an anti-doping rule violation.

784. The decision on the subject of the dispute which decides on all requests of the parties, i.e., determines the existence or non-existence of an anti-doping rule violation is made by the Chamber by a majority vote of the members of the Chamber and sanctions are imposed at the same time. The sanctions imposed by the chamber must be within the limits of the general minimum and maximum and in accordance with the LPDS, World Anti-Doping Code and the rules of the competent national sports federation.

785. The ADAS is obliged, no later than twenty days after making the decision, to publish on the official website information on the identity of the athlete or other person who was found in the first instance or final decision to have violated the anti-doping rules, whereby this information is available for the duration of the sentence. Excluded from this are minors found to have committed an anti-doping rule violation. The ADAS is obliged to send a reasoned decision to the person found to have violated the anti-doping rules and to all anti-doping organizations that have the right to appeal in accordance with the World Anti-Doping Code, no later than twenty days after the decision.

786. If the Chamber finds that the athlete or other person has not committed an anti-doping rule violation, the decision may be made public only with the consent of the athlete or other person. The Anti-Doping Agency of Serbia has the obligation to try to obtain such a consent, and if it does, to publish the decision in whole or in part, as approved by the athlete or other person.

§2. Proceedings in Appeals

787. An appeal may be lodged to the Anti-Doping Committee against the following decisions made in the first instance by the first-instance competent authority:

- a decision establishing the existence of an anti-doping rule violation;
- a decision establishing that there is no violation of the anti-doping rules;
- a decision establishing that there was no jurisdiction for decision-making;
- decisions imposing a temporary suspension on the basis of a previously conducted hearing procedure.

788. If the proceedings are conducted against a person who is an athlete of an international rank, the following have the right to file an appeal to the Arbitration Court for Sports:

- the athlete or person who is the subject of the decision against which the appeal has been lodged;
- the other party to the dispute in which the decision was made;
- the competent international federation or any other anti-doping organization in accordance with whose rules a sanction may have been imposed;
- the IOC, i.e., the IOC for Persons with Disabilities, if the decision may have consequences in connection with the Olympic Games;
- the World Anti-Doping Organization.

789. If the proceedings are conducted against a person who is an athlete of a national rank, the following have the right to file an appeal:

- the athlete or other person who is the subject of the decision against which the appeal is filed;
- the other party to the dispute in which the decision was made;
- the competent international federation;
- the World Anti-Doping Organization;
- other persons determined by the rules of the anti-doping organization.

790. According to Article 30, paragraph 1 item 5) of LPDS, the ADAS decides on an appeal against a measure imposed in the first instance by the OKS or the National Branch Sports Federation for the violation of the anti-doping rules.

791. In the case of athletes of an international rank, appeals are lodged exclusively with the International Court of Arbitration for Sports in Lausanne, in accordance with the rules applicable in this court. Athletes or the anti-doping organization whose decision or approval has been revoked due to therapeutic use may file an appeal with the Arbitration Court for Sports in Lausanne.

792. The deadline for appealing the decision made in the first instance is fifteen days from the day of delivery of the first-instance decision. The decision can be challenged in appellate disputes for the following reasons:

- erroneous or incompletely established factual situation (if there are new facts or new evidence …);
- significant violations of the provisions on the proceedings (if some provisions of the general act have not been applied or have been incorrectly applied, and this is of significant influence for the decision-making …);
- erroneous application of the substantive law (if the facts have been erroneously established or have not been established, if the first instance body has not applied or has incorrectly applied the relevant act or has exceeded its powers …);
- decisions on sanctions (if the sentence has not been properly assessed, given the circumstances that affect the sentence to be either higher or lower, or because no suspended sentence has been imposed if there are conditions for this …).

793. A timely appeal does not postpone the execution of the decision unless there is a request of the appellant for which the President of the Anti-Doping Committee, i.e., the Appeals Chamber, decides not to postpone the execution of the decision due to justified reasons.[218]

794. As a rule, appeals are decided by the Appeals Chamber without a hearing, except when it finds that the facts have been erroneously or incompletely established or that there is a material violation of the provisions of the proceedings or that the proceedings have been suspended due to the incorrect assessment of evidence or misapplication of the substantive law. In this case, it will schedule an oral hearing or order that further proceedings be conducted on the basis of written documents. The Appeals Chamber is obliged to decide within fourteen days after the last oral hearings, i.e., in the case of the written proceedings after the last set date for the exchange of submissions.

795. Deciding on the appeal, the Appeals Chamber may dismiss the appeal as untimely, inadmissible or filed by an unauthorized person if it finds that the

---

218. *See* Art. 75 of the Rulebook on determining the liability of a person who has committed an anti-doping rule violation.

President of the Anti-Doping Committee failed to do so, may reject the appeal as unfounded and confirm the first instance decision, but may also accept the appeal, and change the first instance decision.

796. The decision made in the appellate procedure is final and becomes effective upon delivery to the parties.[219]

797. Article 53, paragraph 7 of LPDS of RS also stipulates that the agreement between the Anti-Doping Agency of Serbia, OKS, PKS and the Sports Federation of Serbia may entrust the final settlement of the dispute to a single PSA court.

798. According to the LPDS of RS, it is exceptionally possible for an international sports arbitration to decide on an appeal, a certain level of judicial protection exists in connection with the judicial examination of the arbitral award on a request for the recognition of the foreign arbitral award.

799. According to the Law on Arbitration of the Republic of Serbia,[220] a foreign arbitral award has the force of a domestic final court decision after it has been recognized by the competent court of the Republic of Serbia.

800. There is also the possibility of a constitutional appeal to the Constitutional Court of Serbia.[221]

801. Supervision over the application of LPDS of RS and the regulations adopted on the basis of this Law, supervision over the performance of entrusted tasks is performed by the Ministry of Youth and Sports of the Republic of Serbia (Article 35, paragraph 1). Inspection is performed through sports inspectors (Article 35, paragraph 2).

802. The rights and duties of sports inspectors are prescribed by LS of RS, but from the scope of the fight against doping in sports, they are in more detail determined by LPDS of RS (Article 36).

803. In performing inspection, the sports inspector has the right and duty to:[222]

(1) control whether organizations and individuals in the field of sports undertake activities to prevent doping in accordance with the Law and sports rules;
(2) control whether doping control measures are undertaken by authorized organizations and persons in accordance with the Law;
(3) control whether the orders issued during the supervision are carried out;
(4) take other measures and actions for which he/she is authorized by law;

---

219. *See* Art. 87 of the Rulebook on determining the liability of a person who has committed an anti-doping rule violation.
220. *See* Art. 64 para. 2 of the Law on Arbitration of the Republic of Serbia.
221. *See* Art. 170 of the Constitution of the Republic of Serbia.
222. *See* Arts 36–37 of the Law on the prevention of doping in sports.

(5) determine the identity of persons who use doping or participate in the doping of an athlete;
(6) temporarily confiscate records, documents and other means of importance for establishing the factual situation and temporarily confiscate prohibited doping substances;
(7) ban a person to whom a measure has been imposed due to a violation of the anti-doping rules from participating in a sports event or in activities in the field of sports, in accordance with this Law;
(8) ban the performance of activities in the organization in the field of sports or performing activities with athletes to a person who has been banned from performing activities in the field of sports due to participation in doping an athlete;
(9) order that the identified irregularities and deficiencies be eliminated within a certain period of time and that the prescribed obligation that has not been performed be performed within a certain period of time;
(10) request the Anti-Doping Agency to conduct a doping control in the event that during the inspection, it suspects that there is a case of doping;
(11) temporarily ban the activities and occupations of an organization in the field of sports, until the deficiencies which are the reason for the ban are eliminated – if: it prevents the inspector from inspecting, fails to pass legally prescribed general acts (sports rules) related to doping or does not implement the order given during the supervision or does not implement the measures imposed due to the violation of the anti-doping rules;
(12) submit a report to the competent authority for the committed criminal offence or submit a request for initiating misdemeanour proceedings;
(13) undertake other measures and actions for which he/she is authorized by law and other regulations.

804. It is also prescribed that an appeal may be lodged against the decision of the sports inspector within fifteen days from the day of delivery of the written decision.

§3. Penalty Provisions

805. The LPDS and the Rulebook on determining the liability of persons who have violated the anti-doping rules prescribe appropriate disciplinary measures for violating the rules on the prevention of doping in sports.

806. Disciplinary measures imposed due to the violation of the anti-doping rules, violation of the imposed measures due to the violation of the anti-doping rules and non-compliance with the obligations established by this Law and the Code, are as follows:

(1) disqualification of sports results;
(2) temporary suspension;
(3) ban on participation in competitions;

(4) ban on performing activities in the field of sports;
(5) other measures determined by the Code and sports rules of the competent national and international sports federations.

I. Criminal Offences

807. The Criminal Code (CC) of the Republic of Serbia does not prescribe criminal offences related to doping in sports. However, LPDS of RS prescribes two criminal offences in this field, and this Law has the character of a secondary or supplementary source of criminal legislation:

(1) criminal offence of facilitating the use of doping agents (Article 38, paragraph 1);
(2) criminal offence of the unauthorized production and distribution of doping agents (Article 38, paragraph 4).

808. The criminal offence of facilitating the use of doping agents is committed by a person who, for the purpose of doping in sports, either prescribes or issues or applies a doping agent to an athlete, or induces, aids, or otherwise enables an athlete to use a doping agent, he/she shall be punished by imprisonment for six months to five years. If the act was committed against a minor or several persons or caused particularly severe consequences, the perpetrator shall be punished by imprisonment for a term between two and ten years.

809. The criminal offence of the unauthorized production and marketing of doping is committed by a person who unauthorizedly produces, processes, sells or offers for sale for the purpose of doping in sports, or for the purpose of sale buys, holds, or transfers, or mediates in the sale or purchase of doping agents, or otherwise, places doping agents on the market without authorization shall be punished by imprisonment for a term between three and twelve years.

810. Whoever, without authorization, makes, procures, possesses, or gives for use equipment, materials or substances for the purpose of doping in sports, which he/she knows are intended for the production or preparation of doping agents, shall be punished by imprisonment for a term between six months and five years. As with the previous criminal offence, the court is obliged to impose a security measure of confiscating the article on the perpetrator of this criminal offence. Taking into account the range of the prescribed penalties (special minimum and maximum) for the mentioned criminal offences, it can be concluded that the legislator correctly noticed that criminal offences related to doping carry a great social danger.

II. Offences

811. Offences in the field of doping in sports, as illegal behaviour of a lesser degree of social danger are prescribed by other provisions of LPDS of RS (Articles

40–42), while the Rulebook on determining the liability of a person who violated the anti-doping rules regulates the procedure for determining the responsibility and imposing disciplinary measures on the person who has violated the anti-doping rules.

812. Liability for the violation of anti-doping rules, violation of measures imposed for the violation of the anti-doping rules and for non-compliance with obligations established by an authorized anti-doping organization in accordance with this Law and the Code is determined by the Anti-Doping Committee of the Anti-Doping Agency and the competent national sports federation.

813. Fines are envisaged for a number of offences.

814. A fine of RSD 400,000–RSD 2,000,000 shall be imposed on the competent national sports federation, sports organization and other legal entity for the offence:[223]

(1) if it interferes with or attempts to interfere with any part of the doping control;
(2) if it without authority sells, transports, sends, delivers or distributes prohibited doping agents (either physically, electronically or otherwise), directly or through a third party, to any person in the field of sports, or attempts such a behaviour;
(3) if it gives or attempts to give, or prescribes or attempts to prescribe doping agents to the athlete;
(4) if it encourages, helps, supports, conceals, creates conditions or otherwise participates in the violation or attempted violation of the anti-doping rules or in the violation of the imposed measure banning participation in sports;
(5) if it takes any action to intimidate or punish another person in order to dissuade them from disclosing information related to doping and non-compliance with the anti-doping rules or to punish them for providing evidence or information related to doping and non-compliance with the anti-doping rules, to an authorized anti-doping organization or competent state body;
(6) if it does not allow, i.e., does not enable the implementation of the doping control;
(7) if it does not store the taken samples, or if it does not handle or analyse them in accordance with the provisions of this Law and the relevant international standards approved by the WADA;
(8) if, within its competencies, it does not take measures and activities to ensure that in the procedure of imposing measures on the persons responsible for doping their personality and the right to appropriate legal protection are observed, or fails not to recognize the sports result in which the athlete under doping participated;
(9) if it fails to comply with the measures imposed by the Anti-Doping Agency;

223. *See* Art. 40 of LPDS of RS.

(10) if, within fifteen days from the day the sports rules enter into force, it does not submit a copy of these rules to the Ministry responsible for Sports Affairs and the Anti-Doping Agency;
(11) if it enables a person to whom a measure has been imposed due to a violation of the anti-doping rules to participate in a sports event or activity in the field of sports, or to perform work, i.e., membership in a body or working body;
(12) without authority, affixes to the product a label with the 'DOPING FREE' sign which was not issued by the Anti-Doping Agency;
(13) if it prevents the sports inspector from performing supervision;
(14) if it does not act on the order of the sports inspector;
(15) if it does not harmonize its organization, work, and general acts with the provisions of this Law within the prescribed period.

815. A responsible person in the national sports federation, i.e., a sports organization and another legal entity will be fined in the amount of RSD 50,000–RSD 150,000 for interfering with or attempting to interfere with any part of the doping control.

816. A fine of RSD 50,000–RSD 150,000 will be imposed on a natural person for the offence:[224]

(1) if he/she uses doping agents as an athlete;
(2) if he/she refuses to give or fails to give without a convincing justification the sample after the notification, or avoids giving the sample in another manner;
(3) if, as an athlete from the registered test group, he/she misses the doping test three times and/or fails to complete the athlete location form, in accordance with the international standards for the management of results approved by the WADA, within a period of twelve months;
(4) if he/she interferes with any part of the doping control;
(5) if he/she associates, in a professional or sport-related capacity, with a person who is banned from participating in sports or has been punished in criminal, disciplinary or other proceedings for an act that constitutes a violation of the anti-doping rules within the meaning of this Law, if his/her sentence still lasts or less than six years have elapsed since the imposition of such sentence or with a person who is the mediator or the representative of such a person;
(6) if he/she does not allow, i.e., does not enable the implementation of the doping control;
(7) if he/she performs the doping control even though he/she is not authorized to do so;
(8) if he/she does not inform the Anti-Doping Agency about the possibility that the athlete was under doping;
(9) if he/she does not inform the athlete who told him/her that he/she is engaged in sports activities that he/she has prescribed an agent containing prohibited doping substances for the purpose of treatment;

224. *See* Art. 41 of LPDS of RS.

(10) if he/she participates in a sports event or in activities in the field of sports, or performs affairs, i.e., membership in a body or working body of the organization in the field of sports;
(11) if he/she prevents the sports inspector from performing supervision;
(12) if he/she does not act on the order of the sports inspector.

817. A fine of RSD 50,000–RSD 150,000 or imprisonment for up to sixty days shall be imposed on a natural person for the offence:[225]

(1) if he/she without authority transports, sends, delivers or distributes prohibited doping agents (either physically, electronically or otherwise), directly or through a third party, to any person in the field of sports, or attempts such a behaviour;
(2) if he/she participates in any way in the violation or attempted violation of the anti-doping rules or in the violation of the imposed measure of the ban on participation in sports;
(3) if in any way threatens or intimidates another person with the intention of discouraging him/her from disclosing information related to doping and non-compliance with the anti-doping rules or acts with the aim of putting a person who has in good faith provided evidence or information related to doping and the non-compliance with the anti-doping rules, an authorized anti-doping organization or a competent state authority.

225. *See* Art. 42 of LPDS of RS.

Chapter 3. Private Regulation

818. The OKS concludes the following agreement with Olympic athletes:

AGREEMENT WITH ATHLETES REGARDING DOPING IN SPORTS

I, the undersigned, certify that I will abide by the rules, regulations and principles set out in the Anti-Doping Code of the Olympic Movement and further respect all applicable anti-doping rules (enter the name of the relevant International Sports Federation and National Sports Federation) and that I will adhere to WADA's instructions for the control and sources of doping in sports.

I certify that:

(1) I will willfully and voluntarily at any time make myself available to any official of the doping testing program conducted by my international federation and/or under the auspices of WADA, either directly or through its duly authorized representatives or agents. In the same way, I will undergo a doping control program conducted by the OCS.
(2) I will immediately and at all times provide accurate information on daily movements, including telephone, mobile and electronic contact, to ensure that the above organizations can contact me quickly over duly authorized persons (with the exception of due to really serious reasons) regarding the testing.
(3) In the case of disagreement regarding the organization of anti-doping programmes and the results of the doping control, I will respect the decisions of the competent authorities in the national sports federation, decisions of my international sports federation, the OCS Arbitration Commission, or if necessary the Court of Arbitration for Sports in Lausanne. I take on all these obligations of my own free will and I consider them binding for me for the entire period of my sports activity.

Date, Signature of the athlete

We enclose the Form for the application of the exemption for therapeutic use, during the completion and submission of which a statement of the athlete is also required.

This Form is submitted to the Anti-Doping Agency of the Republic of Serbia bilingually, in English and Serbian.

ANTIDOPING AGENCIJA REPUBLIKE SRBIJE	www.adas.org.rs test.grupa@adas.org.rs info@adas.org.rs Tel/Fax: (+381) 11 4064 136	
	Молим вас попуните све делове великим штампаним словима или електронски. Спортиста треба да попуни делове 1, 5, 6 и 7; лекар треба да попуни делове 2, 3 и 4. Нечитко написана или непотпуна пријава биће враћена и мораће да се поново пријави читко написана и комплетно попуњена.	
	Please complete all sections in capital letters or typing. Athlete to complete sections 1, 5, 6 and 7; physician to complete sections 2, 3 and 4. Illegible or incomplete applications will be returned and will need to be re-submitted in legible and complete form.	

Формулар за пријаву изузећа за терапеутску употребу (ТУЕ)
Therapeutic use exemption (TUE) application form

1. Информације о спортисти / Athlete Information

Презиме: / Surname: __________ Име: / Given Names: __________

Женско / Female ☐ Мушко / Male ☐ Датум рођења (д.м.г): / Date of Birth (d.m.y): __________

Адреса: / Address: __________

Град: / Town: ________ Држава: / Country: ________ Поштански фах: / Postcode: ________

Телефон: (са међународним кодом) / Phone: (with international code) ________ email: ________

Спорт (и позиција): / Sport (and position): __________

Међународна или национална спортска организација: / International or National Sporting Organization: __________

Ако спортиста има инвалидитет, навести који: / If athlete has disability, indicate disability: __________

2. Здравствене информације / Medical information

Дијагноза: / Diagnosis:

____

____

Ако дозвољен лек може да се користи за лечење наведеног стања, наведите клиничко оправдање за коришћење недозвољеног лека:
If a permitted medication can be used to treat the medical condition, please provide clinical justification for the requested use of the prohibited medication:

____

____

Komentar:

Dokazi koji potvrđuju dijagnozu biće prikupljeni i prosleđeni uz ovu prijavu. Medicinske informacije moraju da obuhvate opsežnu medicinsku istoriju bolesti i nalaze/rezultate određenih ispitivanja, laboratorijskih analiza i dijagnostičkih procedura. Fotokopije originalnih dokumenata ili izveštaja takođe treba da budu poslati uz ovu prijavu. Medicinski dokazi treba da budu što više objektivni, koliko je to u kliničkoj praksi moguće. U slučajevima bez potrebnih dokaza, nezavisno medicinsko mišljenje biće dodato uz ovu prijavu.

WADA raspolaže sa velikim brojem preporuka i smernica da pomogne lekarima u pripremi za popunjavanje i slanje TUE prijava. Ove smernice za lekare mogu se naći na sajtu WADA https://www.wada-ama.org kada se u pretragu nese termin "Medical Information". Smernice se odnose na dijagnoze i lečenje brojnih medicinskih stanja koja se najčešće javljaju kod sportista i zahtevaju lečenje zabranjenim supstancama.

Comment:

Evidence confirming the diagnosis shall be attached and forwarded with this application. The medical information must include a comprehensive medical history and the results of all relevant examinations, laboratory investigations and imaging studies. Copies of the original reports or letters should be included when possible. Evidence should be as objective as possible in the clinical circumstances. In the case of non-demonstrable conditions, independent supporting medical opinion will assist this application.

WADA maintains a series of guidelines to assist physicians in the preparation of complete and thorough TUE applications. These TUE Physician Guidelines can be accessed by entering the search term "Medical Information" on the WADA website https://www.wada-ama.org. The guidelines address the diagnosis and treatment of a number of medical conditions commonly affecting athletes, and requiring treatment with prohibited substances.

3. Детаљи о леку / Medication details

Забрањене материје: генерички назив: Prohibited substance(s): Generic name	Доза Dose	Количина Volume	Начин уноса Route	Учесталост Frequency	Трајање примене лека Frequency
1.					
2.					
3.					

4. Изјава лекара / Medical practitioner's declaration

Potvrđujem da je informacija u odeljku 2 i 3 iznad tačna, i da je iznad pomenuto lečenje medicinski odgovarajuće.
I certify that the information at sections 2 and 3 above is accurate, and that the above-mentioned treatment is medically appropriate.

Име и презиме:
Name: ______

Медицинска специјалност:
Medical Speciality: ______

Адреса:
Address: ______

Телефон:
Phone: ______ Факс:
Fax: ______

E-mail: ______

Потпис лекара опште праксе:
Signature of Medical Practitioner: ______ Датум:
Date: ______

5. Ретроактивна пријава / Retroactive applications

Да ли је ово ретроактивна пријава?
Is this a retroactive application?
да yes ☐ не no ☐

Ако јесте, ког датума је почела примена лека:
If yes, on what date was treatment started?
______

Молимо изаберите једну опцију:

☐ Ургентно лечење или лечење акутног медицинског стања је било неопходно
Emergency treatment or treatment of an acute medical condition was necessary

☐ Због других изузетних (ванредних) околности, није било довољно времена или прилике да се поднесе пријава пре допинг контроле
Due to other exceptional circumstances, there was insufficient time or opportunity to submit an application prior to sample collection

☐ Пријава пре примене лека није обавезна под важећим правилима
Advance application not required under applicable rules

☐ Из разлога праведности (ВАДА и ИФ/НАДО) одобрење се захтева)
Fairness (WADA and [IF/NADO] approval required)

Молимо вас додатно објасните:
Please explain:
______

6. Претходне пријаве / Previous applications

Да ли сте поднели било када ТУЕ пријаву било којој антидопинг организацији? да yes ☐ не no ☐
Have you submitted any previous TUE application(s) to any ADO?

За коју супстанцу или метод?
For which substance or method? ______

Коме?
To whom? ______ Када?
When? ______

Одлука:
Decision: Одобрено Approved ☐ Није одобрено Not approved ☐

7. Изјава спортисте / Athlete's declaration

Ја, ______________________________ тврдим да су информације у одељку 1, 5 и 6 тачне. Сагласан сам да се личне информације проследе одговарајућој антидопинг организацији (АДО) као и WADA овлашћеном особљу, WADA TUEC (WADA Komitet za Izuzeće za terapijsku upotrebu) i druge АДО TUEC и овлашћено особље које може да има право на ове информације према Светском антидопинг коду (Код) и/или Интернационалном стандарду за изузеће за терапеутску употребу. Ове особе су подложне професионалном и поверљивом односу према уговору.

Слажем се да мој лекар проследи особама горе поменутим, било коју здравствену информацију коју они сматрају неопходном у циљу разматрања и прихватања моје пријаве.

Разумем да ће моје информације бити коришћене само за евалуацију моје ТУЕ пријаве и у погледу потенцијалне истраге због повреде антидопинг правила и процедура. Разумем да ако ја икада желим да (1) добијем више информација о располагању са мојим здравственим подацима; (2) остварим своја права као што су приступ, корекцију, забрану, противљење и брисање, или (3) повлачење права ових организација да поседују моје здравствене информације. Морам да обавестим свог лекара и антидопинг организацију о тој чињеници. Разумем и слажем се да је можда неопходно за информације повезане са ТУЕ које су поднете пре одлуке да повучем мој пристанак да буду задржане у циљу истраживања и процесуирања повезаног са потенцијалним антидопинг прекршајем, када је то неопходно због Кода, Интернационалних стандарда или националних антидопинг закона, или да се успостави, спроведе или брани правна тврдња која укључује мене, WADA и/или АДО.

Слажем се са одлуком да ова пријава буде доступна свим АДО, или другим организацијама, са надлежношћу за тестирање и/или организацијом која управља мојим резултатима.

Разумем и прихватам да је особа која прима моје информације може да буду смештена изван земље у којој живим. У неким другим земљама, заштита података и закони о приватности могу да буду различити од оних у мојој земљи. Разумем да моје информације могу да буду чуване у ADAMS која припада WADA на серверима пореклом у Канади, и да ће бити задржани за период који је назначен у WADA Интернационалним стандардима за заштиту приватности и личних података (ISPPPI).

У ситуацији да имам било каквих недоумица или брига око тога како да ли се са мојим подацима у складу са овим захтевом или ISPPPI, могу да поднесем жалбу WADA (privacy@wada-ama.org) или мом националном регулаторном телу одговорном за заштиту података.

Разумем да су ентитети поменути у тексту изнад могу ослонити на и могу бити предмет националних антидопинг закона која имају право да одбаце моју сагласност или других важећих закона који могу да захтевају информација које ће бити доступне локалним судовима, спроводиоцима закона, или другим јавним властима. Могу да добијем више информација о националном антидопинг закону од моје интернационалне федерације или антидопинг агенција.

Потпис родитеља или старатеља (ако је спортиста малолетан или има инвалидитет који га спречава да потпише овај формулар, родитељ или старатељ потписаће овај формулар)

I, ______________________________ certify that the information set out at sections 1, 5 and 6 is accurate. I authorize the release of personal medical information to the relevant Anti-Doping Organization (ADO) as well as to WADA authorized staff, to the WADA TUEC (Therapeutic Use Exemption Committee) and to other ADO TUECs and authorized staff that may have a right to this information under the World Anti-Doping Code ("Code") and/or the International Standard for Therapeutic Use Exemptions. These people are subject to a professional or contractual confidentiality obligation.

I consent to my physician(s) releasing to the above persons any health information that they deem necessary in order to consider and determine my application.

I understand that my information will only be used for evaluating my TUE request and in the context of potential anti-doping rule violation investigations and procedures. I understand that if I ever wish to (1) obtain more information about the use of my health information, (2) exercise any rights I may have, such as my right of access, rectification, restriction, opposition, or deletion, or (3) revoke the right of these organizations to obtain my health information, I must notify my medical practitioner and my ADO in writing of that fact. I understand and agree that it may be necessary for TUE-related information submitted prior to revoking my consent to be retained for the purpose of investigations or proceedings related to a possible anti-doping rule violation, where this is required by the Code, International Standards, or national anti-doping laws, or to establish, exercise or defend a legal claim involving me, WADA, and/or an ADO.

I consent to the decision on this application being made available to all ADOs, or other organizations, with Testing authority and/or results management authority over me.

I understand and accept that the recipients of my information and of the decision on this application may be located outside the country where I reside. In some of these countries data protection and privacy laws may not be equivalent to those in my country of residence. I understand that my information may be stored in ADAMS, which is hosted by WADA on servers based in Canada, and will be retained for the duration as indicated in the WADA International Standard for the Protection of Privacy and Personal Information (ISPPPI).

I understand that if I believe that my Personal Information is not used in conformity with this consent and the ISPPPI, I can file a complaint to WADA (privacy@wada-ama.org), or my national regulator responsible for data protection in my country.

Потпис спортисте: **Датум:**
Athlete's signature: ______________________ **Date:** ______________
Потпис родитеља/старатеља: **Датум:**
Parent's/Guardian's signature: ______________________ **Date:** ______________

(ако је спортиста малолетан или има инвалидитет који га спречава да потпише овај формулар, родитељ или старатељ ће потписати овај формулар)
(If the Athlete is a Minor or has an impairment preventing him/her from signing this form, a parent or guardian shall sign on behalf of the Athlete)

Молимо вас да поднесете попуњен ТУЕ образац Антидопинг агенцији Републике Србије на имејл адресу test.grupa@adas.org.rs (задржавајући своју копију извештаја).

Please submit the completed form to the ADAS email address test.grupa@adas.org.rs or fax and keep a copy for your records.

Part IV. Sport and Commerce

Chapter 1. General Issues

819. Sport is a primordial need, but sport has become a lucrative business today. Sports can bring huge profits not only to companies and sports clubs but also to individuals. Profit is an increasingly powerful driver, so athletes are transformed into modern gladiators, in whom large multinational companies invest money. In the conditions of modern society, large international sports competitions are inconceivable without sponsors, and this trend is present, to a much lesser extent, in school sports competitions, as well as in the organization of recreational activities. The role of the media is immeasurable for the popularization of sports, but it is also immeasurable in terms of the promotion of sports products because sport is a synonym for health and the beauty of life.

820. In the conditions of modern society, sports clubs and other sports organizations independently earn income not only from their core business – participation in competitions and ticket sales to viewers – but also from advertising, sale of TV rights, transfers of top athletes and sponsorships. The influx of money in sports, however, increases the inequality between big and small clubs, between athletes from rich and athletes from poor countries. Making a difference between athletes and sports events of the 'first and second order' is not only out of alignment with the rules of fair play but it is also the basis of discrimination because it is clear that in this case, athletes do not have the same starting points.

821. In the Republic of Serbia, the development of sports for commercial purposes is only partial, largely because of the fact that all sports clubs in Serbia are state-owned, which hinders the development of private initiatives in this area. Sport, as a special branch of the economy, especially top sport, professional one, brings large revenues to the state through various fiscal and parafiscal revenues. However, earnings from TV rights in the Republic of Serbia are still significantly lower in percentage than in developed countries, but a significant turnover of financial resources is achieved through sports transfers. Transfers are especially pronounced within the most popular sports such as football and basketball.

Chapter 2. Public Regulation

822. In the Republic of Serbia, public regulations governing the field of sports within the commercial sector, especially media and television rights, sponsorship, trade and ownership in sports clubs, in addition to the LS, are prescribed by the following laws:

– Law on public Information and media.[226]
– Law on electronic media.[227]
– Law on electronic communications.[228]
– Law on public media services.[229]
– The Law on the temporary regulation of the manner of charging a fee for public media service.[230]
– Law on the Ratification of the European Convention on Transfrontier Television.[231]
– Law on companies.[232]
– Law on endowments and foundations.[233]
– LoAss.[234]
– Law on public enterprises.[235]
– LCT.[236]
– LCIT.[237]
– LPIT.[238]
– Law on value-added tax.[239]
– LoA.[240]

226. *See* 'Official Gazette of RS', Nos 83/2014, 58/2015 and 12/2016 – authentic interpretation.
227. *See* 'Official Gazette of RS', Nos 83/2014 and 6/2016 – other law.
228. *See* 'Official Gazette of RS', Nos 44/10, 60/13 – CC, 62/14 and 95/18 – other law.
229. *See* 'Official Gazette of RS', Nos 83/14, 103/15 and 108/16.
230. *See* 'Official Gazette of RS', Nos 112/15, 108/16, 95/18 and 86/19.
231. *See* 'Official Gazette of RS – International Treaties', No. 42/09.
232. *See* 'Official Gazette of RS', Nos 36/2011, 99/2011, 83/2014 – other law, 5/2015, 44/2018, 95/2018 and 91/2019.
233. *See* 'Official Gazette of RS', Nos 88/2010 and 99/2011 – other law.
234. *See* 'Official Gazette of RS', Nos 51/2009, 99/2011 – other laws and 44/2018 – other law.
235. *See* 'Official Gazette of RS', Nos 119/2012, 116/2013 – authentic interpretation and 44/2014 – other law.
236. *See* 'Official Gazette of SFRY', Nos 29/78, 39/85, 45/89 – Decision of CCY and 57/89, 'Official Gazette of FRY', No. 31/93, 'Official Gazette of Serbia and Montenegro', No. 1/2003 – Constitutional Charter and 'Official Gazette of RS', No. 18/2020.
237. *See* 'Official Gazette of RS', Nos 25/2001, 80/2002, 80/2002-other law, 43/2003, 84/2004, 18/2010, 101/2011, 119/2012, 47/2013, 108/2013, 68/2014 – other law and 142/2014.
238. *See* 'Official Gazette of RS', Nos 24/2001, 80/2002, 80/2002-other law, 135/2004, 62/2006, 65/2006 – corrigendum, 31/2009, 44/2009, 18/2010, 50/2011, 91/2011 – Decision of CC, 7/2012 – adjusted din. amount, 93/2012, 114/2012 – Decision of CC, 8/2013 – adjusted din. amount, 47/2013, 48/2013 – corrigendum and 108/2013, 57/2014, 68/2014-other law.
239. *See* 'Official Gazette of RS', Nos 84/2004, 86/2004 – corrigendum, 61/2005, 61/2007, 93/2012, 108/2013, 68/2014 – other law, 142/2014.
240. *See* 'Official Gazette of RS', Nos 6/2016 and 52/2019 – other law.

- LCRR.[241]
- Law on trade.[242]
- Law on electronic commerce.[243]
- Law on the protection of competition.[244]
- Law on the protection of consumers.[245]
- Law on general administrative procedure.[246]
- Law on special powers for the effective protection of intellectual property rights.[247]
- LoT.[248]
- Law on the Legal Protection of Industrial Design (LID).[249]
- LoP.[250]
- Law on the protection of business secrets.[251]
- Law on republic administrative fees.[252]
- Customs law.[253]
- Law on the organization and competencies of state bodies for the fight against high-tech crime.[254]
- CC.[255]

§1. Media and Television Rights

823. In order to be able to talk about public regulations in the field of media and TV rights, and to understand the public regulations which apply to this field of law, the need to look at the media scene in the Republic of Serbia necessarily arises as a preliminary issue.

241. *See* 'Official Gazette of RS', Nos 104/2009, 99/2011, 119/2012, 29/2016 – Decision of the Constitutional Court and 66/2019.
242. *See* 'Official Gazette of RS', No. 52/19.
243. *See* 'Official Gazette of RS', Nos 41/09, 95/13 and 52/19.
244. *See* 'Official Gazette of RS', Nos 51/09 and 95/13.
245. *See* 'Official Gazette of RS', Nos 62/2014, 6/2016 – other law.
246. *See* 'official Gazette of RS', No. 18/2016.
247. *See* 'official Gazette of RS', No. 46/2006.
248. *See* 'Official Gazette of RS', No. 6/2020.
249. *See* 'Official Gazette of RS', Nos 104/2009, 45/2015 and 44/2018 – other law.
250. *See* 'Official Gazette of RS', Nos 99/2011, 113/2017 – other law, 95/2018 and 66/2019.
251. *See* 'Official Gazette of RS', No. 53/2021.
252. *See* 'Official Gazette of RS', Nos 43/2003, 51/2003 – corrigendum, 61/2005, 101/2005 – other law, 55/2012 – adjusted din. amount, 65/2013 – other law, 57/2014 – adjusted din. amount, 45/2015 – adjusted din. amount, 61/2017 – adjusted din. amount, 113/2017, 3/2018 – corrigendum, 50/2018 – adjusted din. amount, 95/2018, 38/2019 – adjusted din. amount, 86/2019, 90/2019 – corrigendum, 98/2020 – adjusted din. amount, 144/2020 and 62/2021 – adjusted din. amount.
253. *See* 'Official Gazette of RS', Nos 95/2018, 91/2019 – other law and 144/2020.
254. *See* 'Official Gazette of RS', Nos 61/2005 and 104/2009.
255. *See* 'Official Gazette of RS', Nos 85/2005, 88/2005 – corrigendum, 107/2005 – corrigendum, 72/2009, 111/2009, 121/2012, 104/2013, 108/2014, 94/2016 and 35/2019.

824. The basic document for the development of the media scene in the Republic of Serbia is the 2020–2025 Strategy for the Development of the Public Information System.[256]

825. The Strategy states that the regulatory framework and harmonization with European regulations have been established, as well as the transition from analogue to digital television broadcasting in accordance with the deadlines prescribed by international documents which are binding for the Republic of Serbia. At the same time, there is a plan to remove contradictions and mutual inconsistencies of laws, create a legal framework and establish a Media Register to ensure public ownership, as well as prevent excessive ownership concentration which has a dominant or predominant influence on the public opinion.

826. The strategy indicates unclear formulation and insufficient fulfilment of goals in the field of copyright and related rights protection and combating piracy, creation of non-discriminatory conditions for the development of information and communication technologies in the context of the development of freedom of expression.

827. In addition, the strategy envisages the elimination of the conflicts of competencies of two or more bodies over the implementation of regulations, as well as the strengthening of capacities in order to fully enable the control of the implementation of regulations.

828. In addition to the mentioned strategy, public regulations in the field of media and TV rights also include a whole set of by-laws:

- Rulebook on the manner of forming a list of the most important events of special importance for all citizens and exercising the right to access events of great interest to the public.[257]
- Rulebook on advertising and sponsorship in electronic media.[258]
- Rulebook on the procedure for appointing members of the Management Board of the Public Media Service.[259]
- Rulebook on the protection of the rights of minors in the field of media services.[260]
- Rulebook on the manner of imposing measures on media service providers.[261]
- Rulebook on the transition from analogue to digital television broadcasting and multiplex access.[262]
- Rulebook on the protection of human rights in the field of media services.[263]

---

256. *See* 'Official Gazette of RS', No. 11/2020.
257. *See* 'Official Gazette of RS', No. 25/2015.
258. *See* 'Official Gazette of RS', No. 101/2016.
259. *See* 'Official Gazette of RS', No. 143/2014.
260. *See* 'Official Gazette of RS', No. 25/2015.
261. *Ibid.*
262. *See* 'Official Gazette of RS', Nos 86/2014, 18/2015, 30/2015, 50/2015.
263. *See* 'Official Gazette of RS', No. 55/2015.

- Rulebook on the procedure for issuing a licence for the provision of media services on the basis of a conducted public competition.[264]
- Rulebook on the procedure for issuing a licence for the provision of media services on the basis of a request.[265]
- Rulebook on the criteria and manner of increasing the share of European audiovisual works.[266]
- Rulebook on the procedure for issuing consent to the act on the transfer of a licence for the provision of media services and the procedure for reporting a change in the ownership structure.[267]
- Rulebook on minimum conditions for the provision of media services and decision-making criteria in the procedure of issuing a licence for the provision of media services on the basis of a public competition conducted.[268]
- Rulebook on minimum technical and organizational conditions for issuing a licence for the provision of media services on the basis of the request of the media service provider.[269]
- Rulebook on the assignment of unused rights of public media services to broadcast radio, television and other media content of exceptional importance.[270]
- Rulebook on audiovisual commercial communications.[271]
- Instructions on the manner of the application of the provisions of the Law on electronic media regulating own production.[272]
- List of the most important events of special importance for the citizens of the Republic of Serbia.[273]

829. The enumerated set of by-laws regulates in more detail all issues of importance for the media scene in the Republic of Serbia, which are generally regulated by the 2020–2025 Strategy for the Development of the Public Information System.

830. Institutions responsible for the implementation of laws and other legal regulations in the field of public information are:

- Ministry of Culture and Information.
- Provincial Secretariat for Culture, Public Information and Relations with Religious Communities.
- Regulatory Body for Electronic Media (REM).[274]
- Regulatory Agency for Electronic Communications and Postal Services.[275]
- Public media institution 'Radio-televizijaSrbije'.

264. *See* 'Official Gazette of RS', No. 63/2015.
265. *Ibid.*
266. *See* 'Official Gazette of RS', No. 72/2015.
267. *See* 'Official Gazette of RS', No. 93/2015.
268. *See* 'Official Gazette of RS', No. 46/2016.
269. *Ibid.*
270. *Ibid.*
271. *See* 'Official Gazette of RS', No. 69/15.
272. *See* 'Official Gazette of RS', No. 72/2015.
273. *See* 'Official Gazette of RS', No. 45/2016.
274. Hereinafter: REM.
275. Hereinafter: RATEL.

– Public media institution 'Radio-televizijaVojvodine'.
– Business Registers Agency (which maintains the Media Register).

The Ministry of Trade, Tourism and Telecommunications also has a certain competence in its domain.

831. According to the Law on public information and media, a medium is a means of public information that conveys editorially shaped information, ideas and opinions and other content intended for public distribution and an indefinite number of users in words, images or sound.

832. For the purposes of this Law, the media, in particular, includes daily and periodical newspapers, news agency services, radio and television programmes and electronic editions of these media, as well as independent electronic editions (editorially designed websites or internet portals), which are registered in the Media Register, in accordance with this Law. The publisher can be any natural or legal person, who/which must be registered with the competent authority of the Republic of Serbia to perform activities.

833. Apart from the Public Service of Serbia (Radio-televizijaSrbije) and the Public Service of the Autonomous Province of Vojvodina (Radio-televizijaVojvodine), the media cannot, directly or indirectly, be established by the Republic, the Autonomous Province and local self-government units, as well as institutions, companies and other legal entities, which are wholly or partly state-owned, i.e., which are wholly or partly financed from public revenues. Therefore, media services in the Republic of Serbia are provided by the institutions of the Public Media Service, a commercial media service provider and a media service provider of the civil sector.

834. The media market itself consists of publishers (natural and legal persons) of media which are registered for this activity. A media publisher produces the media content making it available to the public but also sells advertising space within its media (advertising market). The services it provides to third parties, such as production, service publishing, etc., are added to this.

835. Media services according to the manner of providing services can be linear and media services on demand, while in terms of the content, they can be general media that include informational, educational, cultural, scientific, sports, entertainment and other programme content, then specialized media services, which include the programme content of the same type (e.g., sports), but may also be entirely dedicated to television sales or self-promotion.

836. According to the Law on electronic media, a media service provider is under the jurisdiction of the Republic of Serbia if it is established on its territory or if it is not established on its territory but uses a terrestrial satellite transmitting station located in the Republic of Serbia and uses satellite capacities belonging to the Republic of Serbia.

837. A media service provider shall be deemed to be established in the Republic of Serbia if:

(1) has its registered office in the Republic of Serbia and editorial decisions on media services are made there;
(2) has its registered office in the Republic of Serbia, and makes editorial decisions on media services in another Member State of the European Union, provided that a significant number of persons are employed in the Republic of Serbia, engaged on the basis of employment contracts or otherwise, involved in activities related to media services;
(3) has its registered office in the Republic of Serbia, and a significant number of persons engaged on the basis of employment contracts or otherwise involved in the performance of activities related to media services, work in the Republic of Serbia and another EU Member State;
(4) has initially started its activity, in accordance with the law, in the Republic of Serbia, provided that it maintains a stable and effective connection with the Serbian economy, and that a significant number of persons engaged under employment contracts or otherwise involved in performing activities in related to media services, do not work in one of the Member States of the European Union;
(5) has its registered office in the Republic of Serbia, and the decisions on media services are made in the country which is not a member of the European Union, or vice versa, provided that a significant number of persons engaged under employment contracts or otherwise involved in activities related to media services, work in the Republic of Serbia.[276]

838. In case it cannot be determined whether the media service provider is under the jurisdiction of the Republic of Serbia or another Member State of the European Union, according to the Law on electronic media, the media service provider is under the jurisdiction of the Member State in which it was established.

839. The Law on electronic media guarantees the freedom to receive and rebroadcast media services from other countries, which is guaranteed in the Republic of Serbia by ratified international treaties.

840. According to the Law on public information and media, everyone is obliged to respect the rights of media publishers and providers of audio and audiovisual media services, and natural and legal persons, domestic and foreign, and have equal rights to publish other rights in the field of public information, in accordance with the law and the ratified international treaty.

841. Legal and natural persons, media publishers, must be registered with the competent authority of the Republic of Serbia to perform activities.

---

276. *See* Art. 45 of the Law on electronic media.

842. The Law on electronic media regulates, in accordance with international conventions and standards, the organization and work of the REM, conditions and manner of providing audio and audiovisual media services, conditions and procedure for issuing licenses for the provision of audio and audiovisual media service, as well as other issues of importance for the field of electronic media.

843. The licence on the basis of which the right to provide the television broadcasting service is acquired, as well as the radio media service, is issued on the basis of a public competition announced by the Regulator in accordance with the law.

844. The REM, established by the Law on electronic media, is an independent regulatory organization with the status of a legal entity, which exercises public authority in order to: effectively implement the established policy in the field of media services in the Republic of Serbia; improve the quality and diversity of electronic media services; contribute to the preservation, protection and development of freedom of opinion and expression; in order to protect the interests of the public in the field of electronic media and the protection of users of electronic media services, in accordance with the provisions of this law, in a manner appropriate to a democratic society.

845. A television broadcasting service provider under the jurisdiction of the Republic of Serbia may not exclusively broadcast events that are on the list of the most important events of special importance to all citizens, in a manner that a significant part of the public in the Republic of Serbia, EU Member State or the signatory of the international agreement which is binding on the Republic of Serbia, is deprived of the possibility of covering these events.[277]

846. REM timely compiles, in a clear and transparent manner, a list of the most important domestic and foreign events, which are of special importance for all citizens (cultural, political, sports, entertainment, etc.) and to which the exclusive broadcasting right can be exercised only by a television broadcasting service provider whose access is free and whose coverage area covers the entire territory of the Republic of Serbia and notifies the European Commission thereof.

847. REM determines which events on the list should be available in whole or in part through a live broadcast, and which in whole or in part through a delayed broadcast if this is necessary for objective reasons or public interest.

848. The television broadcasting service provider, which has the exclusive right to broadcast events of great interest to the public, is obliged to allow and enable all other interested television broadcasting service providers, without discrimination and under equal conditions, to freely choose inserts[278] from the event, take them over and broadcast them for up to ninety seconds, stating the source of the image and tone and with a fee that cannot exceed the amount of the actual costs.

277. *See* Art. 64 of the Law on electronic media.
278. The selected insert is used exclusively for informative programs.

849. If the television broadcasting service provider which has the exclusive right to broadcast events of great interest to the public, as well as the television broadcasting service provider which requires access, are established in the territory of the Republic of Serbia, access is requested from the television broadcasting service provider directly.

850. The Law on special powers for the effective protection of intellectual property rights in Article 5 relating to broadcasting and rebroadcasting, states that the broadcasting and rebroadcasting of a radio or television programme containing copyright works or objects of related rights are prohibited, without regulating the obligation to pay a fee for the use of these rights in accordance with the law governing the collective protection of copyright and related rights. In the event that the broadcaster acts contrary to the provisions of this Article, REM takes measures to which it is authorized by law, regardless of other legal remedies available to the injured party of copyright or related rights.

851. REM also prescribes in detail the manner of forming the list of the most important events of special importance for all citizens and exercising the right to access events of great interest.[279]

852. According to Article 3 of the Rulebook on the manner of forming a list of the most important events of special importance for all citizens and exercising the right to access events of great interest to the public, a specific event (sports, cultural, political, entertainment, etc.) is considered the most important event if it meets at least two of the following conditions:

(1) that the event and its outcome are of special general importance for citizens in the Republic of Serbia, and not only of importance for those citizens who otherwise follow a specific event or other activity to which the event refers;
(2) that the event is traditionally broadcast in the Republic of Serbia within the programme to which access is free, as well as that it is regularly watched by a large number of viewers;
(3) that it is a significant international sports event in which the representatives of the Republic of Serbia participate;
(4) that the event is generally known, i.e., that it has a general cultural significance for the citizens of the Republic of Serbia, as well as significance for the national cultural identity.

853. Article 6 of this Rulebook is considered to be a live broadcast or delayed broadcast of an event, in whole or in part, when it is necessary for objective reasons or in the public interest, and the right to broadcast the event is the right of the television service provider to broadcast the event in a certain area, provided that the right to broadcast the most important event can be acquired only by a television

279. *See* Art. 3 of the Rulebook on the manner of forming a list of the most important events of special importance for all citizens and exercising the right to access events.

broadcasting service provider whose coverage area covers the entire territory of the Republic of Serbia and to whom access is free.

854. It is considered that the coverage area of a television broadcasting service provider covers the entire territory of the Republic of Serbia, if it has a licence to provide media services throughout the Republic of Serbia or if quality reception of its television signal is provided for at least 90% of the population in Serbia. In addition, it is considered that access to the television broadcasting service is not free if it is provided as a protected service, i.e., as a service with conditional access, or if it is necessary to pay an additional fee for its coverage.[280]

855. The list of the most important events of special importance for the citizens of the Republic of Serbia determines the events important for the public of the Republic of Serbia or the Member States of the European Union.

856. The list of the most important sports events of special importance for the citizens of the Republic of Serbia consists of the following events:

- World and European Championship and qualifying matches in which the Serbian national football team participates.
- UEFA Champions League, UEFA Europa League and qualifying matches in which Serbian clubs participate.
- The highest ranks of the domestic competition in football, basketball, volleyball and handball.
- Finals and semifinals of the Serbian Cup in football, basketball, volleyball, handball and water polo.
- International competitions held in the Republic of Serbia in football, basketball, volleyball, handball, water polo, tennis, athletics and swimming.
- World and European Basketball Championship and qualifying matches in which the Serbian national team participates.
- Union of European Leagues of Basketball (ULEB) Euroleague (matches in which the Serbian club participates).
- Finals and semifinals of the ULEB Cup and (matches in which the Serbian club participates).
- ABA Regional League (matches in which Serbian clubs participate).
- World and European Championship and qualifying matches in volleyball in which the Serbian national team participates.
- World Volleyball League (matches in which the Serbian national team participates).
- Finals and semifinals of the European Volleyball Confederation (CEV) Champions League, CEV Cup and CEV Challenge Cup in volleyball (matches in which Serbian clubs participate).
- World and European Championship and qualifying matches in handball in which the Serbian national team participates.

280. The fee for the public media service, as well as the fee for the service package paid to the operator of the electronic communications network, is not considered an additional fee.

- Finals and semifinals of the European Handball Federation (EHF) Champions League, EHF Cup Winners' Cup, EHF Challenge Cup and EHF Handball Cup (matches in which Serbian clubs participate).
- World and European Championship and qualifying matches in water polo in which the Serbian national team participates.
- Super finals of the World League in water polo (if a Serbian club participates).
- Regional League in water polo (matches in which Serbian clubs participate).
- DAVIS Cup and FED Cup (matches in which the Serbian national team participates).
- Wimbledon, Roland Garros, US Open, Australian Open (matches in which Serbian competitors participate).
- ATP and WTA tournaments held in the Republic of Serbia.
- World and European athletics championships (disciplines in which Serbian competitors participate).
- Belgrade Marathon.
- World and European swimming championships (disciplines in which Serbian competitors participate).
- Cycling race 'KrozSrbiju' (Tour of Serbia).
- Round race – Belgrade Prize – auto racing.
- Olympic Games.
- Paralympic Games.
- Special Olympics.

857. Advertising and sponsorship are of special importance for the realization of media and television rights. Certain provisions of the LoA also cover the media.

858. Sponsorship of sports shows/performances and sports news is allowed, but not of informative shows, provided that the sponsorship must be clearly marked as such by stating the name, sign or other symbol of the sponsor at the beginning and end, and possibly during the programme content.[281]

859. The LoA states that media services or programme content cannot be sponsored by state bodies and organizations and political organizations. The content of the notice itself, the manner of broadcasting, the time of broadcasting the notice of the sponsor, as well as the conditions of using the name or other symbol of the sponsor as the name of the sponsored programme content are regulated by the REM.

860. REM has regulated this area in more detail with the Rulebook on advertising and sponsorship in electronic media[282] and the Recommendation on the manner of informing about the placement of goods in shows that are not the own production of the media service provider.[283]

---

281. For example, by marking the name of the good or service or the sign of the sponsor.
282. *See* 'Official Gazette of RS', No. 101/2016.
283. *See also* http://www.rem.rs/ of 7 Oct. 2015.

861. The Rulebook on advertising and sponsorship in electronic media regulates in detail the conditions and manner of displaying and referring to goods or services or other markings in programme content when placing products, as well as the form, duration and place of the notification of product placement, notification content, broadcasting method and time of broadcasting the sponsor notice, conditions of using the name or other symbol of the sponsor as the name of the sponsored programme content, manner, conditions of broadcasting television advertising, television sales, as well as the conditions of broadcasting TV advertising, i.e., TV sales without interrupting the show.

862. Article 10 of the Rulebook on advertising and sponsorship precisely states when a sponsor notice may be broadcast during the sponsored media content, as follows:

- twice in sponsored programme contents lasting less than thirty minutes, and in those lasting thirty minutes or longer twice in each complete part of that programme content whose foreseen duration is at least thirty minutes;
- immediately after the block of advertising messages or TV sales messages, if this block was not broadcast immediately after the beginning, i.e., immediately before the end of the sponsored programme content;
- at the beginning and end of a certain report in the programme content, if the sponsor financed only the production of this report, where this does not exclude the obligation to broadcast the sponsor notice at the beginning and end of the show;
- within the graphics on the screen (subtitle, i.e., signature) which introduces the participant in the programme to the viewer (name, place, occupation, etc.).

863. If the sports news or weather forecast is an integral part of the news programme, the notice of their sponsor is broadcast only at the beginning, during and at the end of the sports news or weather forecast.

864. The REM Recommendation on the manner of informing about the placement of goods in programmes that are not produced by the media service provider specifies how media service providers should inform media service users that a show which is not in their own production contains the placement of goods, in order to establish a single allowed practice and improvements in the provision of media services.

865. Pursuant to the provisions of Article 58, paragraph 2, item 4) of the Law on electronic media and Article 23, paragraph 8 and Article 24, paragraph 3 of the Rulebook on audiovisual commercial communications, the media service provider is obliged to inform media service users that a certain show contains placement of goods only if it is produced in its own production, which means that the obligation of the said notification does not exist if it is a show produced by an independent producer or other media service provider.

866. The media service provider is responsible for the programme content, regardless of whether it was produced by them or another person. Therefore, although the media service provider is not obliged to inform media service users that the placement of goods is present in a show that is not in its own production, it does not affect its responsibility for the published programme content, if it violates other rules governing the placement of goods. It is recommended that media service providers when there are objective possibilities for this, inform the users of media services that the placement of goods is present in a certain show which is not in their own production.

867. Only advertising and sponsorship on electronic media are precisely defined, however, they are an obvious issue in the provision of the services of media content distribution.

868. The situation in the related distribution market, with the lack of adequate supervision (REM and RATEL), can lead to the favourization of certain media service providers, and thus to the discrimination of others, which represents a potential threat to media pluralism. Namely, large operators, in addition to providing media content distribution services, are also active in content production (and are in fact publishers of numerous media through affiliates), so there is a real possibility of favouring such content to the detriment of media that do not operate in the system of the mentioned operators. This situation in the related distribution market makes it impossible for the contents of one large operator to be in the network of another large operator, which is currently the factual situation in terms of sports content, some of which are even on the list of most important events of special importance for citizens in the Republic of Serbia.

869. According to the RATEL analysis,[284] the area of relations between operators (distributors of media services) and providers of media services is insufficiently regulated, and the application of rules concerning the obligation of transmission is inadequate because there is a lack of supervision regarding the application of rules on non-discriminatory treatment. Media laws allow operators to also be media service providers, through affiliates.

870. The Law on electronic media prescribes special obligations for electronic communication network operators for the distribution of media content. Article 100 states that the operator of the electronic communication network for broadcasting and distribution of media services is obliged to obtain the prior written consent of the programme rights holder before including certain media radio services, television broadcasting services or media services on request in its programme package and before the start of its broadcasting and distribution. The application is submitted by REM for registration. Also, the operator is obliged to distribute radio media services or television broadcasting services simultaneously and completely without changes (rebroadcast), in accordance with the obtained written consent. The operator is obliged to adhere to the list of radio media services or television broadcasting

284. *See also* https://www.ratel.rs/en/.

services or media services on request included in the programme package and to notify REM in advance of any change in the number and structure of programme packages.

871. Furthermore, the operator undertakes to distribute media services on request without changes in a fair, transparent and non-discriminatory manner, in relation to media service providers.

872. The law allows the operator to distribute encrypted satellite programmes only if it has entered into a distribution agreement with the holder of rights to such programmes which allows decoding for further public rebroadcasting. However, the media service provider is obliged to timely inform the operator that it does not have the right to publish certain programme content through a certain platform.

873. In accordance with the Law governing free access to information of public importance, REM is obliged to make publicly available the adopted acts, on its website, free of charge, as well as other complete and updated data and information from its scope, especially the Strategy of the development of radio media service and audiovisual media services in the Republic of Serbia, regulations for the application of the Law on electronic media and other general acts of REM, public competitions for issuing licenses, decisions made on public competitions with explanations, data from the register and records, judgments in administrative disputes initiated against the decision of REM and the decision imposing measures in accordance with this law with justifications.

874. REM controls the work of media service providers in terms of the consistent application and improvement of the principles on which the regulation of relations in the field of electronic media is based, in terms of meeting the conditions for providing media services and other rights and obligations under the Law on electronic media.

875. REM may issue a cautioning, warning, temporary ban on the publication of programme content to the media service provider, or may revoke its license, due to the violation of obligations related to the programme content, as well as due to the violation of conditions contained in the licence or approval for media service in accordance with the provisions of this Law. Measures are imposed on the basis of the Rulebook on the manner of imposing measures on media service providers.[285]

876. If the act or omission of a media service provider or a responsible person is characterized by an act punishable by law, REM is obliged to initiate proceedings before a competent court or other state body.

877. According to the Law on electronic media, the following fines are envisaged for economic offences:

285. *See* 'Official Gazette of RS', No. 25/2015.

- A fine of RSD 2,000,000–RSD 3,000,000 shall be imposed on a legal entity for an economic offence if it provides a service without a licence, with the provision that a fine may be imposed in proportion to the amount of damage, unfulfilled obligations or value of goods or other items which is the subject of an economic offence, up to a maximum of twenty times the amount of these values. For the provision of media services without a licence, the responsible person in the legal entity shall be fined from RSD 150,000 to RSD 200,000. For an economic offence – the provision of media services without a licence, a protective measure of banning the performance of a certain activity may be imposed on a legal entity in the duration from one to three years, and on the responsible person in the legal entity, a protective measure of banning the performance of certain tasks for up to one year.[286]
- A fine of RSD 100,000–RSD 1,000,000 shall be imposed on a legal entity, a media service provider that does not act upon the Regulator's warning in the procedure of determining the existence of the violation of media pluralism, while a fine of RSD 10,000–RSD 200,000 shall be imposed on the responsible person in the legal entity, the media service provider.[287]
- A fine of RSD 100,000–RSD 1,000,000 shall be imposed on an entity that fails to comply with its special obligations regarding the protection of media pluralism for an economic offence, and a fine of RSD 10,000–RSD 200,000 will be imposed on the responsible person in the legal entity, the operator.[288]

878. According to the provisions of the Law on electronic media, the following fines are envisaged for violations:

- A fine of RSD 500,000–RSD 2,000,000 shall be imposed on a legal entity for an offence if it does not act in accordance with the provisions of this Law regarding the prohibition of hate speech, as well as if it does not act in accordance with the provisions of this Law regarding obtaining the prior consent from REM in connection with the change of ownership structure, and a fine of RSD 50,000–RSD 150,000 shall be imposed on the responsible person in the legal entity.[289]
- A fine of RSD 10,000–RSD 500,000 shall be imposed on an entrepreneur for an offence if he/she does not act in accordance with the provisions of this Law regarding the prohibition of hate speech or does not act in accordance with the provisions of this Law regarding obtaining the prior consent of the Regulator regarding the change of ownership structure.[290]
- A fine of RSD 500,000–RSD 1,000,000 shall be imposed on a legal entity for an offence if it does not act in accordance with the provisions of this Law regarding special technical obligations and does not act in accordance with the provisions of this Law regarding the protection of minors and if it fails to act in accordance with the provisions of this Law in connection with the special obligations of the

286. *See* Art. 107 of the Law on electronic media.
287. *See* Art. 108 of the Law on electronic media.
288. *See* Art. 109 of the Law on electronic media.
289. *See* Art. 110 of the Law on electronic media.
290. *Ibid.*

operators of electronic communications networks for the distribution of media content, and the responsible person in the legal entity shall be fined from RSD 50,000 to RSD 100,000.[291]

- An entrepreneur, a provider of media services, who does not act upon the warning of the Regulator in the procedure of determining the existence of the violation of media pluralism, shall be fined from RSD 10,000 to RSD 500,000 for an economic offence.[292]

§2. Sponsorship

879. Sponsorship is connecting an organization with an individual or an event, in order to promote the organization itself, its products or services.

880. Sponsorship is a business relationship between organizations that provide funds or services, on the one hand, and individuals, events or organizations, on the other hand, who in turn, for commercial purposes, put their image and resources at their disposal.

881. Athletes, sports organizations and sports events are most often sponsored due to high media visibility, allowing potential sponsors access to a wide audience to promote their products. The very thought of athletes is associated with the values that sport brings with it, and these are, above all, a healthy attitude towards life, a youthful spirit and competition. This is why sports activities attract a large number of spectators who identify with the sports role models or teams they support, which organizations know well and use well.

882. Potential sponsors are aware that a large number of consumers care about their health, and for this reason, they use sports as a model of health and healthy living in order to get closer to them. Consumers identify with successful athletes and sports clubs, and in this manner, the image of the winner from the consumer's point of view is transferred to the organization itself – the sponsor and all this leads to the creation of profit. In addition, sponsorship has its advantages over traditional advertising. It is more favourable for the organization, and the media coverage is higher.

883. It is precisely the great media attention that is one of the most important preconditions for organizations to enter into sponsorship and create an image of a socially responsible company. The growing role of the media in creating public opinion also leads to an increase in investments in sponsorship.

884. In the context of this issue, the situation in the Republic of Serbia is similar to that in the developed world, but there are some differences.

---

291. *See* Art. 111 of the Law on electronic media.
292. *See* Art. 112 of the Law on electronic media.

885. As in most legal systems of different countries, there is no special law in the Republic of Serbia regulating the matter of sponsorship. This matter is partially regulated by laws governing the area that may be the subject of sponsorship interest. The sponsorship agreement itself is not regulated by modern civil codes.

886. In the legal system of the Republic of Serbia, the provisions related to sponsorship are contained in the LS, LoA, Law on the Ratification of the European Convention on Transfrontier Television, which ratified the 1989 European Convention on Transfrontier Television. Sponsorship is also regulated by certain provisions of other legal regulations which regulate the area that may be the subject of sponsorship interest.

887. LS of RS recognizes sponsorship as a possible source of funds. The chapter dedicated to property, in Article 70 of LS of RS states that a sports association may acquire funds and generate income from contributions, membership fees, donations and gifts, subsidies, inheritances, interest on deposits, rents, dividends, services, sponsorships and other commercial, marketing, business and economic activities, in accordance with the Law. The funds acquired in this manner are the property of the sports association.

888. Sponsorship is also mentioned in the chapter of LS of RS which is dedicated to national recognitions, awards and scholarships. Article 128 states that financial aid can be received by a top athlete with special merits for the development of sports who is ranked as a meritorious athlete through the categorization of athletes, in accordance with this Law.

889. Financial assistance may be used to cover expenses that the athlete has personally incurred in preparing for or participating in competitions or for the treatment caused by an injury sustained in the competition, or to cover other particularly eligible costs, provided that these costs are not already covered by expenses of organizations in the field of sports, sponsors or donors, i.e., that the costs of treatment are not covered by health insurance, in accordance with the Law.

890. In this manner, Article 128 limits the possibility of sponsoring a top athlete who is ranked as a meritorious athlete, which may raise the question of the justification and legality of such a rule which restricts the right of an athlete to commercialize their own image without losing their rights on the basis of the status of a top athlete.

891. According to Article 128 of LS of RS, the right of a top athlete is limited if the funds from the sponsorship have been used for preparations or participation in competitions or for the treatment caused by an injury sustained at the competition or to cover other especially justified costs. In this case, although he/she has acquired the right to financial assistance, he/she loses it if he/she has acquired the status of a sponsored athlete. At the same time, this means that if he/she has received financial assistance, he/she cannot acquire the status of a sponsored athlete and his/her right to commercialize his/her own image is limited.

892. This rule unjustifiably collides two different interests – the general interest to finance an athlete in a certain way, who has a certain status and who has met the necessary conditions for receiving financial assistance and the individual interest of an athlete to freely dispose of the image he/she acquired by doing sports.

893. Sponsorship establishes a contractual relationship between two parties, the sponsor and the sponsored.

894. The sponsor can be a natural or legal person.[293]

895. Natural or legal persons can also be sponsored.

896. There are several types of sponsorship: sponsoring athletes, sponsoring a sports club/organization and sponsoring an event.

897. Legal persons can be legal persons of public and private law. Legal persons of public law are the state, autonomous province and local self-government, while legal persons of private law are companies, associations, institutions, endowments and foundations.

898. Legal persons of public law cannot be sponsors or the sponsored because this would create preconditions for corruption. However, in the Republic of Serbia, the biggest sponsors are public companies, although their founder is the Republic of Serbia, i.e., the autonomous province or local self-government. However, in order to create an image and gain profit, public companies sponsor athletes, sports clubs/ organizations and sports events, and the justification may be the fact that according to the Law on public companies, the company is obliged to pay part of the profits to the budget of the founder – the Republic of Serbia, autonomous province or local self-government.

899. Natural and legal persons can be sponsored.

900. Regarding natural persons, athletes and trainers appear as sponsors, but it can be any other natural person, for whom potential sponsors find interest in sponsoring it. An adult but also a minor natural person can be sponsored.[294] On behalf of minor natural persons, athletes, contracts are concluded by their parents, i.e., guardians as legal representatives.[295]

---

293. It is a very rare case that the sponsor in sports is a natural person, so in this monograph, the attention will be focused on legal persons as sponsors.
294. According to the legal regulations in the Republic of Serbia, minors under the age of 14 do not have legal capacity. From the age of 14 to 18, minors have partial legal capacity, and they can also acquire full legal capacity if they have reached the age of 16 by entering into marriage, or if they become parents, with the permission of the court.
295. Minor athletes, from 14 to 18 years of age, have partial legal capacity and these persons can validly conclude contracts only with the consent of their parents or guardians as their legal representatives.

901. A legal person can also be sponsored. As shown in practice, companies, associations and institutions most often appear as sponsors. According to LS of RS, for the purpose of performing sports activities and sports occupations, a sports organization may be established as an association (sports association), as a company (sports company) or as an institution.[296] The sponsorship agreement is concluded on behalf and for the account of the association by the representative of the association, on behalf and for the account of the company by the representative of the company, and on behalf and for the account of the institution by the director of the institution.

902. A special type of sponsorship is event sponsorship, which refers to the sponsorship of sports events. In this case, the contract is concluded with the organizer of the sponsored event, which can again be both a natural person and a legal person. The organizer of the sponsored event concludes the sponsorship agreement in person, or through a proxy if he/she is a natural person, and if it is a legal person, the sponsorship agreement is concluded by their representative in accordance with the law.

903. According to LS of RS, a sports event is a specific, planned and conducted, time-limited sports event, for which there is a public interest and in which several athletes participate.[297] The law stipulates that sports events can be manifestations or sports competitions.

904. A sports competition is a sports event that takes place according to pre-established and known sports rules, which may be generally valid for a specific branch of sport, or only for a specific sports event and whose goal to which each participant strives is either winning the opponent or achieving a certain predetermined sports result. The LPVMS stipulates that the organizer of a sports event is a sports federation, sports association, sports organization-club, as well as another legal or natural person who permanently or occasionally organizes sports events, or who has taken over the organization of certain sports events, or performing certain tasks in organizing the sports event.[298] The organization of sports events must be in accordance with LS of RS and the Law on the prevention of violence at sports events, as well as the rules established by the competent national branch sports federation.

905. In addition to the mentioned laws, in the Republic of Serbia, sponsorship is partially regulated by the LoA[299] The LoA regulates the content of the advertising message, general rules of advertising, special rules and restrictions, direct advertising, sponsorship, legal protection and supervision. The general advertising rules apply to sponsorship accordingly.

296. *See* Art. 33 of LS of RS.
297. *See* Art. 3 para. 1, n. 21.
298. *See* Art. 2 para. 2.
299. *See* 'Official Gazette of RS', Nos 6/2016 and 52/2019 – other law.

906. According to Article 64 of the LoA, sponsorship is any type of financial or other support of a sponsor to another legal or natural person or its activities in order to promote the sponsor's name, title or trademark, activity or product. This Article also defines that sponsorship is not considered when a media service provider participates in the financing of media services or programme content.

907. In any case, the sponsor may not compromise the integrity of the sports content of the sponsored activity by sponsoring it and may not damage the reputation of the sponsored person. However, the sponsored person may not change the name, i.e., the name of the sponsor, its trademark or service mark, nor may it otherwise endanger the reputation or image of the sponsor. It can be concluded that this is a mutually beneficial relationship, which is regulated by the sponsorship agreement.[300]

908. The LoA of the Republic of Serbia precisely defines the publication of messages containing personal property on the basis of which a person can be recognized or a person's identity established. Such an advertisement may not be published without the prior consent of the person to whom it relates personally. Personal property means personal data, personal record or photographic, drawn, graphic, film or digital record of a character, sound recording of the voice and spoken words of a certain natural person.[301]

909. A special part of the LoA refers to restrictions and negative manifestations. Restrictions primarily concern certain manifestations and habits, which are assessed as harmful in society, so there is a fear that the holders of certain activities may negatively affect young people. This is why they are not eligible to be sponsors in sports.

910. The LoA defines three categories of persons who are subject to restrictions regarding sponsorship. In accordance with Article 67, the first category consists of advertisers of alcoholic beverages, the second category of organizers of classic and special games of chance (Article 68) and the third category of advertisers of tobacco products (Article 69).

911. An advertiser of alcoholic beverages may not sponsor athletes, sports clubs, or sports competitions, including sponsorship of individuals or participants in these events unless the alcoholic beverages contain less than 20% alcohol.[302]

912. An advertiser of alcoholic beverages cannot sponsor children and minors, their activities, as well as persons or activities whose audience consists mainly of children or minors.

---

300. *See* Ch. 3, Private regulation.
301. *See* Ch. 2, Public regulation – Merchandising.
302. *See* Art. 67 paras 1, 2, 3. Law on advertising.

913. Any sponsorship of an alcoholic beverage producer must warn of the responsible use of alcoholic beverages or contain a warning message.[303]

914. The organizer of classic and special games of chance cannot sponsor children or minors, their activities, as well as persons or activities whose audience are mostly children or minors.[304]

915. An advertiser of tobacco products cannot sponsor athletes, sports clubs, or sports competitions, including sponsorship of individuals, i.e., participants in these events.[305] Manufacturers of electronic cigarettes are also covered by this ban. The use of the business name and trademark of a tobacco manufacturer is permitted in spaces intended for participants in sponsored gatherings and audiences of sponsored events but is not permitted in any other conspicuous manner which would ensure their visibility during a potential television broadcast or the recording of a sports event.

916. The LoA provides for fines in the amount of RSD 300,000.00–2,000,000.00, if the advertiser of alcoholic beverages, organizer of classic and special games of chance or the advertiser of tobacco products sponsors the media, athletes, sports clubs, sports competitions, including sponsorship of individuals or participants in these events, as well as children or minors, their activities, as well as persons or activities whose audience consists mainly of children or minors contrary to the articles of this Law.[306]

917. In addition, certain restrictions arising from the Law on the Ratification of the European Convention on Transfrontier Television[307] which applies to manufacturers and sellers of tobacco products and to the advertising of medicines and medical treatments and relate to the sponsorship of television programs. The Law on the Ratification of the European Convention on Transfrontier Television stipulates that programmes cannot be sponsored by natural or legal persons whose main activity is the production, or sale of products, or the provision of services whose advertising and teleshopping are prohibited. It is further stated that the advertising and teleshopping of tobacco products shall not be allowed, as well as the advertising of medicines or medical treatments that can be obtained in the contracting state, from whose territory the programme is broadcast, only on a physician's prescription and that teleshopping for medicines and medical treatments are not allowed.

918. In the Republic of Serbia, the tax treatment of the sponsor is also defined. Benefits and receipts earned by the sponsor and the sponsored under the sponsorship agreement are subject to taxation. The tax treatment of sponsorship is regulated by the LCIT, LPIT and the Law on value-added tax.

---

303. *See* Art. 67 para. 6 Law on Advertising.
304. *See* Art. 68 Law on advertising.
305. *See* Art. 69 para. 1 Law on advertising.
306. *See* Art. 78 para. 1, n. 34 Law on Advertising.
307. *See* 'Official Gazette of RS – International Treaties', No. 42/2009.

919. The LCIT stipulates that expenditures for advertising and propaganda in the total amount of up to 10% of the total income are recognized as an expense in the tax balance of the taxpayer.[308]

920. According to the LCIT, for the sponsor, the payment to the sponsored on the basis of the sponsorship agreement represents an expense, while for the sponsored, the monetary payment by the sponsor represents the income. Expenses on behalf of sponsorship, where the recipient of funds has a contractual obligation to provide some kind of counter-service and represents an indirect promotion of the taxpayer's business and is an expense.

921. According to Article 15 of the LCIT, expenditures in the total amount of up to 5% of the total income are recognized as an expense in the tax balance of the taxpayer, among other things, for health, educational, scientific, humanitarian, religious and sports purposes, environmental protection, as well as expenses made for institutions, i.e., providers of social protection services established in accordance with the law governing social protection, if they are performed by persons registered or established for those purposes in accordance with special regulations, which use these expenses exclusively for the performance of a basic activity.

922. Payments by sponsors according to the LPIT have the treatment of personal income on which personal income tax is paid at a rate of 20%, on the basis of gross income less the standard costs in the amount of 20%.[309]

923. According to the Law on value-added tax,[310] it is prescribed that the subject of taxation, of the value-added tax, are deliveries of goods and the provision of services when the sponsor gives the recipient of sponsorship a certain amount of money, and the recipient of sponsorship publicly and in an agreed manner points out that it was sponsored by the sponsor and otherwise advertises the sponsor.[311]

924. The taxpayer of value-added tax, the recipient of the sponsorship, is obliged to calculate and pay value-added tax for the turnover of these services. The basis for the calculation of value-added tax is the total amount of compensation that the taxpayer of value-added tax, the recipient of the sponsorship, receives or should receive for the turnover in question.

---

308. *See* 'Official Gazette of RS', Nos 25/2001, 80/2002, 80/2002 – other law, 43/2003, 84/2004, 18/2010, 101/2011, 119/2012, 47/2013, 108/2013, 68/2014 – other law and 142/2014.
309. *See* 'Official Gazette of RS', Nos 24/2001, 80/2002, 80/2002-other law, 135/2004, 62/2006, 65/2006 – corrigendum, 31/2009, 44/2009, 18/2010, 50/2011, 91/2011 – Decision of CC, 7/2012 – adjusted din. amount, 93/2012, 114/2012 – Decision of CC, 8/2013 – adjusted din. amount, 47/2013, 48/2013 – corrigendum and 108/2013, 57/2014, 68/2014 – other law.
310. *See* 'Official Gazette of RS', Nos 84/2004, 86/2004 – corrigendum, 61/2005, 61/2007, 93/2012, 108/2013, 68/2014 – other law, 142/2014.
311. It is about the turnover of services performed by the recipient of sponsorship to the sponsor, which is subject to value added tax.

925. A sponsor has an obligation, according to the Law on value-added tax when it gives certain goods or services to the recipient of the sponsorship, and in return receives advertising. This is an exchange of goods or services for other services, so the sponsor or value-added taxpayer has the obligation to calculate and pay value-added tax, on the basis of the market value of services provided by the recipient of the sponsorship, which does not include value-added tax.

926. The sponsored person, who is a taxpayer of value-added tax, calculates and pays value-added tax on the turnover of services provided to the sponsor on the basis of the market value of goods or services received from the sponsor, which does not include value-added tax.

927. Due to the fact that the issue of sponsoring athletes, sports organizations and sports activities is a very sensitive issue, many situations are not legally regulated by law but are left to the free will of the contracting parties to regulate certain issues in accordance with the general rule of fair play. The autonomy of the will of the contracting parties is satisfied with the help of the sponsorship agreement. It is extremely important that there is a special sponsorship agreement which should define all the essential elements of the agreement (contracting parties, subject of sponsorship, scope and manner of sponsorship, obligations of the contracting parties, jurisdiction in case of a dispute), as well as irrelevant elements of the agreement relating to the deadlines.

928. The sponsorship agreement is a very important legal instrument because it provides an opportunity to prevent negative manifestations that may manifest themselves and even bring into question the issue of the regularity of the competition if the same person sponsors more than one club participating in the same competition if the sponsor has an interest that one of the teams, contrary to the competition principles, be in a privileged position in relation to the other. In addition, the sponsorship agreement may provide for those situations that are not provided by laws, such as the resulting failure of the athlete or the unsportsmanlike conduct of the sponsored athlete, which could only harm the image of the sponsor. The assumption is that such situations can be foreseen and clearly defined by the sponsorship agreement.

929. Based on the above, it can be concluded that the area of sponsorship in the Republic of Serbia is adequately regulated in those parts concerning public regulations, but there are numerous ambiguities when trying to regulate the same issue from the aspect of private law regulations.

§3. MERCHANDISING

930. The need for sports products is growing, as awareness of healthy lifestyles increases. These needs are quite large, from the need for physical exercise and maintaining psychophysical condition, to the desire to compete and affirm in sports and recreational activities but also the need for achievement in terms of sports results.

Market research identifies these needs, so manufacturers and merchants are directed in which direction they should design and market certain sports products.

931. The commercialization of sports and trade is playing an increasingly important role in the sports industry. The fact is that most of the income in sports, in addition to the sale of the right to broadcast and organize events, is generated through the trade of sports products.

932. In the Republic of Serbia, the same conditions and rules for conducting trade on the single market of the Republic of Serbia, which are regulated by the Law on trade, apply to trade in sports products.[312]

933. In addition to the Law on trade, the most important substantive provisions which regulate trade in sports in Serbia are also contained in: Law on electronic commerce,[313] LoT,[314] LCRR,[315] LoA,[316] Law on consumer protection,[317] Law on the protection of competition,[318] LoP,[319] as well as the Law on special powers for the effective protection of intellectual property rights,[320] LID,[321] Law on the protection of business secrets,[322] Law on republic administrative fees,[323] Law on the organization and competences of state bodies for combating high-tech crime,[324] CC[325] and Customs Law[326] as well as in a number of by-laws.

934. The Law on trade applies to all persons who perform trade activities in the Republic of Serbia, including those who trade in sports products.

935. The basic concepts of commercial law are defined by the provisions of this Law in Article 3, which defines the 'market' as an institutionally regulated relationship between supply and demand, 'goods' as a product of human labour in tangible

312. *See* 'Official Gazette of RS', No. 52/19.
313. *See* 'Official Gazette of RS', Nos 41/09, 95/13 and 52/19.
314. *See* 'Official Gazette of RS', No. 6/2020.
315. *See* 'Official Gazette of RS', Nos 104/2009, 99/2011, 119/2012, 29/2016 – Decision of the Constitutional Court and 66/2019.
316. *See* 'Official Gazette of RS', Nos 6/2016 and 52/2019 – other law.
317. *See* 'Official Gazette of RS', Nos 62/2014, 6/2016 – other law.
318. *See* 'Official Gazette of RS', Nos 51/09 and 95/13.
319. *See* 'Official Gazette of RS', Nos 99/2011, 113/2017 – other law, 95/2018 and 66/2019.
320. *See* 'Official Gazette of RS', No. 46/2006.
321. *See* 'Official Gazette of RS', Nos 104/2009, 45/2015 and 44/2018 – other law.
322. *See* 'Official Gazette of RS', No. 53/2021.
323. *See* 'Official Gazette of RS', Nos 43/2003, 51/2003 – corrigendum, 61/2005, 101/2005 – other law, 55/2012 – adjusted din. amount, 65/2013 – other law, 57/2014 – adjusted din. amount, 45/2015 – adjusted din. amount, 61/2017 – adjusted din. amount, 113/2017, 3/2018 – corrigendum, 50/2018 – adjusted din. amount, 95/2018, 38/2019 – adjusted din. amount, 86/2019, 90/2019 – corrigendum, 98/2020 – adjusted din. amount, 144/2020 and 62/2021 – adjusted din. amount.
324. *See* 'Official Gazette of RS', Nos 61/2005 and 104/2009.
325. *See* 'Official Gazette of RS', Nos 85/2005, 88/2005 – corrigendum, 107/2005 – corrigendum, 72/2009, 111/2009, 121/2012, 104/2013, 108/2014, 94/2016 and 35/2019.
326. *See* 'Official Gazette of RS', Nos 95/2018, 91/2019 – other law and 144/2020.

or intangible form intended for sale on the market, as well as water, gas and electricity, when they are sold in a predetermined quantity, a 'sales facility' when it consists of a space that represents a unique physical, functional and technical and technological unit, of a permanent or temporary construction character, equipped in the prescribed manner, which is intended for trade, a 'sales point' which is a sales facility or other place outside the sales facility where trade is envisaged and approved, in accordance with the law and other regulations, a 'consumer' as a natural person who buys goods or services to meet personal needs or the needs of the household and a 'producer' who is a legal entity, entrepreneur or natural person who make the product or represent themselves in this property by placing their business name, name or title, trademark or other recognizable mark on the product.

936. According to the Law on trade, trade and the provision of services to consumers is performed as: trade at the point of sale, trade by personal offering, and remote trade (electronic trade and other remote trade through other means).[327]

937. Remote trade is the display of an offer and the conclusion of a contract for the sale of goods/services using one or more means of remote communication. A foreign person is considered to perform remote trade in the Republic of Serbia if it is aimed at consumers in the Republic of Serbia.

938. Electronic commerce is a type of remote commerce which is realized in a way that goods/services are offered, ordered and sold through the Internet.

939. In the era of digitalization, remote and electronic commerce become dominant.

940. One of the particularly good sides of the new Law on trade is more clearly defined models of electronic commerce, bearing in mind that an increasing number of people use services in this way on the one hand, while on the other hand, doing business in this way allows many persons to easily enter entrepreneurship.

941. Electronic commerce is performed as the sale of goods/services through an e-shop,[328] sale of goods/services through an electronic platform,[329] sale of goods

327. *See* Art. 13 para. 1, n. 1, 2, 3, Law on trade.

328. An e-shop is an online store through which a merchant offers goods/services. It is a sale where the merchant owns its web shop through which the consumer orders goods directly from the merchant, and the merchant delivers it to the consumer, in its own organization or through a courier service. *See* Art. 17 para. 3 n. 1 Law on trade.

329. An electronic platform is a means by which a person who has the status of an information society service provider, in terms of the law governing electronic commerce, provides a connection service to parties which do trade electronically. The electronic platform connects merchants and consumers (sales through an e-commerce platform through which consumers and merchants are connected, whereby the platform also provides billing services). *See* Art. 17 para. 3 n. 2 Law on trade.

through an electronic shop or through an electronic platform, where the goods are delivered to the consumer directly from the manufacturer/wholesaler – 'dropshipping'.[330]

942. Other remote trade is done through other means of communication (TV sales, catalogue sales, mobile telephony, answering machines, etc.).

943. In Article 3 of the Law on the protection of competition,[331] they apply to all legal and natural persons who directly or indirectly, permanently, occasionally or one-time only participate in the trade of goods or services, regardless of their legal status, form of ownership or citizenship, or nationality.[332]

944. The Law on the protection of competition applies to acts and actions committed in the territory of the Republic of Serbia, i.e., acts and actions committed outside its territory that affect, or could affect competition in the territory of the Republic of Serbia, and, among other things, apply to sports organizations as well as to their sports rules. It is very important to emphasize that the provisions of the Law on the protection of competition refer exclusively to those sports rules that have an economic effect. Competition with solely sports rules implies something completely different.[333]

945. The Law on the protection of competition especially refers to those sports rules[334] which regulate marketing activities in a sports competition. Such activities have an economic effect because the provision of marketing services in a sports competition for a fee is a form of economic activity. The National Branch Sports Federation has a dominant position in performing sports activities of certain branches of sports and if the sports rules prohibit individual marketing activities in sports competitions, it would abuse its dominant position, and the abuse of a dominant position by Article 16 of the Law on the protection of competition is prohibited.

330. It is a form of electronic commerce where goods are delivered to the consumer directly from the manufacturer. In this form of electronic commerce, the goods do not come into contact with the seller. The consumer addresses the merchant regarding the goods he/she wants to procure and makes a payment to the merchant. The merchant forwards the information and data to the manufacturer, and the manufacturer delivers the product to the buyer. *See* Art. 17 para. 3 n. 3 Law on trade.

331. *See* 'Official Gazette of RS', Nos 51/09 and 95/1.

332. In terms of the Law on the protection of competition, participants in trade and legal transactions include both domestic and foreign companies and entrepreneurs, as well as state authorities, bodies of territorial autonomy and local self-government and other natural and legal persons and other forms of association of market participants, public enterprises, companies, entrepreneurs and other market participants that perform activities of general interest, i.e., who have been granted a fiscal monopoly by an act of the competent state authority, unless the application of this Law would prevent the performance of those activities, i.e., the performance of entrusted tasks.

333. Sports rules that have no economic effect relate to the dimension of sports arenas, the number of players participating, etc.

334. In the Republic of Serbia, sports rules in certain branches of sports are prescribed by national branch sports federations.

946. The legislative framework regulating intellectual property is of special importance for the trade of goods in sports. This legal framework is amended, especially in the areas of copyright, patents, and trademarks, and thus harmonized with the Agreement on trade-related aspects of intellectual property rights and European Union standards, as well as other international conventions in this field.

947. With the Stabilization and Association Agreement with the EU, the Republic of Serbia is obliged to the EU to apply the same standards of protection of intellectual property rights as those prescribed by the EU.

948. Regarding sports brands and sports products, the most commonly used intellectual property is certainly trademark. Trademarks contribute to the brand value and identity, and ultimately to the creation of revenues.

949. The LoT[335] regulates the manner of acquiring and protecting the rights to signs used in the trade of goods and services.

950. A trademark is defined as a right which protects a sign (mark) which in trade serves to distinguish goods, i.e., services of one natural or legal person from the same or similar goods, i.e., services of another natural or legal person. The provisions of this law are in accordance with the Madrid Agreement on the International Registration of Trademarks and the Protocol to the Madrid Agreement.

951. In respect of the protection of signs by trademarks in the Republic of Serbia, foreign natural and legal persons enjoy the same rights as domestic natural and legal persons if this arises from international treaties or from the principle of reciprocity.

952. The LoT defines the entire procedure of the protection, international registration of a trademark, acquisition and scope of rights, termination of rights and the annulment of a trademark, civil protection and penal provisions.

953. Article 49 of the LoT stipulates that the holder of a trademark has the exclusive right to use the sign protected by the trademark to mark the goods or services to which the sign refers. At the same time, the trademark holder has the right to prohibit other persons from unauthorized use of a mark that is identical to his trademark. This right also applies to the sign, which is the same or similar to the trademark if there is a probability that due to this sameness, i.e., similarity, confusion will arise on the part of the public.

954. The holder of the trademark, i.e., the applicant may, by the licence agreement, assign the right to use the trademark, i.e., the rights from the application, for all or only for some goods or services. If some issues related to the assignment of the right to use the trademark are not regulated by the LoT, the regulations governing contracts and torts shall apply.

335. *See* 'Official Gazette of RS', No. 6/2020.

955. The rights and obligations of the trademark holder, who is both the licensor on the one hand and the licensee on the other hand are determined in more detail by the licence agreement.

956. If the licensee violates the provisions of the licence agreement relating to the duration of the licence, the form covered by the registration in which the trademark may be used, the scope of goods or services for which the licence is granted, the area where the trademark may be displayed or the quality of goods produced, i.e., the services provided by the licensee, the trademark holder may invoke its rights.

957. The rights of the trademark holder may also be violated by the unauthorized use of the sign by any participant in the trade.

958. Article 97 of the LoT stipulates that a lawsuit for infringement may be filed by the trademark holder, applicant, licensee, collective trademark user with the consent of the collective trademark holder and the guarantee trademark user with the consent of the guarantee trademark holder, provided that the licensee may file a lawsuit only with the consent of the right holder unless otherwise specified in the agreement.

959. The LoT also specifies that the acquirer of an exclusive licence who has formally notified the trademark holder of the trademark infringement, i.e., the rights from the application, may file a lawsuit for the infringement of rights, if the trademark holder, i.e., the applicant, fails to do so within thirty days from the day of the receipt of the notice.

960. In case of the violation of the right, the plaintiff may request the establishment of the violation of the right and the prohibition of actions that violate or actions that pose a serious threat that the right will be violated, as well as the prohibition of repeating such or similar actions under the threat of paying an adequate amount of money to the plaintiff. Also, the plaintiff has, if a violation is proven, the right to compensation and the right to request the publication of the judgment at the expense of the defendant. The plaintiff may also request the confiscation, i.e., permanent exclusion from circulation or the destruction or alteration, free of charge, of the articles by which the violation was committed, as well as the alienation, confiscation or destruction, free of charge, of materials and articles used in the production of the articles by which the violation of rights was committed.[336]

961. In determining the amount of damages, the court takes into account, in particular, the negative economic consequences suffered by the plaintiff, including lost profits, as well as the profits made by the defendant in the violation of rights.

336. *See* Art. 92 of the Law on trademarks.

962. If the violation of the right was not committed intentionally or through gross negligence, the court may award the plaintiff compensation in the amount of the profit that the defendant made by violating the right.

963. The LID[337] regulates the manner of acquiring the right to the external appearance of an industrial or craft product (which means the overall visual impression that the product leaves on the informed consumer or user) and the protection of these rights.

964. The LoP[338] regulates the legal protection of inventions in the field of technology, which are new, have an inventive level and are industrially applicable.

965. Only the implementation of these laws is conditioned by the implementation of laws prescribing organizational and procedural provisions, important for the protection of intellectual property rights and the prosecution of persons who infringe on them. These provisions are contained in the LID, the Law on special powers for the effective protection of intellectual property rights,[339] the Law on the organization and competencies of state authorities for combating high-tech crime[340] and in the CC.[341]

966. The LID regulates the manner of acquisition and protection of the right to the external appearance of an industrial or craft product.[342] The provisions of this Law apply in all matters not regulated by the Hague Agreement and refer to the procedure of the acquisition and protection of industrial design which is internationally registered for the territory of the Republic of Serbia on the basis of the Hague Agreement on the International Industrial Design Registration.

967. The Law on the organization and competencies of state authorities for combating high-tech crime regulates the education, organization, competencies and authorizations of special organizational units of state authorities for the purpose of detection, criminal prosecution and trial, *inter alia*, and for criminal offences against intellectual property. A special department for the fight against high-tech crime is formed in the Higher Public Prosecutor's Office in Belgrade.

968. The Law on special powers for the effective protection of intellectual property rights regulates special powers of state administration bodies and organizations exercising public powers, in order to effectively protect intellectual property rights in accordance with the regulations governing intellectual property rights. The provisions of this Law apply to the production, trade, use and holding of goods and to the provision of services that infringe intellectual property rights.

337. *See* 'Official Gazette of RS', Nos 104/2009, 45/2015 and 44/2018 – other law.
338. *See* 'Official Gazette of RS', Nos 99/2011, 113/2017 – other law, 95/2018 and 66/2019.
339. *See* 'Official Gazette of RS', No. 46/2006.
340. *See* 'Official Gazette of RS', Nos 61/2005 and 104/2009.
341. *See* 'Official Gazette of RS', Nos 85/2005, 88/2005 – corrigendum, 107/2005 – corrigendum, 72/2009, 111/2009, 121/2012, 104/2013, 108/2014, 94/2016 and 35/2019.
342. Visual impression that the product leaves on the consumer or user.

969. The Ministry in Charge of Trade, Tourism and Services, through market inspection, performs inspection supervision over the production and trade of goods which infringe intellectual property rights, including trademarks, designs, patents, copyrights and related rights, as well as supervision over the production and trade of goods protected by copyright or related rights.

970. Institutions dealing with the protection of intellectual property rights in the Republic of Serbia are the Intellectual Property Office,[343] as well as the competent ministries and other state authorities, among which the most important are the courts.

971. The Intellectual Property Office is a special organization in the system of state administration of the Republic of Serbia, which is responsible for matters related to industrial property rights and copyright and related rights. The scope of work of the Intellectual Property Office is prescribed by Article 36 paragraph 1 of the LoM, according to which the Intellectual Property Office performs professional and state administration tasks related to: patent and small patent, trademark, design, indication of geographical origin, integrated circuit topography, copyright and related rights; application of international treaties in the field of intellectual property protection and presentation and representation of the interests of the Republic of Serbia in specialized international organizations for the protection of intellectual property; supervision over the work of organizations for collective management of copyright and related rights; development in the field of intellectual property protection; information and educational activities in the field of intellectual property protection, as well as other activities determined by the Law.

§4. Ownership of Clubs

972. The LS regulates issues related to the legal status, organization and registration of entrepreneurs and legal persons in the sports system.

973. For the purpose of performing sports activities and sports occupations, a sports organization may be established as an association or as a company.[344]

974. This part of the monograph will analyse the legal aspects of club ownership and potential problems related to the announced privatization of sports clubs.

975. Sports clubs in the Republic of Serbia are most often registered as sports associations, i.e., as a voluntary non-profit organizations based on the freedom of association of several individuals and/or legal persons, organized on the basis of the statute and established to achieve a common goal in sports.

343. *See also* https://www.zis.gov.rs.
344. *See* Part I Organization of Sport, Ch. 2 Public Regulation.

976. Although sports associations and sports companies have a similar organizational structure, since they are sports organizations, there are still differences. Namely, a sports company may be established by legal or natural persons with the status of a joint-stock company or a limited liability company, with the primary goal of gaining profit, while this is not the case with a sports association. In addition, sports companies must respect the regulations of commercial law.

977. The provisions of the LoAss apply to all issues of importance for sports associations and sports companies that are not regulated by LS of RS[345] and the provisions of the Law on companies.[346]

978. According to the Law on companies, the persons who establish the company and the persons who subsequently join it are the members with limited liability in the limited liability company and shareholders in the joint-stock company.

979. Although Part I Organization of Sport, Chapter 2 Public Regulation explained in detail how sports associations and sports companies are organized, we will repeat certain specifics that are characteristic of ownership in sports clubs.

980. It is necessary to emphasize that only a sports association can establish a company in order to obtain the funds needed to achieve its sports goals. In this case, the sports association – the founder uses the entire net profit of the established legal entity, but exclusively for achieving its sports goals determined by the statute and has no right to distribute the profit from economic or other activities to its founders, members, members of the sports association bodies, directors, employees or affiliated persons.

981. The net profit realized by the company in the current year must be at least 70% reinvested in the sports activities of that company.

982. A sports association may change its legal form into a sports company as a limited liability company by transferring the founding rights to the local self-government unit on whose territory it has its seat, with the prior consent of that local self-government unit. The process of changing the legal form of current clubs organized as the associations of citizens into sports companies brings certain benefits because, above all, the tradition and image of the sports club are preserved, and the possibility is opened for future domestic or foreign investors to buy the minority or majority shares of these clubs.

983. In the event of the termination of a sports association, only a domestic non-profit organization in the field of sports may be determined, by the statute, as the recipient of its property.

345. *See* 'Official Gazette of RS', Nos 51/2009, 99/2011 – other laws and 44/2018 – other law.
346. *See* 'Official Gazette of RS', Nos 36/2011, 99/2011, 83/2014 – other law, 5/2015, 44/2018, 95/2018 and 91/2019.

984. Article 92 of LS of RS stipulates that a person who has shares or stocks in a sports company, and who is elected or appointed to a public office or a position in a body of a political party is obliged to, within thirty days from the day of the election or appointment, transfer the management rights based on shares or stocks to a legal or natural person who is not an affiliate, to perform them, in its own name, and on behalf of the official, until the termination of the public office, i.e., the position in the body of a political party and to inform the sports company about this transfer.

985. The same person may not directly, indirectly or through affiliates, be the owner, or have shares or stocks in more than one sports company in the same level of competition, and within the same branch of sport may have shares and stocks that account for a maximum of 5% of the share capital of the sports company only in one more sports company.

986. According to LS of RS, shares, i.e., stocks of a sports company cannot, directly, indirectly or through affiliates be held by persons whose jobs and activities can directly affect the competition in the appropriate branch of sport, i.e., the level of competition, such as athletes, trainers, referees/judges, as well as sports betting owners and sports betting employees. If a person acquires shares, i.e., stocks contrary to the provisions, it is obliged to, without delay, alienate its share, i.e., stocks that it acquired even though it was not entitled to them, and until it does so it cannot exercise the rights from acquired shares, i.e., stocks in any sports organization. Until the alienation of the share, i.e., stocks, the rights from the share, i.e., stocks are exercised by the commissioner appointed by the competent national branch sports federation.[347]

987. The provisions of the LS arbitration shall apply accordingly to resolving disputes arising in connection with the performance of sports activities and occupations of a sports company with other participants in the sports system.

988. Certain problems are still expected regarding the announced privatization of sports clubs.

989. The biggest clubs in Serbia (Red Star, Partizan) are actually sports societies, and all sports societies in Serbia are state-owned, which makes it difficult to develop a private initiative in this area.

990. According to LS of RS, Article 179 unequivocally states that the privatization of property and capital in society, i.e., public ownership in organizations in the field of sports, will be regulated by a special law. For now, these are only unofficial announcements and there are no signs as to which model of privatization (from those applied in the EU countries) could be applied.

---

347. *See* Art. 92 of the LSRS.

991. A large number of clubs in the Republic of Serbia that have the right to use social or public property may, until the adoption of the law on the privatization of sports clubs, only with the prior consent of the Government, at the proposal of the competent ministry, dispose of these properties, as well as to make decisions on reducing or increasing the capital, reorganization or restructuring, investing, selling part of the property, pledging things or establishing a mortgage, long-term lease, disposition of receivables, taking or approving loans or issuing guarantees. Clubs themselves will decide about their future status when the law on the privatization of sports clubs is adopted because the Constitution guarantees the freedom of association. So, in this case, clubs will have the opportunity to be privatized, but they can also remain in the status of sports associations.

992. Privatization of sports clubs is one of the solutions, especially for financing football clubs in the Republic of Serbia because the state authorities have less opportunities to finance non-profit sports organizations.[348]

993. The privatization of sports clubs also carries certain dilemmas. The question is whether there would be interested buyers, bearing in mind that the largest and most popular clubs in Serbia are also the biggest losers, whether the privatization is based on the market value of the club or property valuation (business premises, stadium).

994. Also, the issue of denationalization presents certain problems.[349] Prior to the privatization, the issue of the restitution of confiscated property, primarily the land on which the existing sports facilities are located, should be resolved, in accordance with the Law on the return of confiscated property and compensation.[350] This property has legitimate and legal heirs, and a certain number of sports facilities are located on such land.

995. From all the above, we can conclude that the issue of ownership in sports associations and societies is accompanied by many unknowns, especially the announced privatization when a significant change in the ownership structure of sports clubs in the Republic of Serbia is expected.

348. So far, the state has financed one part from the budget, and the other part through sponsorships of state public companies.

349. By applying the regulations on the agrarian reform, nationalization, sequestration, as well as other regulations on the basis of acts on nationalization, in the former Yugoslavia, after 9 Mar. 1945, the property was confiscated from individuals and certain legal persons and transferred to the national, state, social or cooperative property.

350. *See* 'Official Gazette of RS', Nos 72/2011, 108/2013, 142/2014, 88/2015 – Decision of CC, 95/2018 and 153/2020).

Chapter 3. Private Regulation

996. As noted in the previous chapters, private regulations in the field of sports in the Republic of Serbia include various contracts which regulate relations and to which, in principle, the rules of the law of contracts and torts apply. The application of the rules of the law of contracts and torts for the regulation of contractual relations *inter partes* in the domain of sports law is framed by the provisions of LS of RS. In other words, in the Republic of Serbia, sports organizations and athletes themselves regulate relations between themselves and with third parties, but in accordance with the law. A unique and efficient legal system in the field of sports is created by the fact that private regulations must be in accordance with the laws and by-laws of the Republic of Serbia. Indeed, this is one of the important preconditions because it is necessary to strengthen the private initiative for the development of sports in its entirety.

997. In the Republic of Serbia, freedom of agreement is guaranteed, so there are numerous agreements from the world of sports commercialization: Agreement on Television Rights,[351] Trade Agreement, Sponsorship Agreement, Business Cooperation Agreement but also other agreements in the field of media and copyright, as well as other forms such as direct agreements. In this Chapter, due to space constraints, we will mention only some of them.

998. With the development of sports and with the development of its commercialization, sponsorship support is growing. However, the increasingly growing money in the sports market in the Republic of Serbia has not been accompanied by appropriate regulations. The sponsorship agreement still falls into the category of unnamed agreements, which means that no rules have been defined that would regulate these agreements. The general rules of contract law apply to the conclusion and realization of the rights and obligations of the sponsorship agreement.

999. The sponsor, on the one hand, and the sponsored, on the other hand, have complete autonomy of will in terms of regulating their relations. On the other hand, it also means that there is no unique type, i.e., form of the sponsorship agreement. Nevertheless, in practice, certain rights and obligations have been established arising from the sponsorship agreement, which are regularly contracted.

1000. The obligation of the sponsor always consists in paying a certain amount of money, providing certain services, transferring ownership or handing over the use of certain things, while the obligations of the sponsored differ from agreement to agreement.

1001. The Sponsorship Agreement is characterized by the fact that the support provided by the sponsor is equal to the value of the goods on which it acquires the

351. In the Republic of Serbia, in 2021, a three-year Agreement on TV rights of TV Arena Sport was signed for the matches of the Serbian Football Super League worth EUR 24 million, but the details of the Agreement were not announced.

right of use, and it is mostly the image of the sponsored athlete, sports organization or sports event, or the value of services provided by the sponsored.

1002. A potential problem can arise if a sponsor sponsors several sports organizations in the same competition rank and in this case, it may jeopardize the very regularity of the competition. Also, the regularity of the competition can be called into question if the sponsor of the competition also sponsors one of the sports organizations or the athlete participating in this competition.[352]

1003. From this aspect, the autonomy of the will of the contractor can thus lead to problems. These problems can be prevented by adopting special rules that would provide a framework for the effect of the Sponsorship Agreement. In any case, the validity of the agreement cannot be called into question due to non-compliance with sports regulations. For example, the exclusivity clause, when the sponsored person cannot conclude a sponsorship agreement with a third party, is something that may be contrary to the Law on the protection of competition.

1004. In addition, when an athlete, sports organization or event have more than one sponsor, the agreement must clearly define the rights, restrictions and corresponding obligations of each sponsor, as well as of the sponsored parties. Initially, the sponsored person is obliged to inform possible sponsors about what sponsors he/she is already in a contractual relationship with.

1005. However, the sponsor is obliged to refrain from all actions that may negatively affect the image of the sponsor during the term of the sponsorship agreement. If the athlete behaved differently, he/she would prevent the sponsor from making a business profit, which is why it entered the sponsorship. Such an obligation of the athlete is provided by the LoA of the Republic of Serbia, with the provision that this obligation applies to both contracting parties.

1006. Agreements that sports organizations conclude with athletes who perform for them, as a rule, provide for certain restrictions for athletes in terms of concluding individual sponsorship agreements. Also, these agreements contain provisions on the right of the sports organization to use the name and image of the athlete.

1007. According to the Professional Contract on Playing (employment contract) of the Football Association of Serbia,[353] the player undertakes to advertise sponsors or clients of the Club who have concluded a sponsorship agreement or a promotion

352. It is a well-known event from the Olympic Games in Beijing in 2008, when the legendary American swimmer Michael Phelps won the final race in 100 m, ahead of the Serbian competitor Milorad Čavić, although the video clearly showed that Čavić was the first to reach the finish line. '*Omega*' Company which was the official timekeeper, was also one of the sponsors of the American swimmer. The explanation that Čavić was the first to touch the button at the finish line, but that Phelps did it harder, so his touch was the first to be registered, which followed a year later, did not change the result or convince a part of the public that everything was regular.

353. *See also* https://fss.rs/dokumentacija/ugovori-i-dokumenta-vezana-za-registraciju/, site accessed on 22 Sep. 2021.

agreement with the Club, in full compliance with the conditions and the order of the Club. Advertising of other legal or natural persons is not allowed by the player without the written consent of the Club.

1008. In addition, by signing this agreement, the player transfers the right to use the image and name to the Club. This right applies to the use of the player's image in all media and institutions, including multimedia, and in particular to the use of photographs of the player permitted by the Club.

1009. The Football Association of Serbia also prescribes that the club has the right to use the facsimile of the player's signature on club souvenirs, while the player can individually use his/her image and name for marketing purposes by not using the Club's insignia or its official sports equipment.

1010. The player undertakes to participate in all activities aimed at promoting the Club, especially in activities through electronic and printed media, as well as through public events, promotions, etc. The player must not endanger the reputation of the club or football.[354]

1011. In other sports in Serbia, the agreements between sports clubs and athletes regulate the rights and obligations regarding commercial obligations, but this is not expressed to the same extent as in football.

1012. For example, the agreements that basketball clubs conclude with basketball players, according to the contract on professional engagement of players of the Basketball Association of Serbia in this regard contain only a provision which obliges the player to respect the obligations towards club sponsors.[355]

1013. The Volleyball Federation of Serbia, in the agreement between the club and the player and in the agreement between the club and the trainer, only prescribes that the player (trainer) is obliged to participate in the marketing and humanitarian activities of the club.[356]

1014. Regarding the individual image of the athlete, as a personal right, it is protected from violation and unauthorized use by the LCT and the LoA. Regarding personal rights, the athlete decides at his/her own will whether he/she will leave it to others, with or without compensation, which is provided by the clause in the agreement between the sports organization and the athlete.

1015. A special type of sponsorship agreement is equipment agreements, according to which the athlete is obliged to wear the equipment of the sponsor of

354. *Ibid.*
355. *See also* https://kss.rs/dokumenta/, site accessed on 22 Sep. 2021.
356. *See also* https://www.ossrb.org/dokumenta.html, site accessed on 22 Sep. 2021.

the sports organization. The athlete is obliged to wear the sports equipment of a certain manufacturer at all official performances, while outside such events, the athlete has the right to conclude individual sponsorship agreements.

1016. Further below, in the form of an attachment, a model of the Sponsorship Agreement is presented of the sports club from the world of auto racing, like the one applied in the Republic of Serbia:[357]

SPORTS CLUB SPONSORSHIP AGREEMENT
Concluded on _____________, between:

(1) SPONSOR: '__' d.o.o. from __ St. __ no. __ TAX ID __ reg. no. __ represented by ___.
(2) CLUB: ________________________ from __ St. ____________ no. _.

Article 1

In this Agreement, the Contracting Parties regulate the mutual relations arising from the sponsorship relations and on the basis of which they assume certain rights and obligations.

Article 2

The Sponsor shall transfer to the account of the Club the amount of _________ dinars in the name of the sponsorship of the Club and the advertisement of the sponsor that the Club shall perform during the competition season ____.

The Sponsor shall fulfill its obligation to pay the funds according to the following timetable:

(1) by __ the amount of ______ din;
(2) by __ the amount of ______ din.

Article 3

The Club undertakes:

(1) to wear on all competition and other vehicles the protected name and sign of the sponsor as well as its products and activities;
(2) that the competition cars and driver's equipment bear the sign and colours which shall be jointly agreed by the Club and the Sponsor;
(3) that the competition cars are technically, maximally and completely faultless and ready for the competition season __ in the competitions for the Championship of Serbia;
(4) to promote the Sponsor's products and services in an appropriate manner and in interviews and statements for the media;
(5) to submit to the Sponsor, at the request of the Sponsor, all available material on the executed work (video cassettes, photos, etc.);

357. *See also* https://www.overa.rs/ugovor-o-sponzorstvu-2.html.

(6) The Club undertakes not to advertise any competing companies and their products and services on the competition vehicle under this Agreement during the term of this Agreement.

Article 4

The Contracting Parties agree that the Club shall have the right to receive monetary funds and other funds, namely sponsorships and advertisements from other natural and legal persons, with the Sponsor from this Agreement having the primary right to choose the place of advertisement on competition vehicles and the equipment of Club drivers.

Article 5

The Contracting Parties agree that in the case of non-fulfillment of the Sponsor's obligations under this Agreement regarding the timetable of payment, the Club shall not be responsible for fulfilling its obligation – a timely preparation of technical correctness of vehicles for competitions in the Championship of Serbia.

Article 6

In case of a dispute, the Contracting Parties shall try to resolve it by agreement, and if an agreement is not possible, the dispute shall be resolved by a court which is actually and locally competent.
SPONSOR CLUB

Part V. Sport and COVID-19

Chapter 1. General Issues

1017. The famous saying of Roman satirist Juvenal[358] '*mens sana in corpore sano*', the unwritten rule of the ancient games and the Olympics, that mental health is a condition for mental balance, has become inapplicable in the last two years due to the epidemiological situation caused by the coronavirus.[359]

1018. Globally, the current epidemiological situation has led to the stumble of sport with a tendency to fade, both in terms of its active application and monitoring.

1019. Society is increasingly facing a global problem caused by the coronavirus, and as a result, human existence is becoming an increasing concern, and sports and sports activities are getting out of focus. In other words, a person is burdened with problems that one has to solve due to the new situation, while sports become a third-class thing.

1020. This image is present everywhere in the world today.

1021. Sport has been under great temptation in Serbia during the COVID-19 pandemic. At one point, all sports activities completely stopped. There was no competition, no accompanying sports activities. The epidemiological situation changed from day to day. Conditions have changed, measures and activities have been adjusted, and in accordance with this, this chronological overview of the preparation of legal regulations for athletes, sports organizations, organization of sports events and sports, in general, has been prepared.

358. *See* Ivan Klajn and Milan Šipka, *Veliki rečnik stranih izraza*, Novi Sad, 2008.

359. Less than two years ago, one could hardly have imagined postponing the Olympic Games. Only a planetary catastrophe, which just happened as a result of the COVID-19 pandemic, could lead to this.

Chapter 2. Government Institutions in the System of Sports Organization in the Republic of Serbia in the Conditions of COVID-19

1022. The Republic of Serbia did not have prepared protocols and elaborated legal and other mechanisms for reacting in certain epidemiological situations in the field of sports. For this reason, the status of athletes was at one point reduced to the status of citizens, whose rights were restricted.

1023. The situation caused by the COVID-19 pandemic is recognized by the regulations in the Republic of Serbia through the Constitution[360] and through the Law on the Protection of the Population from Infectious Diseases (ZZSZB),[361] as well as through the Law on State Administration (LSA),[362] while the LS does not regulate such situations.

1024. In the Republic of Serbia, the first case of COVID-19 was registered on 6 March 2020, and already on 11 March 2020, the Ministry of Health issued an Order banning gatherings[363] which prohibits public gatherings throughout the country in public places indoors when more than 100 people gather. This decision also applies to sports events.

1025. Two days later, on 13 March 2020, the Ministry of Youth and Sports issued an important notice prohibiting public gatherings throughout the Republic of Serbia, in open sports facilities (stadiums, trim tracks, bike trails, regatta tracks, etc.). However, it was allowed to hold sports competitions in open sports facilities, but only without the presence of the audience.[364]

1026. As time went on and the epidemiological situation worsened, the measures became more and more rigorous.

1027. According to the Constitution, when a public threat endangers the survival of the state or citizens, a state of emergency is declared. The decision to declare and lift the state of emergency is made by the National Assembly, and if they are unable to meet, the decision to declare a state of emergency is made jointly by the President, the President of the National Assembly and the Prime Minister, under the same conditions as the National Assembly.[365]

---

360. *See* 'Official Gazette of RS', No. 98/2006.
361. *See* 'Official Gazette of RS', Nos 15/2016, 68/2020 and 136/2020, Law from 2016 that was amended twice in 2020 during the pandemic.
362. *See* 'Official Gazette of RS', Nos 79/2005, 101/2007, 95/2010, 99/2014, 47/2018 and 30/2018 – other law.
363. *See* 'Official Gazette of RS', No. 30/20 of 11 Mar. 2020 Orders banning gatherings have been issued on several occasions depending on the epidemiological situation. This paper will deal only with those that directly concern the status of sports and athletes.
364. https://www.mos.gov.rs/vest/vazno-obavestenje.
365. *See* Art. 105 and Art. 120 of the Constitution of the Republic of Serbia.

1028. The decision on the state of emergency is valid for a maximum of ninety days. After the expiration of this deadline, the National Assembly may extend the decision on the state of emergency for another ninety days, by a majority of the total number of deputies.

1029. During the state of emergency, according to the Constitution, the National Assembly may prescribe measures derogating from the constitutionally guaranteed human and minority rights, but only to the extent necessary, provided that derogation measures do not lead to discrimination based on race, gender, language, religion, nationality or social origin.

1030. When the decision on the state of emergency has not been made by the National Assembly, the National Assembly shall confirm it within forty-eight hours of its adoption, i.e., as soon as they are able to meet, which in this case happened in Serbia.

1031. Pursuant to Article 200(5) of the Constitution, the President of the Republic, the President of the National Assembly and the Prime Minister made the decision to declare a state of emergency on 15 March 2020.[366]

1032. At the same time, on 15 March 2020, the Government of the Republic of Serbia, with the co-signature of the President, passed the Regulation on Measures during the state of emergency (UMVS),[367] which, among other things, prescribes that it is prohibited to convene and hold rallies and all other gatherings of citizens outdoors. In addition, all gatherings (sports, cultural and other events) are prohibited indoors, except for gatherings that are of special interest for the work and functioning of state bodies and services, for the holding of which a special approval is issued by the Minister of the Interior in accordance with this decision.

1033. In order to prevent the spread of the infectious disease COVID-19, in the territory of the Republic of Serbia, it is not allowed to perform sports activities (training, games, matches, races, etc.) in closed sports facilities, school gyms, halls, gyms, sports centres, institutes responsible for sports, etc.) and in open sports facilities (stadiums, regatta tracks, trim and bicycle tracks, etc.) for the duration of the threat of spreading the infectious disease COVID-19 in the territory of the Republic of Serbia.

1034. Article 16 of the Regulation prohibits movement in all parks and public areas intended for recreation and sports.

1035. This Regulation practically stopped sports in the Republic of Serbia.

366. *See* 'Official Gazette of RS', No. 29 of 15 Mar. 2020, with the fact that this Decision was confirmed by the Decision on the Confirmation of the Decision on Declaring the State of Emergency ('Official Gazette of RS', No. 62/2020), which entered into force on the day of publication in the 'Official Gazette of the Republic of Serbia', i.e., on 29 Apr. 2020.
367. 'Official Gazette of RS', No. 31 of 15 Mar. 2020.

1036. Pursuant to Article 6(2) of the ZZSZB and Article 15(3) of the Law on Public Administration, the Ministry of Health issued an order declaring the epidemic of the infectious disease COVID-19.[368]

1037. The epidemiological situation conditioned that the Government of the Republic of Serbia made decisions according to which sports facilities, and sports halls became temporary COVID-19 hospitals, which separated athletes from training and competition for a longer period.

1038. On 3 April 2020, in the Decision on the opening of a temporary facility for the accommodation and treatment of persons suffering from the infectious disease COVID-19 caused by the SARS-CoV-2 virus – '*Čair Hall*' (OPO Čair)[369] in Niš became a temporary COVID hospital.

1039. The Decision of the Government of the Republic of Serbia, among other things, states that in order to effectively combat the epidemic and treat patients in the Republic of Serbia, OPO Čair Niš, as part of the military health system managed by the Ministry of Defence in the state of emergency in accordance with the law governing the performance of military, labour and material obligations and decisions of the competent authorities relating to labour in the state of emergency.

1040. Afterwards, '*Atenica*' Hall In Čačak was put into function in order to preserve health and combat COVID-19, as well as the largest sports hall in Serbia- '*Štark arena*' in Belgrade.

1041. The state of emergency in the Republic of Serbia was lifted on 6 May 2020 by the Decision on the abolition of the state of emergency.[370] The decision was made by the National Assembly.

1042. The Law on the Validity of Regulations Adopted by the Government during the State of Emergency and Confirmed by the National Assembly was also adopted,[371] as well as the new ZZSZB[372] which regulates the protection of the population from infectious diseases and special health issues, determines infectious diseases that endanger the health of the population of the Republic of Serbia and whose prevention and control is of general interest to the Republic of Serbia, implementation of epidemiological surveillance and measures, implementation and provision of funds for their implementation, supervision over the implementation of this law, as well as other issues of importance for the protection of the population from infectious diseases.

368. *See* 'Official Gazette of RS', No. 37 of 19 Mar. 2020.
369. *See* 'Official Gazette of RS', No. 50 of 3 Apr. 2020.
370. *See* 'Official Gazette of RS', No. 65 of 6 May 2020.
371. *Ibid.*
372. *See* 'Official Gazette of RS', No. 68 of 10 May 2020.

1043. In line with the current epidemiological situation, the Ministry of Health issued a new order banning gatherings in public places indoors and outdoors – when more than fifty people gather at the same time. During the permitted gathering in public places indoors, all preventive measures related to hand disinfection, use of personal protective equipment (masks) and a distance between the persons present of at least two meters must be applied, while during the permitted gathering in public places outdoors, the distance between the persons must be at least two meters, with the use of personal protective equipment (masks).

1044. With lifting the state of emergency and the adoption of the new ZZSZB, the preconditions for initiating the training process of athletes and holding sports competitions in the territory of the Republic of Serbia were met.

1045. Based on the Decision of the Government of the Republic of Serbia and the Crisis Relief Headquarters for the control of the COVID-19 disease,[373] to further relax measures in the fight against coronavirus, which provides for the start of the training process indoors, the Ministry of Youth and Sports issued Recommendations for the continuation of the training process in all sports facilities of top athletes and other athletes in the sports system of the Republic of Serbia for the application of measures to prevent and reduce the risk of transmitting the SARS-CoV-2 virus.

1046. The continuation of the training process of top athletes and other athletes in the sports system of the Republic of Serbia began on 11 May 2020 in all sports facilities.

1047. According to the Recommendation, training of all top athletes and other athletes of the Republic of Serbia in the sports system of the Republic of Serbia that are directly or indirectly under the jurisdiction of national sports federations in the Republic of Serbia can continue after lifting the state of emergency in the Republic of Serbia, if all entities (athletes, trainers, authorized persons of sports clubs, authorized persons of sports facilities) enable compliance with all conditions and measures determined by this Recommendation.

1048. On arrival, departure and during training, athletes should adhere to the following recommended measures:

- athletes and trainers are recommended to come to the training individually in training equipment while avoiding the use of locker rooms (use of common, auxiliary rooms, such as locker rooms, showers, etc., is possible only if there is a possibility to disinfect the room after each use);
- whenever possible, training should be organized in the open field;

373. The Crisis Relief Headquarters was formed by the Conclusions of the Government of the Republic of Serbia No. 53-2449/2020 of 13 Mar. 2020, No. 53-2506/2020 of 16 Mar. 2020, No. 53-2673/2020-1 of 19 Mar. 2020, No. 53-2864/2020 of 26 Mar. 2020 and No. 53-2973/2020 of 1 Apr. 2020.

- during individual training, it is recommended that athletes keep a distance of at least 5 m;
- for training in contact sports where it is not possible to keep a physical distance between trainers and athletes, it is recommended that always the same trainer and athlete do the training;
- athletes should use their personal hygiene products (soaps, towels), and during training, the athlete should use only his/her water bottle, sports drink, protein and should not share it with anyone else;
- when not in training, the athlete should adhere to all measures of physical distance as a prevention measure in the Republic of Serbia in order to prevent the spread of COVID-19.

1049. The Ministry of Youth and Sports also made recommendations regarding the organization of the training itself.

1050. It is recommended that the training organizers in cooperation with the responsible persons and the management of sports facilities provide the following conditions, i.e., to take the following measures:

- for each training, a training record system should be established (data on the trainer, athletes, technical staff and other staff involved in the implementation of the training; training time, place of training) for subsequent and more efficient epidemiological monitoring of contacts in case of COVID-19 occurrence among the persons that attended the training;
- upon arrival at the training, the training organizer should collect information from each athlete, trainer, other technical and other staff involved in the implementation of the training on the existence of any of the symptoms that may indicate infection with SARS-CoV-2 (fever, cough, malaise, difficulty breathing, etc.), and if there is any symptom, the athlete should not be allowed into the facility, i.e., the athlete should leave the training and be referred to the competent physician;
- if during the training, any symptoms indicating COVID-19 infection of any athlete, trainer, technical or other training staff appear, the training should be stopped immediately and the person with symptoms should be referred to the physician;
- the organizer of the training should provide a special basket in which all used plastic and other packaging is thrown, as well as paper handkerchiefs – napkins and whose contents, after the training, are placed in a specially closed plastic bag which is then disposed of as municipal waste;
- in the sports facility where the training is held or this facility is used during the training, hand disinfectants should be installed;
- before the beginning and after the end of the training, the training organizer should disinfect the fixed sports equipment that was used in the training of athletes;
- before and after each training, all balls, as well as other sports equipment used in training, should be disinfected with a product with at least 70% alcohol;
- training organizers in cooperation with the management of sports facilities should ensure that the time interval in the schedule between the two trainings is at least fifteen minutes;

– all closed rooms used by athletes, trainers, technical and other staff should be regularly ventilated naturally, by opening doors and windows, and if weather conditions allow, the windows can be constantly open, to provide natural ventilation;
– the use of central air conditioning is not recommended.

1051. The recommendations of the Ministry of Youth and Sports also apply to the competent national sports federations, as well as to all organizations in the field of sports, to organize, whenever possible, controlled (quarantined) training preparations for their athletes.

1052. In this case, they should take the following measures:

– all athletes, trainers and other persons involved in controlled (quarantined) preparations, as well as training organizers should adhere to all measures set out in this instruction, for the entire duration of the preparations;
– all persons working in facilities used by sports teams (receptionists, waiters, cooks, persons engaged in maintaining cleanliness, etc.), should always wear protective masks and respect all other established prevention measures in the Republic of Serbia to prevent the spread of COVID-19.

1053. Before the start of the training process, it is recommended that athletes and sports experts determine their state of health, which, in addition to the prescribed health examinations, includes a serological test in accordance with the recommendations, and which will be determined in more detail by a by-law of the LS ('Official Gazette of RS', No. 10/16) which regulates the determination of the health ability of athletes and sports experts to perform sports activities and participate in sports competitions.

1054. The Government of the Republic of Serbia and the Crisis Relief Headquarters for the control of the infectious disease COVID-19 also recommended that the Minister in Charge of Health and the Minister in Charge of Sports proceed to adopt the by-law of the LS referred to in item 6 of this instruction, which in more detail regulates the manner, type, scope and deadlines within which health examinations of athletes and sports experts are conducted, which will determine the measure of prevention, prevention of spread and the reduction of the risk of COVID-19 disease through performing health examinations of athletes and sports experts.

1055. As the epidemiological situation became better, on 16 June 2020, the Ministry of Health issued a new Order banning gatherings in the Republic of Serbia in public places indoors and outdoors.[374] According to this Order, the measures were further relaxed so that a ban on public gatherings on the entire territory of the Republic of Serbia in public places indoors and outdoors was introduced – when more than 500 people gather at the same time, with the distance between those

374. *See* 'Official Gazette of RS', No. 60 of 16 Jun. 2021.

present being at least 2 m, i.e., for every 4 m^2 one person can be present, and during the gatherings, the implementation of other established epidemiological measures must be ensured.

1056. Exceptionally, the gathering of more than 500 people was allowed if the permission of the Crisis Relief Headquarters for the control of infectious diseases COVID-19 was obtained beforehand, as well as during the gathering at a sports event organized within the registered official competitions, with the number of people present during a sports event held in an open space not exceeding 50% of the capacity of the facility in which the sports event is held, or 30% of the capacity when a sports event is held indoors.

1057. In such conditions, the Ministry of Youth and Sports left the possibility to the national branch sports federations to decide for themselves how the championships started would be finished.[375]

1058. On 11 August 2020, the Agreement on Free Testing of Athletes and Sports Experts at COVID-19 was signed. By signing the Agreement on the Cooperation between the Institute for Sports and Sports Medicine of the Republic of Serbia and the Directorate for National Reference Laboratories of the Ministry of Agriculture, Forestry and Water Management of the Republic of Serbia, all athletes and sports experts were enabled to undergo COVID-19 testing.

1059. It is not enough to say that in the age of COVID-19, it was difficult to finance sports. In this regard, the Regulation on the establishment of financial support programmes for sports organizations in difficult economic conditions due to the COVID-19 pandemic caused by the SARS-CoV-2 virus was passed[376] with the aim of preserving the stability of the sports system in the Olympic and Paralympic branches. The main goals of the Programme are to provide support to sports organizations that have a general interest in the field of sports in order to improve the sports system, and through mitigating the negative consequences in difficult economic conditions.

375. The decisions were different from federation to federation, so the Handball Federation of Serbia made the decision to terminate the championships and not end them for the 2019/20 competition year, while, for example, the Volleyball Federation of Serbia decided to end the championships with the current situation on the scorecard. The Football Association, for example, changed the propositions of the competition, shortened the championship and when the conditions were met, brought the 2019/20 competition year to an end.

376. *See* 'Official Gazette of RS', No. 144/2020.

Chapter 3. Funding of Sports Organizations in the Age of COVID-19

1060. The programme of financial support to sports organizations refers to the allocation of non-refundable financial resources to sports organizations in the conditions of potential risks caused by the emergency health situation.

1061. The funds for the implementation of the Regulation are provided by the 2020 Law on the Budget of the Republic of Serbia[377] in the amount of RSD 1,100,000,000.00.[378]

1062. Funds in the amount of a total of RSD 802,600,000.00 have been allocated for the financing of four collective sports.

1063. Funds in the amount of a total of RSD 220,000,000.00 have been allocated for the financing of eleven individual sports.

1064. Funds in the amount of a total of RSD 20,000,000.00 have been allocated for the financing of Paralympic sports.

1065. The programme is implemented by the Government through the Ministry of Youth and Sports, in cooperation with the competent national sports federations in the Republic of Serbia.

1066. The right to financial support under this programme has a sports organization performing sports activities and/or activities in Olympic and Paralympic sports that have a long sports tradition in the Republic of Serbia, gather a large number of athletes of all ages and have significant sports results at major international sports competitions. (basketball, volleyball, handball, water polo, wrestling, taekwondo, rowing, kayaking, athletics, shooting sport, swimming, tennis, table tennis, karate and judo).

1067. The funds under this programme can be used for:

- salaries, fees and scholarships of licensed athletes in the competent national sports federation;
- salaries and fees of sports experts who have a work permit issued by the competent national sports federation;
- renting and leasing facilities for performing the training and competition process;
- costs of participation in international competitions and maintaining the fulfilment of conditions for participation in international competitions in the current and next competition season;

---

377. *See* 'Official Gazette of RS', Nos 84/19, 60/20 – other law, 62/20 – other law, 65/20 – other law and 135/20.
378. EUR 9,383,183.63 at the middle exchange rate of the National Bank of Serbia on 1 Sep. 2020. The EUR was RSD 117,231 on this day.

- transport and transportation costs;
- costs of procurement of equipment and props.

1068. Conditions for the financial support under this programme are that the sports organization should:

- be registered in accordance with the LS;
- have membership in the competent national sports federation;
- participate in one of the two highest ranks of national sports competitions; should not be in the process of liquidation, bankruptcy or under a temporary ban on performing activities;
- not have a blocked business account at the time of concluding the contract on the implementation of the Programme and transfer of budget funds to the business account, as well as should not be penalized in the last two years for a misdemeanour or economic offence related to financial operations, use of property and work with children.

1069. The right to financial support under this programme is exercised on the basis of the request of the competent national sports federation. The deadline for submitting requests by sports organizations for the implementation of the Programme to the competent national sports federations was 3 December 2020.

1070. Agreements were concluded between the competent national sports federations and sports organizations and the funds were transferred as of 30 December 2020.

1071. The supervision and control of the intended use of funds by sports organizations on the basis of this programme were performed by the competent national sports federations, which were obliged to submit a report on the implementation of the Programme to the Ministry by 1 September 2021.

1072. The Ministry of Youth and Sports is obliged to submit the final report on the realization of the Programme to the Government of the Republic of Serbia by 15 January 2022 at the latest.

Chapter 4. Application of Measures by Sports Organizations in the Conditions of COVID-19

1073. In the Republic of Serbia, sports activities take place in accordance with the epidemiological situation.

1074. According to Article 10a of the Regulation on Measures for the Prevention and Control of Infectious Disease COVID-19 (UCOVID19),[379] when holding sports competitions indoors, the presence of up to 30% of the total occupancy capacity of the presence of visitors in the facility where the competition is held and with the mandatory wearing of protective masks of visitors is allowed.

1075. When a sports competition is held outdoors, the presence of up to 50% of the total capacity of the presence of visitors in the facility where the competition is held and with the obligatory wearing of protective masks of visitors is allowed.

1076. Article 13 of the Regulation specifies special measures for the protection of the population from infectious diseases if the competent authority has declared a state of emergency in the territory of the local self-government unit. Some of these measures concerning sports, athletes and the organization of sporting events include:

- prohibition of gathering indoors and outdoors of more than five persons, if it is not possible to provide a physical distance of two metres and appropriate personal protection measures;
- up to five people are allowed to gather in public parks and playgrounds, as well as during outdoor exercises, with appropriate personal protection measures;
- in all closed spaces, it is obligatory to wear protective masks and respect the physical distance of 2 metres;
- prohibition of organizing ceremonies, as well as organizing sports and other entertainment events.

1077. Based on the aforementioned measures adopted and applied in the Republic of Serbia, efforts are still being made to stand in the way of the 'plague' that won several rounds in the global match, even in the Republic of Serbia, in order for the sport to strike back and justify the slogan 'the show must go on'.

379. *See* 'Official Gazette of RS', Nos 151/2020, 152/2020, 153/2020, 156/2020, 158/2020, 1/2021, 17/2021, 19/2021, 22/2021, 29/2021, 34/2021, 48/2021, 54/2021, 59/2021, 60/2021, 64/2021, 69/2021, 86/2021, 95/2021, 99/2021 and 101/2021, of 27 Oct. 2021.

Conclusion

1078. The 'Sports Law in the Republic of Serbia' Monograph was drafted as a result of many years of scientific and practical research by the author. It was written, on the one hand, with the desire to familiarize the scientific and professional public with the opportunities in the development of sports law in the Republic of Serbia, on the other hand, it is part of a large project of the International Encyclopaedia of Law within Kluwer Law International. In addition, this Monograph can be solid material for students of faculties and colleges where sports law is studied. Although the Monograph is intended for the scientific and professional public as well as students who show interest in studying sports law in RS, it can also be the subject of interest of a wider readership interested in the development of sports law in the Republic of Serbia.

1079. The purpose of this Monograph determined its content and the method of presenting the matter. The matter of sports law in the Republic of Serbia is presented on almost 200 pages of the monograph, observed through four large units (chapters): 'Organisation of sports', 'Legal status of athletes', 'Doping and sports' and 'Sport and commerce'.

1080. Having in mind the lack of similar works in the domestic legal literature, this monograph is an attempt to consolidate, in one place, and present all legal and statutory solutions to these issues through the analysis of laws and by-laws regulating them in the field of public and private regulation. In order to reach certain conclusions regarding the development of sports law in the Republic of Serbia, it was necessary to draw and present a number of statutory solutions, primarily contained in the LS of the Republic of Serbia, and then solutions of other regulations which are a subsidiary source of sports rights in the Republic of Serbia.

1081. Based on the detailed analysis conducted with the application of appropriate methods of scientific research (primarily normative, sociological, methods of induction and deduction, analysis and synthesis), certain observations were made and in accordance with these observations, certain conclusions were also made.

1082. Regarding the organization of sports in the Republic of Serbia, the conclusion is that the system of sports in the Republic of Serbia is very complex since it consists of three constitutive elements. In order to manage such a complex system, competencies are divided between the governmental and non-governmental sectors. This further points to the conclusion that in sports in the Republic of Serbia, public and private regulations are part of a single legal system. Based on the conducted analysis, a conclusion was reached, which is also a *de lege ferenda* proposal, that it is necessary to strengthen private initiative in sports activities, within the framework provided by law, which is estimated to contribute to greater development and strengthening of sports law in the Republic of Serbia.

1083. The issue of the legal status of an athlete and the rights and obligations arising from a certain status is regulated in detail by the sports legislation of the Republic of Serbia. The LS regulates in detail both the legal status of a professional athlete and an amateur athlete, whereby the legislator does not differentiate between these two types of athletes. In an effort to define the legal status of the athlete, the issues of the qualification of the athlete, rights and obligations arising from it, issue of responsibility of the athlete, his/her employment status, social, health and pension insurance and the issue of tax treatment of the athlete were analysed. Based on the obtained research results, it was concluded that in terms of regulating the legal status, public law regulations are dominant, while private regulation is dominant through the statutory possibility to regulate the rights, obligations and responsibilities of athletes by a collective agreement, with regards to professional athletes, i.e., by an agreement between the athlete and the sports organization with regards to amateur athletes.

1084. In the Republic of Serbia, too, there is a very restrictive legislation regarding the use of doping by athletes or inducing and giving doping to athletes by third parties. The illicit use of doping in the Republic of Serbia is based on two facts: by using doping agents, an athlete in an illicit manner gains an advantage in sports competitions, and on the fact that such use is risky for the athlete's health.

1085. With regards to the use of sports for commercial purposes, it is noticed that in modern society, this use is increasingly noticeable, given the fact that sports in the modern market are an increasingly lucrative business. In the Republic of Serbia, there is an increasing need for the use of sports for commercial purposes, where the source of large earnings can be seen through the transfer of athletes, sale of TV broadcasting rights, sponsorship of athletes, etc. As all sports associations in the Republic of Serbia are owned by the state, we can conclude that the commercial side of sports has not yet gained the meaning it already has in developed countries.

1086. Based on the conducted detailed analysis of the development of sports law in the Republic of Serbia, a general conclusion was reached that sports law in the Republic of Serbia is a multidisciplinary branch of law (sui generis), in which the branches of public and private law meet and intertwine: sports law and civil law (issue of ownership of sports fields), sports and trade (management in sports clubs), sports and copyright (sale of TV broadcasting rights), sports and labour (relationship between a professional athlete and a sports organization), sports and criminal law (existence of illicit and negative manifestations at sports competitions and fields, illicit use of doping), sports and international public (role of international sports organizations in the promotion of sports), sports and international private law (relationships regulating sports activities between foreigners).

Selected Bibliography

Monographs

Đurđević, N. – Commentary on the Law on the Prevention of Doping in Sports, Kragujevac, 2008.

European Sports Charter, https://www.cok.me.

Jorgić, B., Aleksandrović, M., Mirić, F., Čolović, H., Dimitrijević, L. *Holistic Approach to Adapted Phytic Activities,* Faculty of Sports and Physical Education, University of Niš, Niš, 2020.

Klajn, I., Šipka, M. *Veliki rečnik stranih izraza*, Novi Sad, 2008.

Milosavljević, B. Prevention of Violence at Sports Events from the Aspect of Security Guard Services, Archives of Legal and Social Sciences, Belgrade, 2013.

Nešić, B. *Sports Law*, Sports Academy, Belgrade, 2020.

Nešić, B., Fratrić, F. *Basics of Sports Organisation*, Edukons, Sremska Kamenica, 2013.

Periodicals

Andonović, S. *The Right to Sport as a Human Right*, Strani pravni život, No. 61, Belgrade, 2017.

Galantić, M. – *Lex sportiva* – Origin and Meaning of the Term, Topics, XXXIX, No. 2, 2015, 559–577.

Legal Sources

2020 Law on the Budget of the Republic of Serbia, 'Official Gazette of the RS', Nos 84/19, 60/20 – other law, 62/20 – other law, 65/20 – other law and 135/20.

2020–2025 Public Information System Development Strategy. 'Official Gazette of RS', No. 11/2020.

Brković, R., Urdarević, B. *Labor Law with Elements of Social Security*, Official Gazette, Belgrade, 2020.

Code of Criminal Procedure, 'Official Gazette of RS', Nos 72/2011 … 62/2021 – CC Decision.

Conclusions of the Government of the Republic of Serbia No. 53-2449/2020 of 13 March 2020, No. 53-2506/2020 of 16 March 2020, No. 53-2673/2020-1 of 19 March 2020, No. 53-2864/2020 of 26 March 2020 and No. 53-2973/2020 of 1 April 2020.

Criminal Code, 'Official Gazette of RS', Nos 85/2005 … 35/2019.

Customs Law, 'Official Gazette of RS', Nos 95/2018, 91/2019 – other law and 144/2020.
Decision on lifting the state of emergency, 'Official Gazette of RS', No. 65 of 6 May 2020.
Decision on opening a temporary facility for accommodation and treatment of persons suffering from the infectious disease COVID-19 caused by the SARS-CoV-2 virus – '*Čair Hall*', 'Official Gazette of RS', No. 50 of 3 April 2020.
Decision on the confirmation of the Decision on Declaring the State of Emergency, 'Official Gazette of RS', No. 62/2020.
Instructions on the manner of application of the provisions of the Law on Electronic Media regulating own production, 'Official Gazette of RS', No. 69/15.
Labor Law, 'Official Gazette of RS', Nos 24/2005 … 95/2018 – authentic interpretation.
Law on Accounting, 'Official Gazette of RS', Nos 73/2019 … 44/2021 – other law.
Law on Advertising, 'Official Gazette of RS', Nos 6/2016 … 52/2019 – other law.
Law on Advertising, 'Official Gazette of RS', Nos 6/2016 and 52/2019 – other law.
Law on Animal Welfare, 'Official Gazette of RS', No. 41/2009.
Law on Arbitration, 'Official Gazette of RS', No. 46/2006.
Law on Associations, 'Official Gazette of RS', Nos 51/2009, 99/2011 – other laws and 44/2018 – other law.
Law on Broadcasting, 'Official Gazette of RS', Nos 42/2002 … 86/2006.
Law on Budget System, 'Official Gazette of RS', Nos 54/2009 … 149/2020.
Law on Companies, 'Official Gazette of RS', Nos 36/2011, 99/2011, 83/2014 – other law, 5/2015, 44/2018, 95/2018 and 91/2019.
Law on Consumer Protection, 'Official Gazette of RS', Nos 62/2014, 6/2016 – other law.
Law on Copyright and Related Rights, 'Official Gazette of RS', Nos 104/2009 … 66/2019.
Law on Copyright and Related Rights, 'Official Gazette of RS', Nos 104/2009, 99/2011, 119/2012, 29/2016 – Decision of the Constitutional Court and 66/2019.
Law on Corporate Income Tax, 'Official Gazette of RS', Nos 25/2001 … 153/2020.
Law on Corporate Income Tax, 'Official Gazette of RS', Nos 25/2001, 80/2002, 80/2002 – other law, 43/2003, 84/2004, 18/2010, 101/2011, 119/2012, 47/2013, 108/2013, 68/2014 – other law and 142/2014.
Law on Determining Certain Competencies of the Autonomous Province of Vojvodina, 'Official Gazette of RS', Nos 99/2009 … 18/2020 – other law.
Law on Doping, 'Official Gazette of RS', No. 111/2014.
Law on Drugs and Medical Devices, 'Official Gazette of RS', Nos 30/2010, 107/2012, 113/2017 – other law and 105/2017 – other law.
Law on Electronic Commerce, 'Official Gazette of RS', Nos 41/09, 95/13 and 52/19.
Law on Electronic Communications, 'Official Gazette of RS', Nos 83/14, 103/15 and 108/16.
Law on Electronic Media, 'Official Gazette of RS', Nos 83/2014 and 6/2016 – other law.

Law on Employment and Insurance in Case of Unemployment. 'Official Gazette of RS' No. 36/2009 … 49/2021.
Law on Endowments and Foundations, 'Official Gazette of RS Gazette', Nos 88/2010 and 99/2011 – other law.
Law on Free Access to Information of Public Importance, 'Official Gazette of RS', Nos 120/2004 … 36/2010.
Law on Games of Chance, 'Official Gazette of RS', No. 18/2020.
Law on General Administrative Procedure, 'Official Gazette of RS', No. 18/2016.
Law on Government, 'Official Gazette of RS', Nos 55/05, 71/05 – corrigendum, 101/07, 65/08, 16/11, 68/12 – CC, 72/12, 7/14-CC and 44/14.
Law on Health Insurance, 'Official Gazette of RS', No. 25/2019.
Law on Indications of Geographical Origin, 'Official Gazette of RS', Nos 18/2010, 44/2018.
Law on Legal Protection of Industrial Design, 'Official Gazette of RS', Nos 104/2009 … 44/2018.
Law on Legal Protection of Industrial Design, 'Official Gazette of RS', Nos 104/2009, 45/2015 and 44/2018 – other law, 'Official Gazette of RS', Nos 99/2011, 113/2017 – other law, 95/2018 and 66/2019.
Law on Ministries, 'Official Gazette of RS', No. 128/2020.
Law on Misdemeanors, 'Official Gazette of RS', Nos 65/2013 … 91/2019 – other law.
Law on Occupational Health and Safety, 'Official Gazette of RS', Nos 101/2005 … 113/2017 – other law.
Law on Patents, 'Official Gazette of RS', Nos 99/2011 … 66/2019.
Law on Patents, 'Official Gazette of RS', Nos 99/2011, 113/2017 – other law, 95/2018 and 66/2019.
Law on Personal Income Tax, 'Official Gazette of RS', Nos 24/2001 … 44/2021.
Law on Personal Income Tax, 'Official Gazette of RS', Nos 24/2001, 80/2002, 80/2002 – other law, 135/2004, 62/2006, 65/2006 – corrigendum, 31/2009, 44/2009, 18/2010, 50/2011, 91/2011 – Decision of CC, 7/2012-adjusted din. amount, 93/2012, 114/2012 – Decision of CC, 8/2013 – adjusted din. amount, 47/2013, 48/2013 – corrigendum and 108/2013, 57/2014, 68/2014 – other law.
Law on Property Tax, 'Official Gazette of RS', Nos 26/2001 … 114/2020.
Law on Public Enterprises, 'Official Gazette of RS', Nos 119/2012, 116/2013 – authentic interpretation and 44/2014 – other law.
Law on Public Information and Media, 'Official Gazette of RS', Nos 83/2014 … 12/2016 – authentic interpretation.
Law on Public Information and Media, 'Official Gazette of RS', Nos 83/2014, 58/2015 and 12/2016 – authentic interpretation.
Law on Public Media Services, 'Official Gazette of RS', Nos 83/14, 103/15 and 108/16.
Law on Public Order and Peace, 'Official Gazette of RS', Nos 6/2016 … 24/2018.
Law on Public SkiResorts, 'Official Gazette of RS', No. 46/2006.
Law on Republic Administrative Fees, 'Official Gazette of RS', Nos 43/2003, 51/2003 – corrigendum, 61/2005, 101/2005 – other law, 55/2012 – adjusted din. amount, 65/2013 – other law, 57/2014 – adjusted din. amount, 45/2015 – adjusted din. amount, 61/2017 – adjusted din. amount, 113/2017, 3/2018 – corrigendum,

50/2018 – adjusted din. amount, 95/2018, 38/2019 – adjusted din. amount, 86/2019, 90/2019 – corrigendum, 98/2020 – adjusted din. amount, 144/2020 and 62/2021 – adjusted din. amount.

Law on Retirement and Disability Insurance, 'Official Gazette of RS', Nos 34/2003 … 62/2021.

Law on Special Powers for Effective Protection of Intellectual Property Rights, 'Official Gazette of RS', No. 46/2006.

Law on State Administration, 'Official Gazette RS', Nos 79/2005, 101/2007, 95/2010, 99/2014, 47/2018 and 30/2018 – other law.

Law on the Organisation and Competencies of State Bodies for Combating High-Tech Crime, 'Official Gazette of RS', Nos 61/2005 and 104/2009.

Law on the Prevention of Discrimination Against Persons with Disabilities, 'Official Gazette of RS', Nos 33/2006, 13/2016.

Law on the Prevention of Doping in Sports, 'Official Gazette of RS', No. 41/2009.

Law on the Prevention of Violence and Misconduct at Sports Events ('Official Gazette of RS', Nos 67/2003, 101/2005 – other law, 90/2007 – other law, 111/2009, 104/2013 – other law and 87/2018.

Law on the Protection of Competition, 'Official Gazette of RS', Nos 51/09 and 95/13.

Law on the Protection of the Population from Infectious Diseases, 'Official Gazette of RS', Nos 15/2016, 68/2020 and 136/2020.

Law on the Protection of the Population from Infectious Diseases, 'Official Gazette of RS', Nos 68 of 10 May 2020.

Law on the Protection of Trade Secrets, 'Official Gazette of RS', No. 53/2021.

Law on the Ratification of the European Convention against Doping in Sports, 'Official Gazette of SFRY – International Agreements', No. 4/91.

Law on the Ratification of the European Convention on Transfrontier Television, 'Official Gazette of RS – International Agreements', No. 42/09.

Law on the Ratification of the International Convention Against Doping in Sport, 'Official Gazette of RS – International Agreements', No. 38/2009.

Law on the Ratification of the Nairobi Treaty on the Protection of the Olympic Symbol ('Official Gazette of FRY – International Treaties', No. 1/1999.

Law on the Restitution of Confiscated Property and Compensation, 'Official Gazette of RS', Nos 72/2011, 108/2013, 142/2014, 88/2015 – Decision of CC, 95/2018 and 153/2020).

Law on the Temporary Regulation of the Manner of Collecting Fees for the Public Media Service, 'Official Gazette of RS', Nos 112/15, 108/16, 95/18 and 86/19.

Law on the Validity of Regulations Passed by the Government with the Co-signature of the President of the Republic During the State of Emergency and Confirmed by the National Assembly, 'Official Gazette of the RS', No. 65 of 6 May 2020.

Law on Torts and Contracts, 'Official Gazette of SFRY', No. 29/1978 … 'Official Gazette of Serbia and Montenegro', No. 1/2003 – Constitutional Charter and 'Official Gazette of RS', No. 18/2020.

Law on Trade, 'Official Gazette of RS', No. 52/19.

Law on Trademarks, 'Official Gazette of RS', No. 6/2020.

Law on Value Added Tax, 'Official Gazette RS Gazette', Nos 84/2004, 86/2004 – corrigendum, 61/2005, 61/2007, 93/2012, 108/2013, 68/2014 – other law, 142/2014.
List of the Most Important Events of Special Importance for the Citizens of the Republic of Serbia, 'Official Gazette of RS', No. 45/2016.
Order on Declaring an Epidemic of Infectious Disease COVID-19, 'Official Gazette of RS ', No. 37 of 19 March 2020.
Order prohibiting gatherings in the Republic of Serbia in public places indoors and outdoors, 'Official Gazette of RS', No. 60 of 16 May 2021.
Order prohibiting gatherings, 'Official Gazette of RS', No. 30/20 of 11 March 2020.
Regulation on establishing the program of financial support to sports organizations in difficult economic conditions due to the COVID-19 pandemic caused by the SARS-CoV-2 virus, 'Official Gazette of RS', No. 144/2020.
Regulation on Measures During the State of Emergency, 'Official Gazette of RS', No. 31 of 15 March 2020.
Regulation on Measures for the Prevention and Control of the Infectious Disease COVID-19, 'Official Gazette of RS', Nos 151/2020, 152/2020, 153/2020, 156/2020, 158/2020, 1/2021, 17/2021, 19/2021, 22/2021, 29/2021, 34/2021, 48/2021, 54/2021, 59/2021, 60/2021, 64/2021, 69/2021, 86/2021, 95/2021, 99/2021 and 101/2021, of 27 October 2021.
Regulation on National Sports Recognitions and Cash Prizes, 'Official Gazette of RS', no. 22/2016, 83/2017, 74/2021.
Rulebook on advertising and sponsorship in electronic media, 'Official Gazette of RS', No. 101/2016.
Rulebook on audiovisual commercial communications, 'Official Gazette of RS' No. 69/15.
Rulebook on competent national sports federations for sports branches and areas of sports in the Republic of Serbia, 'Official Gazette of RS', Nos 30/2016 … 97/2021.
Rulebook on conditions for performing sports activities and occupations, 'Official Gazette of RS', No. 63/2013.
Rulebook on detailed conditions and criteria for scholarships for top athletes and for the monetary support to top athletes, 'Official Gazette of RS', No. 124/2012.
Rulebook on detailed conditions for performing sports activities and sports occupations, 'Official Gazette of RS', No. 42/2017.
Rulebook on detailed criteria for determining general interest in the field of sports, 'Official Gazette of RS', No. 9/2006.
Rulebook on determining the layout of a stamp with the 'DOPING FREE' sign and the procedure for issuing the stamp, 'Official Gazette of RS', No. 139/2014 Statute of the Anti-Doping Agency of the Republic of Serbia, 'Official Gazette of RS', No. 139/2014.
Rulebook on determining the responsibility of a person who has violated the anti-doping rule, 'Official Bulletin of ADAS', No. 38/2021.
Rulebook on disciplinary measures and the procedure for their imposition in cases of established violation of anti-doping rules.
Rulebook on granting exemptions for therapeutic use, 'Official Bulletin of ADAS', No. 38/2021.

Rulebook on minimum conditions for the provision of media services and decision-making criteria in the procedure of issuing a license for the provision of media services on the basis of a public competition conducted, 'Official Gazette of RS', No. 46/2016.

Rulebook on minimum technical and organisational conditions for issuing a license for the provision of media services based on the request of the media service provider, 'Official Gazette of RS' No. 46/2016.

Rulebook on sports branches and areas of sports in the Republic of Serbia and sports disciplines within sports branches and areas of sports, 'Official Gazette of RS', Nos 51/2016 … 44/2018.

Rulebook on the Assignment of Unused Rights of Public Media Services to Broadcasting of Radio, Television and Other Media Content of Extreme Importance, 'Official Gazette of RS', No. 46/2016.

Rulebook on the content and manner of keeping a single record of associations, organisations and entrepreneurs in the field of sports, 'Official Gazette of RS', No. 108/2017.

Rulebook on the content and manner of keeping the Register of associations, societies and federations in the field of sports, 'Official Gazette of RS', no. 32/2016, 44/2018 – other law.

Rulebook on the control of professional work in the field of sports, 'Official Gazette of RS', No. 92/2011.

Rulebook on the criteria and manner of increasing the share of European audiovisual works, 'Official Gazette of RS', No. 72/2015.

Rulebook on the doping control at sports competitions and out of competitions, Rulebook on determining the responsibility of a person who has violated the anti-doping rule, 'Official Bulletin of ADAS', No. 38/2021.

Rulebook on the doping control at sports competitions and out of competitions, 'Official Bulletin of ADAS', No. 38/2021.

Rulebook on the harmonization of the ADAS anti-doping rules with the World Anti-Doping Code.

Rulebook on the list of prohibited doping agents for horses, 'Official Gazette of RS', No. 23/2021.

Rulebook on the list of prohibited doping agents, Rulebook on determining the responsibility of a person who has violated the anti-doping rule, 'Official Bulletin of ADAS', No. 38/2021.

Rulebook on the manner of establishing a list of the most important events of special importance for all citizens and exercising the right to access events of great interest for the public, 'Official Gazette of RS', No. 25/2015.

Rulebook on the manner of imposing measures on media service providers 'Official Gazette of RS', No. 25/2015.

Rulebook on the national categorization of sports, 'Official Gazette of RS', No. 12/2017.

Rulebook on the nomenclature of sports occupations and titles, 'Official Gazette of RS', No. 86/2020.

Rulebook on the procedure for appointing members of the Management Board of the Public Media Service, 'Official Gazette of RS', No. 143/2014.

Rulebook on the procedure for issuing a license for the provision of media services on the basis of a public competition, 'Official Gazette of RS', No. 63/2015.
Rulebook on the procedure for issuing a license for the provision of media services based on the request, 'Official Gazette of RS', No. 63/2015.
Rulebook on the procedure for issuing consent to the act on the transfer of a license for the provision of media services and acting upon the application for a change in the ownership structure, 'Official Gazette of RS' No. 93/2015.
Rulebook on the protection of human rights in the field of media services, 'Official Gazette of RS', No. 55/2015.
Rulebook on the protection of the rights of minors in the field of media services, 'Official Gazette of RS', No. 25/2015.
Rulebook on the transition from analogue to digital television broadcasting and access to the multiplex, 'Official Gazette of RS', Nos 86/2014, 18/2015, 30/2015, 50/2015.
Rulebook on the use of public sports facilities and the performance of sports activities in public sports facilities, 'Official Gazette of RS', No. 55/2013.
The Constitution of the Republic of Serbia, 'Official Gazette of RS', No. 98/2006.

Internet Addresses

Anti-Doping Agency of the Republic of Serbia, http://www.adas.org.rs/.
Anti-Doping Convention – Strasbourg, 16.XI.1989 – Coe https://rm.coe.int.
Aritonović, G. *What Taxes Must a Sports Organisation Pay*?, http://poreskisavetnikkv.rs/koje-sve-poreze-mora-da-placa-sportska-organizacija/, 2017.
Intellectual Property Office, https://www.zis.gov.rs.
Ministry of Youth and Sports of the Republic of Serbia, Sector for Sports, https://www.mos.gov.rs/o-ministarstvu/sektor-za-sport.
Ministry of Youth and Sports, https://www.mos.gov.rs/.
Notification of the Ministry of Youth and Sports of the Republic of Serbia, https://www.mos.gov.rs/vest/vazno-obavestenje.
Organization and composition of the Permanent Sports Arbitration OCS, https://oks.org.rs/stalna-sportska-arbitraza/organizacija-i-sastav-stalne-sportske-arbitraze/.
Procedure and applicable law before the Permanent Sports Arbitration OCS, https://oks.org.rs/stalna-sportska-arbitraza/pravila-postupka-i-merodavno-pravo/.
Procedure and applicable law before the Permanent Sports Arbitration OCS, https://oks.org.rs/stalna-sportska-arbitraza/pravila-postupka-i-merodavno-pravo/.
RATEL, https://www.ratel.rs/en/.
Rulebook on Permanent Sports Arbitration of OCS, https://oks.org.rs/akti-oks/pravilnik-o-stalnoj-sportskoj-arbitrazi-oks/.
Statute of the Olympic Committee of Serbia, https://oks.org.rs/akti-oks/statut-olimpijskog-komiteta-srbije/.
Statute of the Paralympic Committee of Serbia, https://paralympic.rs/assets/documents/docs/Paraolimpijski%20komitet%20Srbije%20-Statut.pdf.
World Anti-Doping Agency, www.wada-ama.org.

Selected Bibliography

Index

The numbers here refer to paragraph numbers.

www.ingramcontent.com/pod-product-compliance
Lightning Source LLC
Chambersburg PA
CBHW071437230926
51846CB00001B/266
9789403537078